The Westminster Shorter Catechism

INTERIOR OF WESTMINSTER ABBEY.

FOR BIBLE CLASS AND FAMILY INSTRUCTION.

THE

WESTMINSTER

SHORTER CATECHISM.

WITH

ANALYSIS, SCRIPTURAL PROOFS, EXPLANATORY
AND PRACTICAL INFERENCES, AND
ILLUSTRATIVE ANECDOTES.

BY

REV. JAMES R. BOYD,

AUTHOR OF "ELEMENTS OF RHETORIC," AND "ECLECTIC MORAL PHILOSOPHY,"
EDITOR OF "ENGLISH POETS, WITH NOTES," ETC.

SECOND EDITION.

NEW YORK:
PUBLISHED BY M. W. DODD
BRICK CHURCH CHAPEL, CITY HALL SQUARE.

1856.

Entered, according to Act of Congress, in the year 1854,
BY M. W. DODD,
In the Clerk's Office of the Southern District of New York.

STEREOTYPED BY
THOMAS B. SMITH,
216 William St. N. Y.

TO A GREAT ADMIRER

OF THE WESTMINSTER SHORTER CATECHISM,

THE WIFE OF A BELOVED AND VENERATED PASTOR

OF MY EARLY YEARS,

This Little Volume,

UNDERTAKEN AT HER EARNEST REQUEST,

FOR THE BENEFIT OF

THE YOUTH OF CHRISTIAN CONGREGATIONS,

IS MOST AFFECTIONATELY AND GRATEFULLY

INSCRIBED;

WITH THE PLEASING HOPE

THAT IT MAY GAIN HER APPROVAL,

AS TO ITS PLAN AND EXECUTION,

AND SERVE THE IMPORTANT PURPOSE

ABOVE SUGGESTED.

INTRODUCTORY REMARKS.

The Westminster Shorter Catechism has now fairly entered upon its Third Century of existence and of usefulness; and, like the writings of Shakspeare and Milton, composed not far from the same period, remarkably retains its high and deserved reputation, amidst the ever-flowing and overflowing issues of the press. Many excellent works have at different times appeared, in explanation and amplification of this admirable compend of Christian doctrine. Some of these have been consulted, and others largely used, in the preparation of the work now submitted,—particularly those of Vincent and Paterson; the Rev. Dr. Green's Lectures, and the works of Doolittle and Watson have been occasionally referred to. All these publications have their respective merits and appropriate fields of usefulness; yet it is supposed, that neither they nor others in common use, supersede the experiment of presenting the Catechism in still another form, somewhat original, and with some accompaniments that may render the systematic study of divine truth more attractive and useful than heretofore, to the youth connected with Christian congregations.

PECULIARITIES OF THE PRESENT WORK.

With this view the Answers of the Shorter Catechism are, for the most part, presented, by way of inference, in other words, more plain and less technical—conveying the same truth, but in modern and easy style of speech, so that the subject may be readily and agreeably laid hold of, and understood, before an attempt is made to commit to memory the concise, condensed, and theological forms of thought presented in those Answers.

In the Second place, the doctrinal instructions of the original answers are *analysed* and presented in a distinct and separate form, and are *supported by appropriate passages of Scripture*, which may easily and profitably be committed to memory. The study of this portion will show that the Catechism is not a mere human composition, not "a cunningly-devised fable," but that it derives its being, its vitality, its beauty, its grandeur, its high authority, from the very words of Divine inspiration.

In the Third place, it seemed desirable to turn the doctrinal instructions of the Catechism to a practical account; to make them instrumental in rousing the conscience, and impressing the heart, and influencing the every-day life of the student.

For this purpose I have represented him as *drawing for himself*, from the Answers, *Practical Lessons* for the guidance of his own future conduct, and the control of his own mind and heart. The Catechism, thus enlarged, and carried out into a form personally and practically useful, loses its abstract, and much of its repulsive aspect; and, when committed to memory, under such advantages, cannot fail to exert a more valuable influence, not only intellectual, but moral and practical, even upon comparatively young minds.

In the Fourth place, from the field of Christian aud General Biography, have been selected many *useful, impressive, and entertaining Anecdotes*, which serve to throw light, and to spread no small degree of attractiveness, around each successive doctrine and duty, and also to impress them more vividly upon the understanding and upon the heart. These illustrative Anecdotes may be regarded as a delightful commentary, furnished by Divine Providence, for leading the popular, as well as the youthful mind, into a larger knowledge, appreciation, and love of the sublime doctrines and holy precepts of the Christian Faith.

In these various methods have I sought to allure my young readers, and perhaps others beyond the period of youth, to study this good old Catechism, and to examine and draw out, as for themselves, the rich treasures of divine wisdom and counsel and saving influences, which they will find embodied and consolidated in its compact, scholar-like, enduring, and noble structure.

ORIGIN OF THE SHORTER CATECHISM.

It may serve to excite a deeper interest in this theological composition itself, to be informed that it was produced and published under the sanction of an assembly, consisting of one hundred and twenty-one divines, and thirty laymen from England, and of five commissioners from Scotland, convened in 1643, by order of the British Parliament, in a part of the celebrated Westminster Abbey. This assembly embraced, as will not be denied, some of the most godly and learned men that ever adorned the British empire. Richard Baxter, from personal acquaintance with the greater part of them, avows that the Christian world, since the days of the Apostles, never had a Synod of more excellent divines. In the striking language which he employs:—"The divines there congregated, were men of eminent learning, godliness, ministerial abilities, fidelity; and being not worthy to be one of them myself, I may the more freely speak the truth, even in the face of malice and envy, that as far as I am able to judge, by the information of all history of that kind, and by any other evidence left us, the Christian world, since the days of the Apostles, had never a synod of more excellent divines than this and the Synod of

Dort." It is remarkable that this assembly was engaged for more than five years and a half in preparing a Form of Church Government, and summaries of religious doctrine and practice for England and Scotland. "It was felt," says Dr. Belfrage, "by the leading men in the struggle with superstition and arbitrary power, in the seventeenth century, that a scheme of doctrine, church government and worship, pure and scriptural, would be a most excellent means of establishing the rights for which they were contending, and forming the virtues by which freedom is blest. It was with this view that the Westminster Assembly was convened; and that its proceedings were honored with the countenance of the first and best man in the land—the first in influence, and the best in true worth." While the Confession of faith was still under discussion, able committees were appointed to present its substance in the form of the Larger and Shorter Catechism, which, after careful examination, received the solemn sanction of the Assembly. In the latter part of 1647, they were presented for approval to the House of Commons, and adopted by the General Assembly of the Church of Scotland, in 1648. They were not adopted by the ecclesiastical authorities in England. These documents, with slight emendations in the Confession of Faith and Larger Catechism, relative to civil government, were adopted by the Presbyterian Church in this country, as standards of doctrine and church government and discipline, in the city of Philadelphia, in May 1788.

TESTIMONIES TO THE UNRIVALLED EXCELLENCE OF THE SHORTER CATECHISM, AND THE ADVANTAGES OF AN EARLY STUDY OF IT.

The above historical sketch will prepare us to assent to the high but deserved eulogium, which the Rev. Dr. Humphrey (in his work on Domestic Education) has pronounced in the following terms: —" In calling the particular attention of heads of families to that admirable compendium of Christian doctrine, the Westminster Shorter Catechism, I do not mean to speak disparagingly of the Catechisms of those evangelical Christians, who dissent from some of its statements; but only to express my own admiration of it, as the most lucid, guarded, and comprehensive epitome of Bible truth which I have ever seen; and as, in my judgment, the best family manual that the wisdom and piety of any body of uninspired men has ever yet given to the church. And however the advocates of other creeds may differ from me in opinion, I cannot well see how any of the enlightened members of that very large body of Christians, Presbyterian and Congregational, who embrace the Westminster Confession of Faith, can dissent."

I cannot forbear to add, in conclusion, the equally valuable testimony of the late venerable and reverend Dr. Ashbel Green, who, in his Introductory Lecture, thus speaks of the advantages to be derived from an early and thorough study of the Shorter Catechism :—" The catechetical or questionary form of religious summaries, renders them most easy and interesting to children and youth, and, indeed, to Christians of all ages and descriptions. For myself, I have no reluctance to state here publicly, what I have frequently mentioned in private, that in the composition of sermons one of the readiest and best aids I have ever found, has been my Catechism. Let me add, further, that long observation has satisfied me, that a principal reason why instruction and exhortation from the pulpit are so little efficacious, is, that they presuppose a degree of information, or an acquaintance with the truths and doctrines of divine revelation, which, by a great part of the hearers, is not possessed; and which would best of all have been supplied by catechetical instruction. It is exactly this kind of instruction which is at the present time most urgently needed, in many, perhaps in most, of our congregations. It is needed to imbue effectually the minds of our people with "the first principles of the oracles of God;" to indoctrinate them soundly and systematically in revealed truth; and thus to guard them against being "carried about with every wind of doctrine;" as well as to qualify them to join in the weekly service of the sanctuary with full understanding, and with minds in all respects prepared for the right and deep impression of what they hear."

THE WESTMINSTER CATECHISM.—THE FIRST UNION QUESTION BOOK.

It is deserving of remark, that the authors of this compend consisted of various denominations, not only Presbyterians and Congregationalists, but Episcopalians and Erastians also. The Westminster Assembly (as the Puritan Recorder observes) gave the world *the first example of a union of different denominations in an effort to produce a Question Book, approved by them all, for the religious instruction of children and youth;* and so singularly successful was their endeavor, that after the lapse of more than two centuries, no compend of the doctrines and duties of Christianity can be found, better adapted to strengthen the minds of the young, to teach them the truth as it is in Jesus, to preserve them from error, and to make them wise unto salvation.

The Shorter Catechism was not an abridgment of the Larger: the latter was an expansion of the former. Both were prepared under the influence of that impression which each member had taken at the outset of his labors: "I do sincerely and solemnly protest, in the presence of Almighty God, that in the Assembly, of which I am a member, I will not maintain anything in matters of doctrine, but what I think in my conscience to be truth; or in point of discipline, but what I consider to conduce most to the glory of God, and to the good and peace of the church."

Such men deserve our confidence, and their arduous labors have been duly appreciated by multitudes of the wise and good. The *Puritan Recorder* remarks that *this little manual has undoubtedly contributed more than any other book, except the Bible, to the religious intelligence and piety of the children and descendants of the Puritans.* The same may be affirmed of all the families in Britain and America, in which the Shorter Catechism has been faithfully used.

ANALYSIS OF THE SHORTER CATECHISM.

GENERAL INTRODUCTION.

The chief design of man's being created, p. 19.
The Scriptures the only rule of faith and duty, 22.
The two principal topics treated of in Scripture, and explained in the Two Divisions of the Catechism, 25.

FIRST DIVISION.
What we are to believe concerning God.

Chap. I.
Concerning God considered in himself.

I. Concerning the Nature and Perfections of God, 27.
II. ————the Oneness of God, 30.
III. ————the Trinity and Unity of the Godhead, 31.

Chap. II.
Concerning God's Doings with respect to his Creatures.

I. Concerning the *Nature* and *Character* of God's decrees, 35.
II. ————the *Execution* of God's decrees, 38.
    I. In Creation.
        [1.] In the Creation of the world, 39.
        [2.] In the Creation of man, 41.
    II. In Providence.
        [1.] In God's General Providence. Its nature and character, 43.

[2.] In God's Special Providence towards man, —first in his creation and fall,—and then in the plan of redemption, 46.

SECT. 1. *Concerning the Execution of God's Decrees, in his Special Providence towards Man in his Creation and Fall.*

(1.) Concerning the covenant of works, its parties and terms, 46.
(2.) ———— Man's disobedience and fall by sin, 47.
    1. The nature of sin in general, 48.
    2. The nature of Adam's sin in particular, 50.
(3.) ———— the *extent* of the fall, 51.
(4.) ———— the *consequences* of the fall, 53.
    1. The sinfulness of man's estate by the fall, 54.
    2. The misery of man's estate by the fall, 56.

SECT. II. *Concerning the Execution of God's Decrees, in his Special Providence towards Man in Redemption.*

[1.] The PLAN of redemption by a Redeemer, 60.
    (1.) The Redeemer's person and character, 63.
    (2.) His assumption of human nature, 66.
    (3.) His *offices* as a Redeemer, 67.
        1. His office of a prophet, 69.
        2. His office of a priest, 71.
        3. His office of a king, 73.
    (4.) The *states* in which these offices are executed.
        1. His state of Humiliation, 75.
        2. His state of Exaltation, 78.

[2.] The APPLICATION of redemption.
    (1.) The *Agent* by whom redemption is applied, 80.
    (2.) The *means* used for its application in effectual calling, 82.
    (3.) The *manner* and *order* of applying redemption in effectual calling, 83.

[3.] The BENEFITS of redemption.
    (1.) The benefits of redemption in *this life*, 86.

1. Justification, 88.
2. Adoption, 91.
3. Sanctification, 92.
4. Additional benefits of redemption, 96.

(2.) The benefits of redemption at *death*, 99.
(3.) The benefits of redemption at the *resurrection*, 102.

SECOND DIVISION.
Of the Duty which God requires of Man.

INTRODUCTION.

Of the nature of man's duty in general, p. 105.

CHAP. I.

Of the Moral Law, binding on all Rational Creatures, as summed up in the Ten Commandments, 107.

INTRODUCTION.

The sum of the ten commandments, 108.
The Preface to the ten commandments, 113.

The COMMANDMENTS divided into two tables.

THE FIRST TABLE.

Containing the Duties which we owe to God.

1. The first commandment, 116.
2. The second commandment, 125.
3. The third commandment, 137.
4. The fourth commandment, 144.

THE SECOND TABLE.

Containing the Duties which we owe to Man.

1. The fifth commandment, 159.
2. The sixth commandment, 169.
3. The seventh commandment, 174.
4. The eighth commandment, 177.
5. The ninth commandment, 181.
6. The tenth commandment, 187.

Chap. II.
Of the special Duties which God requires from Man under the Gospel Dispensation.

Introduction.
Inability of man to keep the law, 193.
Different degrees of guilt in breaking the law, 197.
The deserts of every breach of the law, 199.

Section I.
Of Faith in Jesus Christ, 202.

Section II.
Of Repentance unto Life, 205.

Section III.
Of Diligent Use of the Means of Grace, 209.
I. Of the *Word of God* as a means of grace.
    [1.] Of the effects of the Word of God, 212.
    [2.] Of the proper use of the Word of God, 215.
II. Of the use of the *Sacraments* as a means of grace.
    [1.] Of the efficacy of the Sacraments, 218.
    [2.] Of the nature of the Sacraments, 221.
    [3.] Of the New Testament Sacraments, 223.
        (1.) Of Baptism.
            1. Of the nature and use of Baptism, 224.
            2. Of the subjects of Baptism, 227.
        (2.) Of the Lord's Supper.
            1. The nature and use of the Lord's Supper, 234.
            2. The proper observance of the Lord's Supper, 235.
III. Of *Prayer* as a means of grace.
    [1.] Of the nature of prayer, 238.
    [2.] Rule of direction as given in the Lord's Prayer, 241.
        (1.) The *Preface* to the Lord's Prayer, 242.
        (2.) The *Petitions* in the Lord's Prayer, 245.

GENERAL INTRODUCTION,

SHOWING THE PRINCIPAL END OF MAN'S CREATION; THE RULE BY WHICH MAN MAY ATTAIN TO THAT END; AND THE TWO PRINCIPAL TOPICS TREATED OF IN SCRIPTURE.

Q. 1. WHAT IS THE CHIEF END OF MAN?

Man's chief end is to glorify God, and enjoy him for ever.

What Truths are embraced in this Answer?

1. *The chief design of Man's creation, in reference to God, was actively to spread abroad his glory.*—1. *Cor.* x. 31. Whether therefore ye eat or drink, or whatsoever ye do, do all to the glory of God.

2. *The chief design of Man's creation, in reference to himself, was the enjoyment of God.*—*Deut.* xii. 18. Thou shalt rejoice before the Lord thy God in all that thou puttest thine hands unto.

3. *The foundation and end of every duty, should be the glory of God.*—*Rom.* xiv. 8. Whether we live, we live unto the Lord; and whether we die, we die unto the Lord: whether we live therefore, or die, we are the Lord's.

4. *All happiness here and hereafter must be derived from the enjoyment of God.*—*Psal.* lxxiii. 25, 26. Whom have I in heaven but thee? and there is none upon earth that I desire besides thee. My flesh and my heart faileth: but God is the strength of my heart, and my portion for ever.

From the above Truths what Lessons do you draw ?

I learn (1.) That I must make it my daily aim to honor God and to secure his favor, and to seek my chief happiness in so doing. (2.) That my greatest happiness is not to be found in this world, but in the everlasting ages of the next. (3.) That I have no right to make the gaining of worldly goods my chief desire and labor. (4.) That most men mistake the true business and proper use of this short life, since they take no proper pains to honor God or to secure his favor. (5.) It must be a sad and fearful event to die before one has begun to live for God and for eternity.

What Illustrations can you relate ?

1. *President Humphrey* says:—"For myself, though I confess with shame, that when my mother used to give me my little task, and teach me *The chief end of man*, I would gladly have been excused from both, and wondered what good thing they could ever do me; I subsequently found abundant cause to be thankful for her fidelity and perseverance. I was astonished when I began to read the Bible seriously, and to collect and arrange its doctrines, to find what a fund of definitions and important scriptural truths I had got treasured up for the occasion. This, I doubt not, accords with the experience of thousands, who, like myself, once loathed the Assembly's Catechism. And how delightful it is to hear, as we sometimes do, the aged disciple, just on the verge of heaven, repeating, with thrilling interest, and feasting his soul upon the definitions of *justification, adoption, sanctification,* and the like, which, three quarters of a century before, were imprinted indelibly upon his memory in the nursery!"

2. The Rev. *Dr. Payson*, after months of severe suffering on a sick bed, remarked:—"God has been cutting off

one source of enjoyment after another, till I find that I can do without them all, and yet enjoy more happiness than ever in my life before. There can be no such thing as disappointment to me, for I have no desire but that God's will may be accomplished."

3. "Two things," (said the late Rev. *Samuel Pierce*,) "are causes of daily astonishment to me:—The readiness of Christ to come from heaven to earth for me; and my backwardness to rise from earth to heaven with him. But, oh! how animating the prospect! A time approaches when Christians shall rise to sink no more: to 'be forever with the Lord.' To be with *the Lord* for a week, for a day, for an hour; how sweetly must the moments pass! But to be *forever* with the Lord,—*that* enstamps salvation with perfection; that gives an energy to our hopes, and a dignity to our joy, so as to render it *unspeakable and full of glory!*"

He also said:—"It has pleased God lately to teach me more than ever that HIMSELF is the *fountain* of happiness; that likeness to him, friendship for him, and communion with him, form the basis of all true *enjoyment*. The very disposition which, blessed be my dear Redeemer! he has given me, to be anything, do anything, or endure anything, so that his name might be glorified,—I say, the *disposition* itself is heaven begun below."

4. Lady Glenorchy, of Edinburgh, offering one day to read to her minister, (then upon his death-bed,) a passage in one of Hill's Sermons, he said:—"O, no; read the Bible; all other writings are insipid to me—they are the words of men, and some of them are good; but the words of God are my delight. *One promise* gives me more comfort than all the writings of men. I have no relish for any book or conversation that does not bring them to my remembrance."

Q. 2. WHAT RULE HATH GOD GIVEN TO DIRECT US HOW WE MAY GLORIFY AND ENJOY HIM?

The Word of God, which is contained in the Scriptures of the Old and New Testament, is the only rule to direct us how we may glorify and enjoy him.

What Truths are embraced in this Answer?

1. *A rule of faith and duty was necessary for man.—Jer.* x. 23. The way of man is not in himself: it is not in man that walketh to direct his steps.
2. *The Bible, though written by men, is the word of God.—* 2 *Pet.* i. 21. For the prophecy came not in old time by the will of man: but holy men of God spake as they were moved by the Holy Ghost.
3. *The Old Testament Scriptures are the word of God.—Rom.* iii. 2. Unto them were committed the oracles of God.
4. *The New Testament Scriptures are the word of God.—* 1 *Thess.* ii. 13. When ye received the word of God which ye heard of us, ye received it not as the word of men, but (as it is in truth) the word of God.
5. *The Bible is the only rule of faith and duty.—Isa.* viii. 20. To the law and to the testimony: if they speak not according to this word, it is because there is no light in them.
6. *The Bible is a complete and sufficient rule of faith and duty.—Psal.* xix. 7. The law of the Lord is perfect, converting the soul: the testimony of the Lord is sure, making wise the simple.

What Lessons do you derive from the above Doctrines?

I learn (1.) That the Bible is of more value, and of greater excellence, than all other books. It has God for its author; it teaches things the most important to Him and to me: it may safely be relied upon. I could not do without it, for it shows me the only true method of honoring God and of becoming happy in his favor. (2.) When I read it, therefore, I must bear in mind that God is therein speaking to me, and expects me to give my best regard and obedience to what he teaches and enjoins. (3.) That the Apocrypha, though it contains some very good things, is a merely human composition, and is not to be regarded or obeyed as of divine authority. (4.) That the pretended revelations of Mohammed, Mormon, and others, are to be rejected as impostures. (5.) That the entire Bible should be read; should be translated into every language, and sent to every family on earth. (6.) I have read the Bible almost in vain, if I have not been so impressed by it, as to have formed the habit of properly honoring God, and of seeking my chief happiness in his favor.

THE BIBLE.

"Most wondrous book! bright candle of the Lord!
Star of eternity! the only star
By which the bark of man could navigate
The sea of life, and gain the coast of bliss."—POLLOK.

What Illustrations can you relate?

1. THE GOLD MINE.—A certain Spaniard had a gold mine of very great value; but, instead of working it in a proper manner, he contented himself with digging over the surface and removing a little of the earth, but never went half deep enough to get the gold; so that, although he was the owner of a mine, he lived and died poor, never having got so much from his mine as to keep him from poverty.

Now, the Bible is more valuable than a gold mine; and the truth it contains, that "God so loved the world that he gave his only begotten Son, that whosoever believeth in him should not perish, but have everlasting life," (*John*, iii. 6) is more precious than the choicest gold. If, then, we go deep enough into our Bibles, to discover the Saviour for sinners, and to acknowledge, trust in, and love him as our Saviour, happy are we; but if we rest contented in reading the Bible without discovering, and thus acting upon this truth, we shall get no more profit from the Bible than the Spaniard got from his gold mine.

2. "Men are *Atheistical*, because they are first *vicious;* and question the *truth* of Christianity, because they hate the *practice* of it."—*South.*

3. THE SCRIPTURES AT THE HERVEY ISLANDS.—For some years English missionaries had labored there, and with great success. The noble work of translating the entire Bible into the native language has just been accomplished. These Bibles were printed in England, and for a long time the natives had been anticipating the arrival of the ship John Williams, bringing them this greatly-desired treasure. Their joy was unbounded when she arrived. Every able-bodied church member at once engaged in transporting the cases of books from the seaside to the Mission House.

These simple-minded natives, with their own earnings, have now furnished themselves with this inestimable treasure.

At a public meeting, held in commemoration of the arrival of the finished Scriptures, one of the natives said:—

"Let us read the whole book. Let us go to the missionary by day and by night, and inquire into the meaning of the new parts which we have not read. Let us be at his door when he rises. Let us stop him when we meet him, that he may tell us of these new books." And he added, with the excited energy of a feeble old man, "My brethren and sisters, this is my resolve. The dust shall never cover my new Bible; the moths shall never eat it; the mildew shall never rot it. My light and my joy!"

THE PRINCIPAL TOPICS OF SCRIPTURE.

Q. 3. WHAT DO THE SCRIPTURES PRINCIPALLY TEACH?

The Scriptures principally teach what man is to believe concerning God, and what duty God requires of man.

What Truths are embraced in this answer?

1. *The Scriptures teach us other things besides the knowledge of God, and the duty and happiness of man.*—*Matt.* xiii. 23. Wo unto you, Scribes and Pharisees, hypocrites! for ye pay tithe of mint, and anise, and cummin, and have omitted the weightier matters of the law, judgment, mercy, and faith: these ought ye to have done, and not to leave the other undone.

2. *The Bible teaches what we are to believe about God.*—*Deut.* xxxi. 12. That they may learn, and fear the Lord your God, and observe to do all the words of this law.

3. *The Bible teaches us what is our duty to God and man.*—*Luke*, x. 25, 26. And, behold, a certain lawyer stood up, and tempted him, saying, Master, what shall I do to inherit eternal life? He said unto him, What is written in the law? How readest thou?

What Lessons do you derive from the above Doctrines?

I learn (1.) That the most important things taught in the Bible are—what God is, has done, and will do; and also, what he has commanded man to do and to be. (2.) That in reading the Bible, these subjects claim my chief attention and regard. (3.) I must gain the best knowledge I can of God and of my duty, with a view to serve Him and to secure my own everlasting happiness.

What Illustration can you relate?

1 I adopt it," (says the late Professor B. B. Edwards,) " as my settled resolution, that THE BIBLE is my book, and that I will never let any other book take that place in my affections which the Bible ought to have. I will read it twice a day devotionally."

2. PUNGENT REPLY.—To a young infidel, who scoffed at Christianity, on account of the misconduct of some of its professors, Dr. Mason said, "Did you ever know an uproar made because an infidel went astray from the paths of morality?" The infidel admitted he had not. "Then," said the Doctor, "don't you see that you admit that Christianity is a holy religion, by expecting its professors to be holy; and that thus, by your very objection, you pay it the highest compliment in your power?"

3. CLEMENTINE CUVIER.—This lovely young Christian once said to a friend:—" I experience a pleasure in reading the Bible, which I have never felt before; it attracts and fixes me to an inconceivable degree, and I seek sincerely there, and only there, the truth. When I compare the calm and the peace which the smallest grain of faith gives to the soul, with all that the world alone can give of joy, or happiness, or glory, I feel that the least in the kingdom of heaven is a hundred times more blessed than the greatest and most elevated of the men of the world." And yet she lived in the full enjoyment of the comforts and luxuries of life—was beloved, caressed, and flattered.

4. HOW TO READ THE SCRIPTURES.—The Rev. *R. McCheyne*, in writing to a young boy of his parish, who had just left his father's roof, says:—" You read your Bible regularly, of course; but do try and understand it; and still more, to *feel* it. Read more parts than one at a time. For example, if you are reading Genesis, read a Psalm also; or if you are reading Matthew, read a small bit of an Epistle also. *Turn the Bible into prayer.* Thus, if you love reading the first Psalm, spread the Bible on the chair before you, and kneel and pray. 'O Lord, give me the blessedness of the man,' &c. 'Let me not stand,' &c. This is the best way of knowing the meaning of the Bible and of learning to pray."

FIRST DIVISION.

WHAT WE ARE TO BELIEVE CONCERNING GOD

CHAPTER I.

CONCERNING GOD CONSIDERED IN HIMSELF.

I.—*The nature and perfections of God.*

Q. 4. WHAT IS GOD?

God is a Spirit, infinite, eternal, and unchangeable, in his being, wisdom, power, holiness, justice, goodness, and truth.

What Truths are embraced in this Answer?

1. *God is a Spirit.—John,* iv. 24. God is a Spirit: and they that worship him, must worship him in spirit and in truth.
2. *God is infinite in his being and perfections.—Job,* xi. 7. Canst thou by searching find out God? canst thou find out the Almighty unto perfection?
3. *God is eternal in his being and perfections.—Psal.* xc. 2. From everlasting to everlasting, thou art God.
4. *God is unchangeable in his being and perfections.—Mal.* iii. 6. I am the Lord, I change not.
5. *God is infinitely wise.—Psal.* cxlvii. 5. His understanding is infinite.
6. *God is infinitely powerful.—Job,* xlii. 2. I know that thou canst do everything.

7. *God is infinitely holy.—Rev.* xv. 4. Thou only art holy.

8. *God is infinitely just.—Zeph.* iii. 5. The just Lord is in the midst thereof; he will not do iniquity.

9. *God is infinitely good and merciful.—Exod.* xxxiv. 6. The Lord, the Lord God, merciful and gracious, long-suffering, and abundant in goodnes and truth.

10. *God is infinite in truth.—Deut.* xxxii. 4. A God of truth, and without iniquity; just and right is he.

What Lessons do you derive from the above Doctrines?

I learn (1.) That there is a God—a Supreme Being. (2.) That God has not a body, as man has, neither can I see Him. (3.) That in the largest measure he always was, and ever will be, a Being who knows all things, and how to act for the best; a Being who is able to do all that he judges it best to do; a Being who has no sinful or improper thoughts or feelings, and is opposed to all such; Being who wrongs none of his creatures, but is ever engaged in bestowing undeserved favors; and a Being who always declares what is true, and most strongly hates what is false. Hence I learn,—That such a Being is altogether worthy of my highest respect, adoration, and love and that to secure his friendship and love must contribute more to my happiness than anything else I can acquire. (4.) That the knowledge of God will avail me but little, if he be not *my* God: if I have not his wisdom to teach me, his holiness to sanctify me, his Spirit to comfort me, his mercy to save me. (5.) Hence I must choose Him for my portion and my happiness, before all other beings or things, and give myself, soul and body, wholly to Him, to be used in his service, and to promote his glory. (6.) As God is an infinitely intelligent spirit, I must give him the worship of my mind and heart.

What Illustrations can you relate?

1. In one of the earliest meetings of the Committee appointed to prepare the Shorter Catechism, the subject of

deliberation was to frame an answer to the question, "*What is God?*" Each man felt the unapproachable sublimity of the divine idea suggested by these words; but who could venture to give it expression in human language! All shrunk from the too sacred task in awe-struck reverential fear. At length it was resolved, as an expression of the Committee's deep humility, that the youngest member should first make the attempt. He consented; but begged that the brethren would first unite with him in prayer for divine enlightenment. Then, in slow and solemn accents, he thus began his prayer:— "O God, Thou art a Spirit, infinite, eternal, and unchangeable, in thy being, wisdom, power, holiness, justice, goodness, and truth." When he ceased, the first sentence of his prayer was immediately written down and adopted, as the most perfect answer that could be conceived; as, indeed, in a very sacred sense, God's own answer, descriptive of Himself. The youngest member of that Committee was George Gillespie—the man, therefore, who was thus guided to frame this marvellous answer.— [Presbyterian's Armory, Vol. 1, p. 28.]

2. *Simonides*, a heathen poet, was asked by Hiero, king of ancient Syracuse, *What is God?* but after many days of anxious investigation of the question, he was unable to give a more satisfactory answer than this:—"The more I think of God, he is still the more dark and unknown to me."

3. A dignified clergyman once asked a little boy of an acute mind, "Where God was?" promising an orange upon getting a reply. "Tell me," answered the boy, "where he is not, and I will give you two?"

4. A visitor at the Deaf and Dumb Asylum, in Paris, having proposed to the pupils the question, "What is Eternity?" received from one of them the beautiful reply —"It is the life-time of the Almighty."

II.—*The Oneness of God.*

Q. 5. ARE THERE MORE GODS THAN ONE?

There is but one only, the living and true God.

What Truths are embraced in this Answer?

1. *There is but one God.*—1 *Cor.* viii. 4. There is none other God but one.

2. *God is the only living and true God.*—*Jer.* x. 10. But the Lord is the true God, he is the living God, and an everlasting King.

What Lessons do you derive from the above Doctrines?

I learn (1.) That God is altogether unlike the *things* which the heathen call gods, and which they worship: those gods are many, and are destitute of life; He is alone as God, and not only lives, and always has lived, but He also gave life to all things that have it. (2.) I discover that the heathen are to be greatly pitied for their stupidity as to the worship of God, and need to have the Bible, to teach them that there is but one God, and he a living One. (3.) That there is great occasion for earnest prayer in their behalf, at the Monthly Concert, and at other times. (4.) That I am unspeakably indebted to the grace of God, in casting my lot among those who have the Bible, by which I have been raised above the darkness, and sottishness, and debasement, and perils, of Heathenism.

What Illustrations can you relate?

1. A Hindoo child, about eight years old, who had been instructed in the Christian religion, was ridiculed on that account, by some of his heathen acquaintances, older than himself. In reply, he informed them what he had learned concerning God. "Show us your God!" said they. "I cannot do that," answered the child, "but I can soon

show you yours." Upon which, taking up a stone, and daubing it with some resemblance of a human face, he placed it very gravely upon the ground, "There," said he, "is such a God as you worship."

2. The Rev. *Pliny Fisk*, previous to going out as a Missionary to Palestine, thus examined his own heart:— "*Do I believe there is a God?* My understanding assents to the evidence of his existence; but with my heart and soul do I believe, that there is one Supreme Being who created, who upholds, and who governs all things? I think I am not deceived when I answer, Yes. Much of the time during the past eight years I have had a very different sense of Divine existence, from what I formerly had. I now think of God as a Being, of whose existence I feel as well assured as of my own. I think of Him as the Governor of the universe, and I realize a calm and secret confidence in his government. I never confided so implicitly in my best friend, as I sometimes am enabled to confide in God. He is my Supporter in trouble; my Light in darkness; my Guide in doubt; my Refuge in danger; my Benefactor; my All. This evening I feel a sweet peace in my soul, while I commit whatever respects my education, character, health, life, usefulness, and salvation, to the hands of God. I can place unbounded confidence in his government, and leave all to his disposal."

III.—*The Trinity and unity of the Godhead.*

Q. 6. HOW MANY PERSONS ARE THERE IN THE GODHEAD?

There are three persons in the Godhead, the Father, the Son, and the Holy Ghost; and these three are one God, the same in substance, equal in power and glory.

What Truths are embraced in this Answer?

1. *There are three persons in the Godhead.*—1 *John*, v. 7. For there are three that bear record in heaven, the Father, the Word, and the Holy Ghost.

2. *The Father is God.*—*John*, i. 18. No man hath seen God at any time; the only begotten son, which is in the bosom of the Father, he hath declared him.

3. *The Son is God.*—*Heb.* i. 8. But unto the Son, he saith, Thy throne, O God, is for ever and ever.

4. *The Holy Ghost is God.*—*Acts*, v. 4. (Compared with ver. 3.) Thou hast not lied unto men, but unto God.

5. *The Father, Son, and Holy Ghost are but one God.*—*Deut.* vi. 4. Hear, O Israel; the Lord our God is one Lord.

6. *The Father, Son, and Holy Ghost, though distinct persons, are the same in substance.*—1 *John*, v. 7. These three are one.

7. *The Father, Son, and Holy Ghost, are equal in power.*—*John*, v. 21. As the Father raiseth up the dead, and quickeneth them; even so the Son quickeneth whom he will.

8. *The Father, Son, and Holy Ghost, are equal in glory.*—*Matt.* xxviii. 19. Go ye, therefore, and teach all nations, baptising them in the name of the Father, and of the Son, and of the Holy Ghost.

What Lessons do you derive from the above Doctrines?

I learn (1.) To think of the Godhead as embracing Father, Son, and Holy Spirit, each having the same power, excellence, dignity, and essence, and entitled, therefore, to the same reverence and worship as God. They are so united as to form but one being, yet the Father is God, the Son is God, the Holy Spirit is God. In one sense they are three; in another, and different sense, they are one. "They are *one* in respect to the divine nature; while they are *three* in respect of their mutual and necessary relations to each other, and their relations to men as elected, redeemed, and sanctified. The word *God* is not applied to three separate beings, but to a being which is essentially one, so that each person is God, and all three are but one God." Hence the term *Trinity*, which means Three in One; and the word *Person* is not here to be understood in its ordinary sense, as we apply it to one another. (2.) That in my worship I may address either the Father, or the Son, or the Holy Spirit, according to the parts which these severally perform in relation to the salvation of man; but the more regular method is to call upon the Father, in the name of the Son, and through the gracious aid of the Holy Spirit. (3.) The error of the Jews and of the Turks, who acknowledge only the first person of the Godhead, and thus deny an adequate Redeemer, and Sanctifier. (4.) I discover the great and ruinous error of the Socinians or Unitarians, who consider the Son of God to be only a creature of exalted worth. (5.) The doctrine of the Trinity is above my reason, though not contrary to it, and never could have been known, had not the Scriptures revealed it.

What Illustrations can you relate?

1. The three Persons (or differences in the Divine Nature), were distinguished at Christ's baptism (*Matt.* iii. 17); which made some in ancient times say to those who denied this doctrine, "*Go to Jordan, and there see a Trinity;*" yet though the Father is not the Son, nor the Son the Father, and neither Father nor Son are the Holy Ghost, the three Persons are equally possessed of the one divine nature.

2. The Rev. Thomas Doolittle says:—"May I not, for my admonition, make use of what I have read of AUGUSTINE, who, as he was walking by the sea-side, and meditating on the Trinity, saw a child pouring the water of the sea into a shell having a hole in the midst thereof, and demanded of the child what he was doing? The child said, "I am putting all the sea into this shell." Augustine answered, "Thou playest the child; can a shell,

thinkest thou, comprehend all this sea?" The child replied, "So, good sir, do you, who would by reason comprehend the Trinity." The child vanished. Augustine perceived it was an angel, and was instructed by it, that this doctrine was above the reach of reason.

3. "The renewed man," says *Jeremy Taylor*, "that feels the power of the Father, and to whom the Son is become wisdom, righteousness, sanctification, and redemption—in whose heart the love of the Spirit of God is shed abroad—this man, though he understand nothing of what is unintelligible, yet *he alone truly understands the Christian doctrine of the Trinity.*"

4. The Rev. THOMAS SCOTT, the celebrated commentator on the Scriptures, some years after he became a preacher, thus writes of himself, in his "Force of Truth:"—"The doctrine of a trinity of co-equal persons in the unity of the Godhead, had been hitherto no part of my creed. I had long been accustomed to despise this great mystery of godliness. I had quarelled with the articles of the Established Church about this doctrine; I had been very positive and open in my declarations against it; and my unhumbled reason still retained objections to it. * * * * * * After much reading and meditation upon this subject (afterwards), together with a careful examination of the Scriptures, which I then understood to relate thereto, accompanied with a hearty prayer for Divine teaching, I was at length constrained to renounce, as utterly indefensible, all my former sentiments, and to accede to that doctrine which I had so long despised. I could no longer avoid seeing that the offices and works attributed in Scripture to the Son and Holy Ghost are such as none but the infinite God could perform. * * * * * * And being assured, from reason, as well as from Scripture, that there is not, and cannot be, more Gods than one, I was driven from my reasonings, and constrained to submit my natural understanding to di-

vine revelation; and allowing that the incomprehensible God alone can fully know the unsearchable mysteries of his own Divine nature, and manner of his own existence, to adopt the doctrine of a Trinity in Unity, in order to preserve consistency in my own scheme.".

CHAPTER II.

CONCERNING GOD'S DOINGS WITH RESPECT TO HIS CREATURES.

I.—*Of the nature and character of God's decrees.*

Q. 7. WHAT ARE THE DECREES OF GOD?

The decrees of God are his eternal purpose, according to the counsel of his will, whereby, for his own glory, he hath foreordained whatsoever comes to pass.

What Truths are embraced in this Answer?

1. *God has formed certain purposes and decrees.*—*Eph.* i. 11. Being predestinated according to the purpose of him who worketh all things after the counsel of his own will.

2. *God's purposes were formed in his mind from eternity.* —*Eph.* iii. 11. According to the eternal purpose which he purposed in Christ Jesus our Lord.

3. *God's decrees are exclusively the purposes, or counsels of his own will.*—*Rom.* ix. 18. Therefore hath he mercy on whom he will have mercy, and whom he will he hardeneth.

4. *All things which are agreeable to the counsels or purposes of God have been predestinated by him.*—*Acts*, iv. 28. To do whatsoever thy hand and thy counsel determined before to be done.

What Lessons do you derive from the above Doctrines?

I learn (1.) That the decrees of God are the wise plans which God has always had with respect to what He would himself do, or not hinder to be done by other beings; that these plans were formed by himself alone, and not by the aid or influence of other beings; that He had in view thereby to gain the highest honor to himself; and that whatever takes place among the creatures of God, He determined either to bring about, or not to hinder. (2.) That nothing occurs by chance; that nothing occurs beyond the knowledge or control of God; that nothing occurs differently from what it was certain, according to the settled and wise plan of God, would take place. (3.) That this doctrine of decrees is by no means to be considered as teaching that God is the author of sin; nor that he interferes with the free agency of man, so as to destroy or impair the accountability of man. (4.) I learn, also, that there is nothing in this doctrine to authorize the charges of its opponents, that it implies that God formed a large part of our race on purpose to damn them; that it involves the damnation of infants; and represents the blessed God as an arbitrary, severe, and cruel tyrant. With just abhorrence the Rev. Dr. Green repels these odious charges, and says:—"Whenever you hear Calvinists or Calvinism charged with these, or any similar sentiments, remember that the party who does it is either ignorant or malignant—he either does not know what we believe, or he wilfully misrepresents our sentiments. He draws his own terrific consequences from our principles, and then charges us with them. But we ourselves draw no such consequences; and we earnestly contend that they do not, necessarily or fairly, follow from anything we hold. (5.) I learn that

"Here, not a scene of life comes on—
Of gladness or of tears—

GOD'S DECREES.

Where not the hand of Him that rules
  Our mortal state appears;
Each change that comes of joy or woe,
  Is fixed by heaven's decree—
Nor could we alter aught that God
  Wished from eternity.

"O no, we would not alter aught
  That wisdom hath designed
To train for everlasting bliss
  The wandering, wayward mind.
It is our joy that He we love
  Will be our Judge forever;
Nor aught from his paternal care
  Our interests shall sever."—S. T. SMITH.

What Illustrations can you relate?

1. When King *William the Third* of England was asked, whether he could believe in this doctrine of foreordination, his reply was, "I cannot help believing it: for I cannot degrade my Maker below the character of a wise man, by thinking that he acted without a plan, and without regarding the consequences of what he did."

2. Cowper has truthfully and beautifully said:—

"HAPPY the man, who sees a God employed
In all the good and ill that checker life!
Resolving all events, with their effects
And manifold results, into the will
And arbitration wise of the Supreme.
  Did not his eye rule all things, and intend
The least of our concerns (since from the least
The greatest oft originate); could chance
Find place in his dominion, or dispose
One lawless particle to thwart his plan;
Then God might be surprised, and unforeseen
Contingence might alarm him, and disturb
The smooth and equal course of his affairs."

3 The late Rev. *Samuel Pierce*, in a letter to a friend, thus writes:—"I thank God I never, I think, rejoiced habitually so much in him as I have done of late. I re-

joice that God reigns; that he reigns over all; that he reigns over *me*; over my crosses, my comforts, my family, my friends, my senses, my mental powers, my designs, my words, my preaching, my conduct; that he is God *over all*, blessed for ever.

4. A person in humble circumstances, at Lochwinnoch, whose life had not been consistent with that of a genuine Christian, was nevertheless a great speculator in divinity. Even on his death-bed he was wont to perplex and puzzle himself and his visitors with knotty questions about the doctrines of the Bible. Thomas Orr, a person of a very different character, was sitting at his bedside, endeavoring to turn his attention to what more particularly concerned him: "Ah, William," he said, "this is the *decree* you have at present to do with—'He that believeth shall be saved; he that believeth not shall be damned.'"

II.—*The execution of God's decrees.*

Q. 8. HOW DOTH GOD EXECUTE HIS DECREES?

God executeth his decrees in the works of creation and providence.

What Truths are embraced in this Answer?

1. *God executes his decrees in the works of creation.*—Rev. iv. 11. Thou hast created all things, and for thy pleasure they are and were created.

2. *God executes his decrees in the works of Providence.*—Psal. ciii. 16. His kingdom ruleth over all.

What Lessons do you derive from the above Doctrines?

I learn (1.) That what God always designed, or intended, to do, he actually does in the works of creation and providence. (2.) That, in God's plans, the means as well as the results are embraced, and rendered certain to be employed. (3.) That I can come to a knowledge of

God's decrees, only by the acts which he performs, and by the events which he brings about or suffers to take place, in relation to myself and to other beings.

What Illustration is given?

TROUBLOUS TIMES.—When Whitelocke was embarking, in 1653, for Sweden, he was much disturbed in his mind, as he rested at Harwich on the preceding night, which was stormy, while he reflected on the distracted state of England. It happened that a good and confidential servant slept in an adjacent bed, who, finding that his master could not sleep at length said, "Pray, sir, will you give me leave to ask you a question?" "Certainly." "Pray, sir, don't you think that God governed the world very well before you came into it?" "Undoubtedly." "And pray, sir, don't you think he will govern it quite as well when you are gone out of it?" "Certainly." "Then, sir, don't you think you may trust Him to govern it properly as long as you live?" To this last question Whitelocke had nothing to reply; but turning himself about, soon fell fast asleep, till he was called to embark.

The Creation of the World.

Q. 9. WHAT IS THE WORK OF CREATION?

The work of creation is, God's making all things of nothing, by the word of his power, in the space of six days, and all very good.

What Truths are embraced in this Answer?

1. *God made all things.*—*John*, i. 3. All things were made by him; and without him was not anything made that was made.
2. *God made all things of nothing.*—*Heb.* xi. 3. Through faith we understand that the worlds were framed by the word of God, so that things which are seen were not made of things which do appear.

3. *God made all things by his word.*—*Psal.* xxxiii. 6. By the word of the Lord were the heavens made; and all the host of them by the breath of his mouth.

4. *God made all things in the space of six days.*—*Exod.* xx. 11. In six days the Lord made heaven and earth.

5. *God made all things very good.*—*Gen.* i. 31. And God saw everything that he had made, and behold it was very good.

What Lessons do you derive from the above Doctrines?

I learn (1.) That the work of creation was that of making all things, when as yet there was no material to make them out of; that at the time when he willed them to be, they arose into being; that they were made in the best manner, and fitted to answer the purposes for which God made them. (2.) To adore the almighty power and unsearchable wisdom of God as my Creator, and to look upon all the objects around me with a new interest, considered as his works. (3.) That I am a creature of God, indebted to him for all my powers, and therefore bound to use them in his service; indebted to him for all my sources of enjoyment, and therefore bound to consult his will in all my enjoyments, and to be highly grateful for them to their Great Author. (4.) The great mistake of the ancient Greek philosophers who held that the world always existed. (5.) If God created all things, then it is rational to believe that he can and will perform all that he has promised in his holy word. (6.) Since God hath created all things, they belong to him, and he has therefore a perfect right to dispose of them, and of myself among the rest, as best suits his wise purposes and plans.

What Illustration can you relate?

1. A gentleman being asked to go and examine a magnificent building, erected by a skilful builder, desired to be excused and to remain where he was, looking on a flower which he was admiring—"For," said he, "I see

more of God in this flower, than in all the beautiful edifices in the world."

2. We are told that *Plato*, the Greek philosopher, was convinced of the existence of a Deity, upon observing that all the world could not make even so insignificant a creature as a fly.

3. *Dean Swift* (borrowing the idea from Cicero) says, that he will no more believe that the universe was formed by a fortuitous concourse of atoms, than that the accidental jumbling of the letters of the alphabet would fall by chance into an ingenious and learned treatise of philosophy.

The Creation of Man.

Q. 10. How did God create man?

God created man male and female, after his own image, in knowledge, righteousness, and holiness, with dominion over the creatures.

What Truths are embraced in this answer?

1. *God created man.*—Gen. i. 7. The Lord God formed man of the dust of the ground, and breathed into his nostrils the breath of life.

2. *Man was created male and female.*—Gen. i. 27. Male and female created he them.

3. *Man was created in the image of God.*—Gen. i. 27. God created man in his own image, in the image of God created he him.

4. *God's image in man consisted in knowledge.*—Col. iii. 10. And have put on the new man, which is renewed in knowledge, after the image of him that created him.

5. *God's image in man consisted in righteousness.*—Eccles. vii. 29. God hath made man upright; but they have sought out many inventions.

6. *God's image in man consisted in holiness.*—Eph. iv. 24. Put on the new man, which after God is created in righteousness and true holiness.

7. *God created man with dominion over the creatures.*—

Gen. i. 28. And God blessed them, and God said unto them, Be fruitful, and multiply, and replenish the earth, and subdue it; and have dominion over the fish of the sea, and over the fowl of the air, and over every living thing that moveth upon the earth.

What Lessons do you derive from the above Doctrines?

I learn (1.) That Adam and Eve were made like God in respect to the knowledge which he gave them, and their being right in all their feelings and thoughts; their being free from all disposition to do wrong; and also in their being placed at the head of all the other creatures on earth, and exercising authority over them. (2.) To praise God for the high rank and great excellence which he gave to man at his first creation. (3.) That it is my duty to pursue an upright and worthy course of conduct. (4.) That sin has produced a sad change in man's character and mode of life.

What Illustration can you relate?

I will draw it from Pollok's "Course of Time"— Book I.

> BUT MAN He made of angel form erect,
> To hold communion with the heavens above,
> And on his soul impressed his image fair,
> His own similitude of holiness,
> Of virtue, truth, and love; with reason high
> To balance right and wrong, and conscience quick
> To choose or to reject; with knowledge great,
> Prudence and wisdom, vigilance and strength,
> To guard all force or guile; and last of all,
> The highest gift of God's abundant grace,
> With perfect, free, unbiased will. Thus man
> Was made upright, immortal made, and crowned
> The king of all; to eat, to drink, to do
> Freely and sovereignly his will entire;
> By one command alone restrained, to prove,
> As was most just, his filial love sincere,
> His loyalty, obedience due, and faith."

God's general Providence.

Q. 11. WHAT ARE GOD'S WORKS OF PROVIDENCE?

God's works of Providence are, his most holy, wise, and powerful preserving and governing all his creatures, and all their actions.

What Truths are embraced in this Answer?

1. *God preserves all his creatures.—Psal.* cxlv. 15. The eyes of all wait upon thee: and thou givest them their meat in due season.
2. *God governs all his creatures.—Psal.* ciii. 19. His kingdom ruleth over all.
3. *God directs and governs all the actions of his creatures.—Prov.* xvi. 9. A man's heart deviseth his way: but the Lord directeth his steps.
4. *God's works of providence are most holy.—Psal.* cxlv. 17. The Lord is righteous in all his ways, and holy in all his works.
5. *God's works of providence are most wise.—Isa.* xxviii. 29. The Lord of hosts, which is wonderful in counsel, and excellent in working.
6. *God's works of providence are most powerful.—Psal* lxvi. 7. He ruleth by his power for ever.

What Lessons do you derive from the above Doctrines?

I learn (1.) That there is no such thing as blind fate; that there is a divine agency which guides, and protects, and governs; that it reaches to all places, beings, and events. (2.) To commit myself and all other creatures to the care and guidance of my Creator, and to endeavor at all times to act in obedience to his supreme will. (3.) That events which seem accidental, are nevertheless ordered by the Lord, as when the Bible informs us (1 *Kings,* xxii. 34) of a certain man who drew a bow at a venture, and smote the king of Israel between the joints of the harness. God's providence directed the arrow to the mark. (4.) That the providence of God is merely the accomplishment of his eternal purposes concerning his creatures, and that all the circumstances of my life are regulated by his wisdom and power. Hence (5.) I must not murmur or complain when affliction befalls me, nor be ungrateful to God when he prospers me and gladdens me in my course. (6.) That the cause of religion—the church of Christ—is safe. (7.) That even the wickedness of man is overruled for good, as in the case of the envy of Joseph's brethren, the crucifixion of our Saviour, and the sensuality of Henry VIII. of England.

What Illustrations can you give?

1. There is a habit of saying, "Such a thing will TURN UP," as if it depended on chance; whereas nothing will turn up but what has been ordered. When a man becomes a Christian, he is written upon, "TO BE PROVIDED FOR," and he ought, therefore, to notice, as he goes on, how Providence does provide for him.

2. When the Protestants in Rochelle were besieged by the French king, God, by his providence, sent in a number of small fishes that fed them, such as were never seen before in that harbor.

3. The raven, a bird that has not natural affection enough to feed its own young, yet providentially carried nourishment to the Hebrew prophet Elijah.

4. The Book of Esther details a series of the most wonderful providences in behalf of the Jewish people, when in great danger of a universal massacre.

5. The Rev. Richard Cecil has correctly observed, that "we are too apt to forget our actual dependence on Providence, for the circumstances of every instant. The most trivial events may determine our state in the world. Turning up one street instead of another, may bring us into company with a person whom we should not otherwise have met; and this may lead to a train of other

events, which may determine the happiness or misery of our lives."

6. OVERRULING PROVIDENCE.—"All these things are against me," thought good old Jacob, when he exclaimed in the bitterness of his soul, "Joseph is not, Simeon is not, and will ye take Benjamin away?" And it did seem as if these bereavements would "bring down his gray hairs with sorrow to the grave." But it was all cleared up when "he saw the wagons" which Joseph had sent to carry him and all his numerous family down to Egypt, and save them alive, during the terrible seven years' famine. So Joseph himself must have thought, when his brethren cast him into the pit; when they sold him as a slave to the Ishmaelites; and when, upon the false charge of an adulterous woman, he was thrown into prison, without any hope of relief, or any prospect of it, except by a violent and ignominious death. But how was it, when he found himself suddenly raised to the vice-royalty of Egypt, and that God had sent him down to preserve the life of his venerable father, and of the very brethren who had so cruelly sold him to the passing caravan? "All things are against us," undoubtedly, thought our Puritan ancestors, when they were persecuted from city to city, and could find no secure resting-place short of this great Western wilderness; but God sent his angel before them, and what glorious foundations of civil and religious liberty did they lay upon these shores, for the building up of a great nation. We see in all these and numberless other striking examples, how much better care God takes of his people than they could take of themselves, and how he overrules the most adverse and trying events for their highest good. Indeed, this is a matter of every-day experience. Almost any person who has arrived at the age of forty, can recollect times when his favorite plans were thwarted, and it did seem as if the course of Providence was against him, when, as it proved in the end, it

was all in his favor, and saved him from losses or calamities, in which the carrying out of his plans would inevitably have involved him.—*Dr. Humphrey.*

THE SPECIAL PROVIDENCE OF GOD TOWARDS MAN IN HIS CREATION AND FALL.

Covenant of Works—Its Parties and Terms.

Q. 12. WHAT SPECIAL ACT OF PROVIDENCE DID GOD EXERCISE TOWARD MAN IN THE ESTATE WHEREIN HE WAS CREATED?

When God had created man, he entered into a covenant of life with him upon condition of perfect obedience; forbidding him to eat of the tree of the knowledge of good and evil, upon the pain of death.

What Truths are embraced in this Answer?

1. *God entered into a covenant with Adam.*—Hos. vi. 7. *With Margin.* They like Adam have transgressed the covenant.
2. *The terms of the covenant of works were perfect obedience.*—Gen. iii. 3. God hath said, ye shall not eat of it, neither shall ye touch it.
3. *Obedience was required from our first parents under the pain of death.*—Gen. ii. 17. In the day that thou eatest thereof, thou shalt surely die.

What Lessons do you derive from the above Doctrines?

I learn (1.) That soon after the first man was created, God made a law that he should not eat of a certain tree, called *the Tree of the Knowledge of Good and Evil;* that to secure his obedience to this law, God threatened that the greatest evil, namely death, would come upon him should he fail to keep it; that it would thus be understood, that while he continued obedient, he should enjoy life and all the benefits of his Creator's approbation and love. (2.) That this law, with its threatenings and implied promise of life, is called a *Covenant of Life*, that is, *an agreement* by which life and happiness would have been permanently secured to our first parents had they continued to obey this particular command—a command most easy to be kept, and for transgressing which no excuse can be made.

[This arrangement, proposed to our first parents as the one party, by God as the other, is sometimes called the *Covenant of Works*, because it was a method of securing the perpetual favor of God by the *works* or doings (in reference to this law) of our first parents, and is distinguished from the *Covenant of Grace*, or the method of securing God's favor simply on the ground of what Christ has done and suffered for us.]

I learn (3.) That my highest duty is to obey God, as my sovereign Lord, in every particular, and that this is perfectly reasonable. (4.) That happiness or misery is appointed to follow my actions according to their nature. This tree derives its name, from the fact that Adam would come to a knowledge of the *good* of innocence on his losing it, and of the *evil* of disobedience by the sufferings to which he then should become liable.

Man's Disobedience and Fall.

Q. 13. DID OUR FIRST PARENTS CONTINUE IN THE ESTATE WHEREIN THEY WERE CREATED?

Our first parents being left to the freedom of their own will, fell from the estate wherein they were created, by sinning against God.

What Truths are embraced in this Answer?

1. *Our first parents were left to the freedom of their own will.*—Gen. iii. 13. And the woman said, The serpent beguiled me, and I did eat.

2. *Man by sin fell from the estate in which he was created* —Rom. v. 12. By one man sin entered into the world, and death by sin.

What Lessons do you derive from the above Doctrines?

I learn (1.) That our first parents being allowed to choose for themselves whether they would obey or disobey the particular law which God had given them, chose to disobey it, and thus ceased to be the holy and the happy beings which previously they were, for they had thus become sinners, and had fallen from a state of innocence and happiness. Their moral character was changed. (2.) That disobedience to God is a bad thing for me as well as for others, and that in all cases I must guard against and avoid it. (3.) That I must never cease to watch against the power of temptation; for, by neglecting this, our first parents became sinners.

What Illustration can you relate?

THE DIFFICULTIES OF SCRIPTURE.—An old man once said, "For a long period I puzzled myself about the difficulties of Scripture, until at last I came to the resolution that reading the Bible was like *eating fish*. When I find a difficulty, I lay it aside and call it a *bone*. Why should I choke on the bone, when there is much nutritious meat to use? Some day, perhaps, I may find that even the bones may afford me nourishment."

The Nature of Sin.

Q. 14. WHAT IS SIN?

Sin is any want of conformity unto, or transgression of the law of God.

What Truths are embraced in this answer?

1. *Any want of conformity to God's law is sin.*—*Gal.* iii. 10. Cursed is every one that continueth not in all things which are written in the book of the law to do them.

2. *Any transgression of the law of God is sin.*—1 *John,* iii. 4. Sin is the transgression of the law.

THE NATURE OF SIN.

What Lessons do you derive from the above Doctrines?

I learn (1.) That a refusing, or even a neglect to think, to feel, and to do as God in his law requires, is sin; that sin is also committed when I think, feel, or act differently from what God requires. (2.) That it is my solemn duty and interest carefully to study the Bible (which is God's law), that I may be ignorant of nothing which he requires of me, and do nothing which he forbids. (3.) I learn the great evil of sin: it involves direct opposition to the greatest and best of beings, of whose just and beneficial law it is a violation.

What Illustrations may be cited?

1. It is reported of the Emperor PHOCAS, that having built a wall of prodigious strength around his city, a voice was heard proclaiming: "Sin is within the city, and that will throw down the wall."

2. SATAN AND THE SINNER.—The Rev. JOHN NEWTON said of a certain clergyman, that he had never heard him preach but once; on which occasion he had observed, "If you wish to know what a sinner is, he is a young devil; and if you wish to know what a devil is, he is an old sinner."

3. The last audible prayer of the good Archbishop USHER, was: "Lord forgive my sins, especially my sins of *omission*."

4. It was a remarkable trait in the character of COUNT GODOMAR, according to his own oft-repeated declaration, that *he feared nothing in the world more than sin*, and whatever liberties he had taken in earlier life, he would suffer any form of violent death rather than knowingly or willingly commit any sin against God.

5. DOING NOTHING.—"He made me out a sinner for doing nothing!" said one under the conviction of sin, and who, in a revival, had been asked, "How were you

awakened ?" It was a new thought to the poor man, who had been comforting himself with the plea that he had done nothing very bad. But now he saw that his greatest sin was the very thing in which he had been comforting himself—*doing nothing.*

Adam's Sin, in particular.

Q. 15. WHAT WAS THE SIN WHEREBY OUR FIRST PARENTS FELL FROM THE ESTATE WHEREIN THEY WERE CREATED ?

The sin whereby our first parents fell from the estate wherein they were created, was their eating the forbidden fruit.

What Truths are embraced in this Answer ?

1. *The first and particular sin of Adam was eating the forbidden fruit.—Gen.* iii. 6. She took of the fruit thereof, and did eat; and gave also unto her husband with her, and he did eat.

2. *Eating the forbidden fruit was the cause of Adam's fall.—Rom.* v. 17. By one man's offence death reigned by one.

What Lessons do you derive from the above Doctrines ?

I learn (1.) That in small matters as well as in great, I may show whether I have a spirit of obedience to God, or otherwise. (2.) That I must indulge in nothing that God has forbidden. (3.) That the enormity of the first sin does not appear in looking at the mere outward act performed, but at all the circumstances of the case and consequences. Hence (4.) I learn to beware of, and watch against sin, though it may at first appear to be insignificant. (5.) That, like our first parents, I am exposed to be tempted by Satan, to the ruin of my character and happiness. (6.) That I cannot trust my own powers for obeying God or resisting temptation, but must depend on the grace of God as revealed in Jesus Christ to penitent sinners.

What Illustrations can you relate?

1. The Rev. Thomas Doolittle occupies more than nineteen large folio pages to show the greatness of this first sin, however trivial it may seem to a careless and worldly mind. He shows its greatness (1.) By the ten sins of the woman, which went before the eating of that fruit. (2.) By ten sins of Adam and Eve included in it. (3.) By ten great evils, to them and their descendants, that followed after it. (4.) By ten aggravating circumstances attending it. (5.) By the Ten Commandments all being broken by it.

2. "There are FOUR THINGS," says Philip Henry, "we must not make a mock of—Sin (*Prov.* xiv. 9), people's natural infirmities, the Word of God, and good people."

3. In the West Indies there is said to grow a tree of very attractive appearance, bearing a kind of fruit resembling the golden pippin. It is beautiful to the eye, and fragrant, but, when eaten, produces instant death. So poisonous is the juice of it that the Indians dip the points of their arrows in it for the purpose of poisoning their enemies when they wound them. It is remarkable that in the neighborhood of this fatal tree is always found, through the kind providence of God, a white wood, or a fig tree, the juice of either of which, if applied soon, is an antidote to the poisonous influence of the tree first spoken of—the Manchaneel. This latter may be regarded as a symbol of the pleasing but destructive nature of sin; while the other trees symbolize the precious Word of Christ, which God in his mercy has provided as the only antidote.

The Extent of the Fall.

Q. 16. DID ALL MANKIND FALL IN ADAM'S FIRST TRANSGRESSION?

The covenant being made with Adam, not only for himself, but for his posterity; all mankind, descending from him by ordinary generation, sinned in him, and fell with him, in his first transgression.

What Truths are embraced in this Answer?

1. *The covenant of works was made for the posterity of Adam as well as for himself.—Rom.* v. 14. Nevertheless, death reigned from Adam to Moses, even over them that had not sinned after the similitude of Adam's transgression, who is the figure of him that was to come.

2. *All men are the descendants of Adam and Eve.—Gen.* iii. 20. And Adam called his wife's name Eve, because she was the mother of all living.

3. *All men being the children of Adam sinned in him.— Rom.* v. 12. By one man sin entered into the world, and death by sin; and so death passed upon all men, for that all have sinned.

4. *All men fell with Adam.—*1 *Cor.* xv. 22. In Adam all die.

What Lessons do you derive from the above Doctrines?

I learn (1.) That the covenant, or law, given to Adam, in Paradise, was designed to affect not only himself, but likewise all who should come after him in the ordinary mode of birth; so that if Adam had done what God required of him in that law, or covenant, all the human race would have been thereby rendered obedient to God, and happy; but on the other hand, his disobedience would render them as a race disobedient and miserable. (2.) Deeply to lament Adam's first sin as the beginning and occasion of all the numberless sins that have since been committed on earth, and as the occasion of our loss of all the unmixed happiness and holiness we would have enjoyed as a race, if Adam had not transgressed the law under which, as a means of trial, God had placed him, and us virtually through him.

" Man sinned: tempted, he ate the guarded tree:
Audacious, unbelieving, proud, ungrateful,
He ate the interdicted fruit, and fell;

And in his fall, his universal race;
For they in him by delegation were,
In him to stand or fall—to live or die."—POLLOK.

What Illustrations can you relate?

1. THE ORIGIN OF SIN.—Two American divines were once conversing together about the various theories concerning the origin of sin, when one interrupted them by saying, "It seems to me that it would be far better for ministers, instead of puzzling themselves to know how sin ENTERED INTO the world, to unite their efforts, and try how much of it, with God's blessing, they can drive out." "You remind me, madam," said one of the clergymen, "of my aged deacon, who, after listening to a sermon, in which I had endeavored to explain why God suffered sin to enter the world, being asked what he thought of my theory, shook his head, and replied, "Ah, sir, all I know about it is, I am a sinner, and WISH I WASN'T."

2. "The fact is plain," says Pliny Fisk, "that God governs the world, and controls every event; and yet the world is full of sin and woe. I cannot discover the reasons why it is so; though I can see that by this means God will have an opportunity to make manifest his abhorrence of sin, his justice, and his mercy. Had it not been so, there had been no displays of punitive justice, no ransomed sinners, no bleeding Saviour, no songs of redeeming love in heaven. Still, much darkness overspreads the subject. Restless curiosity starts many questions, to which no answer can be found. Is my heart, nevertheless, filled with love to this Supreme Governor, 'whose judgments are unsearchable, and whose ways are past finding out?'"

Consequences of the Fall.

Q. 17. INTO WHAT ESTATE DID THE FALL BRING MANKIND?

The fall brought mankind into an estate of sin and misery.

What Truths are embraced in this Answer?

1. *The fall of Adam brought mankind into an estate of sin.*—*Rev.* v. 7. By one man's disobedience many were made sinners.

2. *The fall of Adam brought mankind into an estate of misery.*—*Rom.* v. 17. By one man's offence death reigned by one.

What Lesson do you derive from the above Doctrines?

I learn to abhor and dread sin, as the greatest of all evils—as that which "brought death into the world, and all our woe."

What Illustration is given?

WHAT IS OUR OWN?—A heathen girl was once asked by her teacher if there was anything which she could call her own. She hesitated for a moment, and then, looking up, replied:—"I think there is." "What is it?" inquired the teacher, with some surprise. "I think," said the girl, "that my sins are my own." And this is the conclusion of the whole matter.—*Day Spring.*

Sinfulness of Man's State by the Fall.

Q. 18. WHEREIN CONSISTS THE SINFULNESS OF THAT ESTATE WHEREINTO MAN FELL?

The sinfulness of that estate whereinto man fell, consists in the guilt of Adam's first sin, the want of original righteousness, and the corruption of his whole nature, which is commonly called Original Sin; together with all actual transgressions which proceed from it.

What Truths are embraced in this Answer?

1. *The sinfulness of our fallen state consists in the guilt of Adam's first sin.*—*Rom.* v. 18. By the offence of one, judgment came upon all men to condemnation.

SINFULNESS OF MAN'S STATE BY THE FALL. 55

2. *The sinfulness of our fallen state consists in the want of original righteousness.*—*Rom.* iii. 10. There is none righteous, no, not one.

3. *The sinfulness of our fallen state consists in the corruption of our whole nature or of original sin.*—*Psal.* li.5. Behold, I was shapen in iniquity; and in sin did my mother conceive me.

4. *The sinfulness of our fallen nature is shown in our actual transgressions.*—*Eccles.* vii. 20. There is not a just man upon earth, that doeth good, and sinneth not.

5. *Actual transgressions proceed from original sin.*—*Mark*, vii. 21. For from within, out of the heart of men, proceed evil thoughts, adulteries, fornications, murders, &c.

What Lessons do you derive from the above Doctrines?

I learn that the sinfulness which man has acquired through Adam includes (1.) Our liability to suffering, or to be treated as transgressors on his account, as our representative. (2.) That we are born destitute of that pious and righteous state of mind which Adam had when God first made him. (3.) That we are naturally prone to make a wrong and wicked use of our minds and bodies. (4.) That the sinfulness thus far described, is called *Original Sin,* because we have it at our origin or birth. (5.) That as a consequence of this we actually transgress the law of God from day to day (when left to ourselves). (6.) That the "guilt of Adam's sin" is a phrase used in a peculiar, and not in a common sense; that it does not mean that I am to blame for Adam's first sin; yet I am to blame for all my own sins, though committed by me, as a result of that first sin. (7.) The necessity of my being "born again," or of receiving from God an entirely new state of mind and feeling, that my actions may be made to conform to the law of God. (8.) What is meant by the doctrine that man is *totally depraved.* It is not that all men are alike sinful; nor that any man is as bad as he can be; but that *all the human powers are depraved* by sin; and that every person, by nature, is *entirely destitute of holiness*—that state of mind which is essential to the acceptable service of God. At the same time, this doctrine does not deny that men, by nature, may possess some very amiable and useful characteristics.

What Illustration can you relate?

A CAVILLER once asked the shrewd Dr. Nettleton, "How came I by my wicked heart?" "That," he replied, "is a question which does not concern you so much as another, namely: how you should get rid of it. You have a wicked heart, which renders you entirely unfit for the kingdom of God; and you must have a new heart, or you cannot be saved; and the question which now most deeply concerns you, is, how you shall obtain it?" As the man manifested no wish to hear anything on that subject, but still pressed the question how he came by his wicked heart, Dr. Nettleton told him that his condition resembled that of a man who is drowning, while his friends are attempting to save his life. As he rises to the surface of the water, he exclaims, "How came I here?" "That question does not concern you now; take hold of this rope." "But how came I here?" he asks again. "I shall not stop to answer that question now," replies his friend. "Then I'll drown," says the infatuated man, and, spurning all proffered aid, sinks to the bottom.

Misery of Man's State by the Fall.

Q. 19. WHAT IS THE MISERY OF THAT ESTATE WHEREINTO MAN FELL?

All mankind, by their fall, lost communion with God, are under his wrath and curse, and so made liable to all the miseries in this life, to death itself, and to the pains of hell for ever.

MISERY OF MAN'S STATE BY THE FALL.

What Truths are embraced in this Answer?

1. *All men, since the fall, hate God and have lost communion with him.—Rom.* viii. 7. The carnal mind is enmity against God.

2. *Man, by nature, is under the wrath of God.—Eph.* ii. 3. And were by nature the children of wrath, even as others.

3. *Man, by nature, is under the curse of God.—Gal.* iii. 10. For as many as are of the works of the law, are under the curse.

4. *Man, by the fall, is made liable to all the miseries of this life.—Job,* v. 7. Man is born unto trouble, as the sparks fly upward.

5. *Man, by the fall, is made liable to death.—Rom.* vi. 23. The wages of sin is death.

6. *Man, by the fall, is made liable to the pains of hell.—Psal.* ix. 17. The wicked shall be turned into hell, and all the nations that forget God.

7. *The pains of hell shall be for ever.—Isa.* xxxiii. 14. Who among us shall dwell with everlasting burnings?

What Lessons do you derive from the above Doctrines?

I learn (1.) That the wretchedness of that state into which sin has brought me, lies in two things:—First, I have lost the happiness of friendly intercourse with God. Secondly, I am brought under his great displeasure, and a sentence to punishment, which begins to be carried out against me in the pains and troubles of the present life, is continued in the agonies of death, and, if fully carried out, will subject me to the everlasting pains of the world to come. (2.) That all the miseries in life, in death, and in hell, are the result simply of sin, which may thus be seen to be the chief of evils, and never should be thought of as a trifling matter (3.) That my first care should be to seek to be set free from sin, and from all its just but terrible consequences. (4.) That I should welcome, and embrace at once, the offer of deliverance through the Lord Jesus Christ. (5.) That although sorrow, in various forms, comes indiscriminately upon the righteous and the wicked in this life, yet the Scriptures teach me that to the righteous these sorrows are converted into fatherly chastisements from God, tending to their spiritual good; whereas, to the wicked, they are of the nature of punishment for their sins, and are the forerunners of eternal sorrow.

What Illustrations may be given?

1. AN AGED CLERGYMAN, when preaching in New England, some few years since, raising his voice with each succeeding word, and bringing down his clenched hand with amazing force upon the Bible at the last word of the sentence, exclaimed—"A deceitful, wicked man is not fit to serve either God, man, or the devil!" Then, after a pause, he added, "And I'll tell you why. He is not fit to serve God, because he is unholy; he is not fit to serve man, because he is deceitful; and he is not fit to serve the devil, because he's not content with his wages. No," said the old man, "*he's not content with his wages.* No, no, my friends, the sinner is not satisfied with the wages which the devil gives, and he never will be—'for *the wages of sin is death!*' Sinners! sinners! strike for higher wages."

2. Mrs. SUSAN HUNTINGTON, of Boston, in a letter to a friend, thus writes:—"I am afraid I have never been brought truly to submit all things to the disposal of God, especially to submit to his *righteousness in the condemnation of sinners.* I fear I have never yet seen aught of the dreadful evil of sin, and that this is the source of the *misgivings I sometimes experience as to its just desert of eternal punishment.* But Jehovah *is,* I know he is, righteous in all his ways, and holy in all his works; and he has said that the wicked shall be turned into hell, where the worm dieth not, and the fire shall never be quenched.' Hush, then, every murmuring, doubting thought, every rebellious discontented feeling! Oh, for deeper views of *the vileness, the exceeding vileness of sin—*

for stronger and more abiding confidence in the rectitude and the goodness of God!"

3. A pious member of Rev. Mr. James' church, in Birmingham, amid the severe sufferings of her last sickness, said to her husband:—"I could not have thought that any one could have suffered so much, and yet live, and if God inflicts such sufferings upon his own children, what must the pains of hell be to the wicked! O, sin! sin! Remember, all sorrow and suffering are the fruits and effects of sin. I cannot think what the wicked do on a death-bed, when the horrors of the mind are added to the pains of the body."

4. THE MISERY OF THE HEATHEN.—A missionary, speaking of the Hindoos, says:—"They traverse the burning plains, and sandy deserts, and fatal jungles of Hindostan, for thousands of miles, measuring their way through mud and water by the length of their bodies, to bathe in some sacred stream, with the vain hope of washing away their sins, or of beholding the car of Juggernaut. They stretch themselves on planks pierced with sharp iron spikes, and there lie till the blood oozes from every pore. They suspend themselves from large iron hooks, thrust through the muscles of the back, and there sometimes hang until life is extinct. They pierce their tongues with spears, and are led about for hours by the inserted weapon. Yet, after enduring all these modes of torture, I have heard them exclaim:—'*We have no peace,—we have not yet found God,*—where is he, that we may find him?'"

5. Damocles ascended the throne of Sicily at the bidding of the tyrant Dionysius; but while he gazed with delight upon the splendor and wealth that surrounded him, on looking up he perceived a sword hanging over his head by a single hair—a sight that filled him with terror, and made all his expected happiness to vanish. So the sword of God's wrath hangs by a small thread

over every impenitent and careless sinner, and should alarm him, and lead him to abandon his sinful condition.

OF THE SPECIAL PROVIDENCE OF GOD TOWARDS MAN IN REDEMPTION.

Plan of Redemption.

Q. 20. DID GOD LEAVE ALL MANKIND TO PERISH IN THE ESTATE OF SIN AND MISERY?

God having out of his mere good pleasure, from all eternity, elected some to everlasting life, did enter into a covenant of grace, to deliver them out of the estate of sin and misery, and to bring them into an estate of salvation by a Redeemer.

What Truths are embraced in this Answer?

1. *God has ordained, or elected some men to everlasting life.*—*Acts*, xiii. 48. As many as were ordained to eternal life, believed.

2. *God's purpose of election was from eternity.*—*Eph.* i. 4. According as he hath chosen us in him before the foundation of the world.

3. *The election of God is the result of his own good pleasure.*—*Eph.* i. 5. Having predestinated us unto the adoption of children by Jesus Christ to himself, according to the good pleasure of his will.

4. *God entered into a covenant of grace with Christ for the elect.*—*Psal.* lxxxix. 3. I have made a covenant with my chosen.

5. *The people of God are by Christ delivered out of their original state of sin and misery.*—*Rom.* viii. 1. There is therefore now no condemnation to them which are in Christ Jesus, who walk not after the flesh but after the Spirit.

6. *The people of God, by Christ, are brought into a state of complete salvation.*—*Rom.* v. 18. By the righteousness of one, the free gift came upon all men unto justification of life.

What Lessons do you derive from the above Doctrines?

I learn (1.) That God is so merciful that he does not leave, as justly he might, all men to perish in their state of sinfulness, but has ever designed to save some of them by means of a Redeemer: has not only determined with himself to save, by Christ, all those who do believe, obey, and persevere unto the end, but has also appointed who those persons shall be, that he will cause to believe, obey, and persevere. (2.) That the plan he has adopted for this end is called the *Covenant of Grace*, because the safety and happiness thus provided are not in the least degree deserved by any man. (3.) I am to understand that a *Redeemer* is one who frees persons from punishment, and brings them into a happy condition, by suffering the penalty due to them, or performing some service which they were not in a condition to render. (4.) That if I am saved, I shall be altogether indebted to the compassion and grace of God, against whom I have sinned, having no right to salvation, but being exposed justly, for my sins, to everlasting misery. (5.) That God did not elect or choose any because he foresaw that they would believe in Christ, and persevere in religion; but the true doctrine is, that those who believe and persevere, do so because God had chosen them to salvation, and therefore inclined and enabled them to enter upon and pursue the Christian life. Their faith and holy life were not the *cause* of election, but the *result* of it.

How may these Doctrines be Illustrated?

1. A pious old woman, in Albany, once remarked, concerning the doctrine of predestination, "Ah, I have long settled that point, for if God had not chosen me before I was born, I am sure he would have seen nothing in me afterward, to have chosen me for."

2. JONATHAN EDWARDS.—"From my childhood up," says

he, "my mind had been full of objections against the *doctrines of God's sovereignty*, in choosing whom he would to eternal life, and rejecting whom he pleased, leaving them eternally to perish, and be everlastingly tormented in hell. It used to appear a horrible doctrine to me. But I remember the time very well, when I seemed to be convinced and fully satisfied as to this sovereignty of God, and *his justice* in thus eternally disposing of men according to his sovereign pleasure. But I never could give an account how, or by what means, I was thus convinced; not in the least imagining at the time that there was any extraordinary influence of God's Spirit in it. However, my mind rested in it; and it put an end to all these cavils and objections."

3. A UNIVERSALIST MINISTER was travelling, and, agreeably to a notice sent on, preached in a certain place the Doctrine of Universal Salvation. After the sermon, he informed his hearers that he should be that way on his return, at such a time, and, if they desired it, he would preach again. No one replied till he had twice repeated the statement. At last, an old *Friend*, in the back part of the congregation, rose, and said, "If thee hast told the truth this time, we do not *need* thee any more, and if thee hast told us a lie, we do not *want* thee any more"—an answer which, although somewhat grotesque, was yet very much to the purpose.

4. A certain individual said to the Rev. Dr. Nettleton, "I cannot get along with the doctrine of election." "Then," said he, "get along without it. You are at liberty to get to heaven the easiest way you can. Whether the doctrine of election is true or not, it is true that you must repent, and believe, and love God. Now, what we tell you is, that such is the wickedness of your heart, that you never will do these things, unless God has determined to renew your heart. If you do not believe

that your heart is so wicked, make it manifest by complying with the terms of salvation. Why do you stand cavilling with the doctrine of election? Suppose you should prove it to be false; what have you gained? You must repent and believe in Christ after all. Why do you not immediately comply with these terms of the gospel? When you have done this, without the aids of divine grace, it will be soon enough to oppose the doctrine of election. Until you shall have done this, we shall still believe that the doctrine of election lies at the foundation of all hope in your case."

5. To a man, who manifested great opposition to the doctrine of election, he once said, "If I should go to heaven, I feel as if I should wish to say, in the language of the apostle, 'Who hath saved us and called us with an holy calling; not according to our works, but according to his own purpose and grace, which were given us in Christ Jesus, before the world began.' Now, if we should meet in heaven, and I should make use of this language, will you quarrel with me there?"

The Person and Character of the Redeemer.

Q. 21. WHO IS THE REDEEMER OF GOD'S ELECT?

The only Redeemer of God's elect is the Lord Jesus Christ, who, being the eternal Son of God, became man, and so was, and continueth to be, God and man, in two distinct natures, and one person for ever.

What Truths are embraced in this answer?

1. *Christ, the Son of God, is the Redeemer of his people.* —*Gal.* iv. 4. 5. God sent forth his Son, made of a woman, made under the law, to redeem them that were under the law.

2. *Christ is the only Redeemer of man.—Acts,* iv. 12. Neither is there salvation in any other.

3. *Christ is the Son of God.—*1 *John,* v. 20. We know that the Son of God is come.

4. *Christ is the eternal Son of God.—Heb.* i. 8. Unto the Son, he saith, Thy throne, O God, is for ever and ever.

5. *Christ became man.—Heb.* ii. 16. He took not on him the nature of angels: but he took on him the seed of Abraham.

6. *Christ is both God and man.—*1 *Tim.* iii. 16. And without controversy, great is the mystery of godliness: God was manifest in the flesh.

7. *Christ possesses the natures of God and man in one person.—Col.* ii. 9. For in him dwelleth all the fulness of the Godhead bodily.

8. *Christ will continue to be both God and man for ever.— Heb.* vii. 24. But this man, because he continueth ever, hath an unchangeable priesthood.

What Lessons do you derive from the above Doctrines?

I learn (1.) That the only Redeemer of those whom God has chosen to bring to heaven, is the Lord Jesus Christ, who, having always been the Son of God, at the appointed and proper time also became man, and so was, and continues to be, and ever will be, God and man,—the divine and human natures not being mixed, but merely united, so as to form one person. Each nature retains its own properties; those of the one nature are not to be ascribed to the other nature, but those of both belong alike to the person of Christ, the Redeemer. (2.) That God the Son has greatly humbled himself by this union to the man Jesus, for the purpose of saving me and other sinners, and that the wonderful and altogether singular constitution of his person is worthy of my deepest study and worship. Hence, I learn (3.) The great error of those professed Christians who assert that Jesus is not God, but a man only, or at best possessed of some higher nature than the human, though still lower than that of the

PERSON AND CHARACTER OF THE REDEEMER.

Supreme God. (4.) That my natural state is that of slavery—to sin—to the world—to Satan—to death and hell, from all which to deliver me the blessed Saviour, God-man, gave his own life as a ransom, or price of redemption. Finally, that I am under the most pressing obligations to free myself from that degrading slavery, by accepting gratefully and ardently of the deliverance which the Redeemer has thus provided for sinners.

What Illustrations are at hand?

At a weekly meeting for religious conversation, some *South Sea Island* converts (as Rev. John Williams informs us) thus talked with each other concerning Christ: "Give us some other proof that he was God," said another. "The various miracles that he wrought," was the reply. "But did not Peter and all the apostles work miracles?" "Yes, but they did their miracles with borrowed power; and when they returned, did they not tell Jesus that they did all in his name, and not in their own?" Another said, "Is not the star that led the wise men from the East a proof of the divinity of Jesus?" "But, if really God, would he have been laid in a manger?" "Yes, said another, for did he not humble himself and lay aside his glory as God? If he had come in his glory, would not man have exceedingly feared? We know what Moses said." Another said, "He believed he was God, because he said, 'I and my Father are one; and I am the Alpha and Omega, the First and the Last.'" Another believed it "because he is to judge the world, and must therefore be God." Another said, "He himself has promised, where two or three are met in my name, there am I in the midst of them, and I will be with you always even to the end of the world.' Now, how can he fulfil these promises? While we are gathered here to worship and pray, others are gathered in distant lands—some in Britain; and how can he be with them all if he is not God?"

The Redeemer assuming Human Nature.

Q. 22. How did Christ, being the Son of God, become man?

Christ, the Son of God, became man, by taking to himself a true body, and a reasonable soul, being conceived, by the power of the Holy Ghost, in the womb of the Virgin Mary, and born of her, yet without sin.

What Truths are embraced in this Answer?

1. *Christ took to himself a true body.—John*, i. 14. The Word was made flesh, and dwelt among us.
2. *Christ took to himself a reasonable soul.—Matt.* xxvi. 38. My soul is exceedingly sorrowful, even unto death.
3. *Christ was conceived by the power of the Holy Ghost. —Luke*, i. 35. The Holy Ghost shall come upon thee, and the power of the highest shall overshadow thee.
4. *Christ was born of the Virgin Mary.—Luke*, ii. 7. And she brought forth her first-born son, and wrapped him in swaddling-clothes, and laid him in a manger.
5. *Christ was born and continued to be without sin.— Heb.* iv. 15. But was in all points tempted like as we are, yet without sin.

What Lessons do you derive from the above Doctrines?

I learn (1.) The mysterious greatness of the God-man, Christ Jesus. (2.) His unsullied holiness, and my obligation to imitate his holiness. (3.) His full ability to atone for my sins, having no sins of his own to suffer for, and having a divine nature to give infinite value to the sufferings of which his human nature made him capable.

What Illustration can you add?

Conversation between converted South Sea Islanders. —The excellent missionary, Rev. John Williams, relates the following conversation on the Divinity of Christ, which took place in his presence at a weekly meeting for religious inquiry. "I firmly believe," said the first speaker, "that Jesus Christ is God as well as man." "Are you not mistaken?" was the reply, "was not Jesus man, and man only?" "I believe," rejoined the first, "that Jesus was really man, for he had both the body and soul of man; but he was God as well as man, for he took on himself the form of man. If he had been only man he could not have died for sinners." "Is not that a proof," said another, "that he is not God? If God, why die?" First speaker: "His dying only proves him to be man; his rising again proves him to be God." "And if," added another, "he was only man, why so much ado about his death? Many have died cruel deaths: Paul was beheaded, and Peter was crucified, but there is not so much said about their deaths." "Ah, but," rejoined another, "Tuihe died among us, and there was a great ado about his death—what he said, and how happy he died." "But stop," cried one, "did the sun hide himself in darkness at Tuihe's death? Did the rocks rend at Tuihe's death?" "But did not Jesus eat food while on earth, and will God eat food?" "I say," was the answer, "he was man as well as God, therefore did he eat food."

The Offices of the Redeemer.

Q. 23. WHAT OFFICES DOTH CHRIST EXECUTE AS OUR REDEEMER?

Christ, as our Redeemer, executeth the offices of a prophet, of a priest, and of a king, both in his estate of humiliation and exaltation.

What Truths are embraced in this Answer?

1. *Christ is the prophet of his people.—John*, vi. 14. This is of a truth that prophet that should come into the world.

2. *Christ is the Priest of his people.—Psal.* cx. 4. Thou art a priest for ever after the order of Melchizedek.

3. *Christ is the King of his people.—Matt.* xxi. 5. Tell ye the daughter of Sion, Behold, thy King cometh unto thee, meek, and sitting upon an ass, and a colt the foal of an ass.

What Lessons do you derive from the above Doctrines?

I learn (1.) That Christ, the *Anointed* of God, redeems us, by acting as a teacher, as an offerer of sacrifice and intercession, and as a ruler and protector, not only during his humble condition while he dwelt amongst men, but also ever since he returned to his high and glorious state in heaven. (2.) I owe him unbounded confidence and love in these relations, of Prophet, Priest, and King.

What Illustrations are given?

1. Many years ago, at an assemblage of ministers, the late Drs. Mason and Channing were present. The latter was strongly suspected—rather more than suspected—of Unitarian tendencies, and some degree of confident challenging had already taken place. "Dr. C.," said Dr. M. to him, "may I ask how long you have been in the ministry?" "Eleven years," was the reply. "May I ask you once more, sir, what are your views of the Lord Jesus Christ?" There was a little hesitation and flush, and the reply, "I have pondered the subject deeply, but have not exactly made up my mind." Lifting up both hands in holy amazement, and with deep emotion, Dr. M. ejaculated—"What! eleven years a preacher of the gospel, and not know what to think of Jesus Christ!"

CLEMENTINE CUVIER.—This lovely, honored, and accomplished young lady, says, in a letter to a friend, "I want to tell you how happy I am: my heart has at length felt what my mind has long understood. *The sacrifice of Christ answers to all the wishes, and meets all the wants of my soul;* and since I have been enabled to embrace with ardor all its provisions, my heart enjoys a sweet and incomparable tranquillity. Formerly, I vaguely assured myself that a merciful God would pardon me; but now I feel that I have obtained that pardon; that I obtain it every moment; and I experience inexpressible delight in seeking it at the foot of the cross."

The Prophetical Office of Christ.

Q. 24. HOW DOTH CHRIST EXECUTE THE OFFICE OF A PROPHET?

Christ executeth the office of a prophet, in revealing to us, by his word and Spirit, the will of God for our salvation.

What Truths are embraced in this Answer?

1. *Christ, as the Prophet of his people, makes known to them the will of God.—John,* xv. 15. All things that I have heard of my Father, I have made known unto you.
2. *Christ reveals the will of God by his Word.—*2 *Cor.* v. 19. God was in Christ, reconciling the world unto himself, not imputing their trespasses unto them; and hath committed unto us the word of reconciliation.
3. *Christ reveals the will of God by his Spirit.—John,* xiv. 26. But the Comforter, which is the Holy Ghost, whom the Father will send in my name, he shall teach you all things.
4. *The purpose for which Christ reveals to men the will of God is their eternal salvation.—John,* xx. 31. These are written, that ye might believe that Jesus is the Christ, the Son of God; and that believing ye might have life through his name.

What Lessons do you derive from the above Doctrines?

I learn (1.) That Christ makes known to me outwardly, by the Holy Scriptures, and inwardly, by the workings of the Holy Spirit, whatever God would have me know, believe, and do, in order to the religious safety and comfort of my soul. Therefore (2.) It becomes me to prize more highly the Scriptures of divine truth, and to encourage and follow the workings of the Holy Spirit in my soul, tending to my salvation and comfort. It becomes me, also, to confess to Christ my great negligence and disobedience concerning the ways of salvation which he has so kindly made known to me, and so wonderfully urged upon my hearty attention.

What Illustrations can you relate ?

1. In a letter to Dr. Ryland, the Rev. *Samuel Pierce*, of Birmingham, thus writes:—"I have never felt so deeply my need of a Divine Redeemer, and seldom possessed such solid confidence that he is mine. I want more and more to become a little child, to dwindle into nothing in my own esteem, to renounce my own *wisdom*, power, and goodness, and simply look to, and live upon Jesus for *all*."

2. THE DIVINE ENCYCLOPEDIA.—"The Bible is a divine encyclopedia in itself. It contains *history* the most authentic and ancient, tracing it back to the first creation of our world; and *prophecy*, the most important and interesting, traced forward to its final consummation; *journeys*, surpassing all others in the marvellousness of their adventures and the dignity of their guide, for they were marked by miracles at every step, and in every movement directed by God; the *travels* of the most distinguished missionaries, the first preachers of the gospel; and the *lives* of the most illustrious personages, including the biography of the Son of God; *events* more wonderful than romance ever imagined, and *stories* more fascinating than fancy ever sketched; the finest specimens of *poetry* and *eloquence*—of sound *philosophy* and solid *argument;* *models of virtue* the most attractive, and *maxims of wisdom* the most profound; *prayers* the most appropriate in every

variety of spiritual experience, and *songs of praise* that would not be unworthy an angel's tongue; *precepts* of unparalleled importance, and *parables* of unrivalled beauty; *examples* of consistent piety, suited to every situation; and *lessons* of divine instruction, adapted to every age."—*White.*

Christ's Priestly Office.

Q. 25. How doth Christ execute the office of a priest?

Christ executeth the office of a priest, in his once offering up himself a sacrifice to satisfy divine justice, and reconcile us to God; and in making continual intercession for us.

What Truths are embraced in this Answer?

1. *Christ as our Priest offered himself in sacrifice to God.* —Heb. ix. 26. In the end of the world hath he appeared to put away sin by the sacrifice of himself.

2. *Christ as our Priest only once offered himself to God.* —Heb. vii. 27. This he did once, when he offered up himself.

3. *Christ as our Priest offered himself to satisfy divine justice for our sins.*—1 John, ii. 2. He is the propitiation for our sins.

4. *Christ offered up himself to reconcile us to God.—Eph.* ii. 16. That he might reconcile both unto God in one body by the cross, having slain the enmity thereby.

5. *Christ as our Priest makes continual intercession for us.*—Heb. vii. 25. He ever liveth to make intercession for them.

What Lesson do you derive from the above Doctrines?

I learn (1.) That Christ, as my great High Priest, has given himself—his human body and soul—once to death, as an offering for me, or in my place; (2.) That he might pay all that divine justice could claim in the way of punishment, or suffering, for my sins; and (3.) That he might bring me into a state of friendship with God, and hearty devotion to his service.

As a Priest also, he ever prays for me, that through the merit of his death in my behalf, I may have pardon, holiness, and everlasting life, and may be accepted in the worship and service which I render to God, in his name.

Hence, I learn (2.) To depend exclusively on the death of Christ, as a sufficient sacrifice, and not upon my own religious acts or feelings, for salvation.

I learn, also, that I need not the intercession of angels, or of any saints in heaven, since that of Christ alone is perfectly sufficient, and alone availing and constant.

What Illustrations do you offer?

1. The sight of Cæsar's bloody robe incensed the Romans against them that slew him. So (says Thomas Watson) the sight of Christ's bleeding body should incense us against sin.

2. When Esculus was accused for some act of impiety (says the same author), his brother stood up for him, and showed the magistrates how he had lost his hand in the service of the State, and so obtained his pardon. Thus, when the justice of God lays anything to the charge of saints, Christ shows his own wounds, and by virtue of his blood shed on the cross, he answers all the demands of the violated law.

3. THE CHILD AND THE QUEEN.—The gardener of Elizabeth (consort of Frederick II.), had one little daughter, with whose religious instruction he had taken great pains. When she was five years old, the Queen met her one day, and was so much pleased with her that a short time after, the artless child, at the Queen's request, was brought to the palace. She approached the Queen with

intaught courtesy, kissed her robe, and modestly took her seat, which had been placed for her, by the Queen's order, near her own person. From this position she could overlook the table at which the Queen was dining with the ladies of the Court, and they watched with interest to see the effect of so much splendor on the simple child. She looked carelessly on the costly dresses of the guests, the gold and porcelain on the table, and the pomp with which all was conducted, and then folding her hands, she sang, with her clear, childish voice, these words:—

> " Jesus, thy blood and righteousness
> Are all my ornament and dress;
> Fearless, with these pure garments on,
> I'll view the splendor of thy throne.

All the assembly were struck with surprise at seeing so much feeling, penetration, and piety, in one so young. Tears filled the eyes of the ladies, and the Queen exclaimed: "Ah, happy child! how far are we below you!"

Christ's Kingly Office.

Q. 26. HOW DOTH CHRIST EXECUTE THE OFFICE OF A KING?

Christ executeth the office of a king, in subduing us to himself, in ruling and defending us, and in restraining and conquering all his and our enemies.

What Truths are embraced in this Answer?

1. *Christ as a King subdues his people to himself.*—*Psal.* cx. 3. Thy people shall be willing in the day of thy power.

2. *Christ as a King rules his people.*—*Isa.* xxxiii. 22. The Lord is our law-giver, the Lord is our King; he will save us.

3. *Christ as a King defends his people.*—*Psal.* lxxxix. 18. The Lord is our defence; and the holy One of Israel is our King.

4. *Christ as a King restrains the enemies of his people.*—*Psal.* lxxvi. 10. The wrath of man shall praise thee; the remainder of wrath shalt thou restrain.

5. *Christ as a King will at last destroy all his enemies.*—1 *Cor.* xv. 25. He must reign, till he hath put all enemies under his feet.

What Lessons do you derive from the above Doctrines?

I learn (1.) To submit myself to Christ as my Supreme Ruler, to trust in him as my great Protector and Guardian, and to honor him as such. (2.) To endeavor to bring others to cease from rebelling against his rightful authority, and from resisting his gracious endeavors to make them good and to do them good. (3.) That those who continue enemies to Christ must be overthrown, and that his friends have occasion to rejoice in their own safety and permanent happiness.

What Illustrations have you to give?

1. THEODOSIUS THE EMPEROR.—Worldly persons often look with a sort of contempt upon Christians for their piety, but without cause, for they are engaged in the service of him who is KING OF KINGS, and thus enjoy a high honor. Theodosius himself said that he regarded it as a greater honor to be a servant of Christ, than to be the head of the Roman empire.

2. The Rev. Thomas Watson shrewdly asks,—"Have earthly kings their image stamped upon the public coin? but doth not Christ, as King, do a greater thing than that, in causing his image to be drawn upon the heart of every one of his subjects? Is it not also the prerogative of this King above all, to engrave his laws upon the hearts of his subjects, and to rule his voluntary subjects by his laws?"

3. In a missionary speech, an old native *convert of Rarotonga*, among other things, observed: "I have lived

during the reign of four kings. In the first I was but young; we were continually at war, and a fearful season it was; watching and hiding with fear were all our engagements. During the reign of the second, we were overtaken with a severe famine, and all expected to perish. * * * * * * * During the third, we were conquered, and became the prey of two other settlements in the island; then if a man went to fish he rarely ever returned, or if a woman went any distance to fetch food, she was rarely ever seen again. * * * * * * * But, during the reign of this third king, we were visited by another king—a great king—a good king—a powerful king—a king of love—Jesus, the Lord from heaven. He has gained the victory—he has conquered our hearts; we are all his subjects; therefore we now have peace and plenty in this world, and hope soon to dwell with him in heaven."

THE STATES IN WHICH THE REDEEMER PERFORMED HIS THREE-FOLD OFFICE.

His State of Humiliation.

Q. 27. WHEREIN DID CHRIST'S HUMILIATION CONSIST?

Christ's humiliation consisted in his being born, and that in a low condition, made under the law, undergoing the miseries of this life, the wrath of God, and the cursed death of the cross; in being buried and continuing under the power of death for a time.

What Truths are embraced in this Answer?

1. *Christ humbled himself by becoming man.—Phil.* ii. 6, 7. Who, being in the form of God, thought it not

robbery to be equal with God: but made himself of no reputation, and took upon him the form of a servant, and was made in the likeness of men.

2. *Christ, in becoming man, humbled himself by being born a child.—Luke,* i. 35. That Holy thing which shall be born of thee, shall be called the Son of God.

3. *Christ humbled himself by being born in a low condition. Luke,* ii. 7. She brought forth her first-born son, and wrapped him in swaddling-clothes, and laid him in a manger.

4. *Christ humbled himself by submitting to be made under the law.—Gal.* iv. 4. God sent forth his Son, made of a woman, made under the law.

5. *Christ humbled himself by enduring the miseries of life.—Isa.* liii, 3. He is despised and rejected of men; a man of sorrows, and acquainted with grief.

6. *Christ humbled himself by enduring the wrath of God in our stead.—Mat.* xxvii. 46. Jesus cried with a loud voice, saying, My God, my God, why hast thou forsaken me?

7. *Christ humbled himself by submitting to the cursed death of the cross.—Phil.* ii. 8. He humbled himself and became obedient unto death, even the death of the cross.

8. *Christ humbled himself by submitting to be buried—Luke,* xxiii. 53. He took it down, and wrapped it in linen, and laid it in a sepulchre that was hewn in stone.

9. *Christ humbled himself by remaining in the grave for a time.—Mat.* xii. 40. As Jonas was three days and three nights in the whale's belly; so shall the Son of man be three days and three nights in the heart of the earth.

What Lessons do you derive from the above Doctrines?

I learn (1.) How much I owe to Christ for the amazing love which urged him so to humble himself for us sinners—enemies to God, and unworthy of his favor. (2.) How great an evil our sins are, which required such unusual sacrifices from Christ, on our account. (3.) The duty of hating and forsaking all my sins, as this was the result which Christ had in view, when enduring so much degradation and suffering from wicked men, and from God as Moral Governor of the world.

What Illustrations may be given?

1. THE LITTLE SUNDAY-SCHOOL GIRL.

"Mamma," a little maiden said,
Almost with her expiring sigh,
"Put no sweet roses round my head,
When in my coffin-dress I lie."
"Why not, my dear?" the mother said,
"What flower so well a corpse adorns?"
"Mamma," the innocent replied,
"They crowned our Saviour's head with thorns."
JAMES MONTGOMERY

2. AN INDIAN'S GIFT TO CHRIST.—In a portion of the Southern territory, from which the red man has now been driven, at a protracted meeting, held in the wild forest, the subject of "Christ and him Crucified" was illustrated with surpassing beauty and grandeur. The preacher spoke of the good Shepherd, who came into the world to seek and to save the lost. He drew a picture of Gethsemane, and the unbefriended stranger who wept there. He told of the rude buffetings which he met from the heartless soldiers. He pointed to Him as he hung bleeding on the cross. The congregation wept. Soon there was a slight movement in the assembly, and a tall son of the forest, with tears on his red cheeks, approached the pulpit and said: "Did Jesus die for me—die for poor Indian? Me have no lands to give to Jesus, the white man take them away: me give him my dog and my rifle." The minister told him Jesus could not accept these gifts. "Me give Jesus my dog, my rifle, and my blanket; poor Indian, he got no more to give—he give Jesus all." The minister replied that Jesus could not accept them. The poor, ignorant, but generous child of the forest, bent his head in sorrow, and meditated. He raised his noble brow once more, and fixed his eye on the preacher, while he sobbed out, "*Here is poor Indian, will Jesus have him?*" A thrill of unutterable joy ran through the souls of min-

ister and people, as this fierce son of the wilderness now sat, in his right mind, at the feet of Jesus. The Spirit had done his work, and he who had been so poor, received the earnest of his inheritance.

3. THE TWO-FOLD NATURE OF CHRIST.—At the grave of Lazarus, He weeps *like a man!* and then says, "Come forth," *like a God!* Approaching the barren fig-tree, he hungers, *like a man!* And then, with a word, withers the fig-tree away, *like a God!* During a raging storm on the sea of Tiberias, he lay in the hinder part of the ship, and slept, *like a man!* being called upon, he arose, and rebuked the winds and the sea, *like a God!* Having wrought a stupendous miracle, he goes into a mountain apart, to pray, *like a man!* and, at the fourth watch of the night, he comes to his disciples, walking upon the water, *like a God!* On yonder bloody tree he suffers *like a man!* then opens the gates of Paradise to the dying thief, *like a God!* In yonder sepulchre, wrapped in his winding-sheet, the blessed Jesus lies, pale and cold, in death, *like a man!* but on the morning of the third day, by his own immortal energies, he burst the bands of death, and rose triumphant, *like a God!* After his resurrection, meeting with his disciples, he takes a piece of broiled fish, and of an honey comb, and did eat with them, *like a man!* and then leads them out to Bethany, and blesses them; and, as he blesses them, he ascends, in radiant majesty, far above all heavens—a *God confessed!* "God is gone up with a shout!"—*Rev. D. Baker.*

Of Christ's State of Exaltation.

Q. 28. WHEREIN CONSISTETH CHRIST'S EXALTATION?

Christ's exaltation consisteth in his rising again from the dead on the third day, in ascending up into heaven, in sitting at the right hand of God the Father, and in coming to judge the world at the last day.

What Truths are embraced in this Answer ?

1. *Christ was exalted by his rising from the dead.*—1 *Cor.* xv. 4. He rose again the third day, according to the Scriptures.
2. *Christ was exalted by ascending up into heaven.*—*Luke,* xxiv. 51. While he blessed them, he was parted from them, and carried up into heaven.
3. *Christ is exalted by his now sitting at the right hand of God.*—*Col.* iii. 1. Seek those things which are above, where Christ sitteth on the right hand of God.
4. *Christ will be exalted in his coming at last to judge the world.*—*Acts,* xvii. 31. He hath appointed a day, in the which he will judge the world in righteousness, by that man whom he hath ordained: whereof he hath given assurance unto all men, in that he hath raised him from the dead.

What Lessons do you derive from the above Doctrines ?

I learn (1.) To rejoice in the highest possible honor which Christ so deservedly receives in heaven. (2.) To place my affections on heavenly things. (3.) To prepare myself with all care (by the grace of God) for the solemn account which I must render, after death, to the Lord Jesus Christ, of all my feelings and conduct in the present life. (4.) To exalt Christ in my thoughts and affections above all created things.

What Illustration can you give ,

1. CHRIST AT THE RIGHT HAND OF GOD.—To speak properly, God hath no right hand or left; for, being a Spirit, he is void of all bodily parts; but it is a borrowed speech, a metaphor taken from the manner of kings, who were wont to advance their favorites next to their own

persons, and set them at their right hand. Solomon caused a seat to be set for the Queen, his mother, and placed her at his right hand. So for Christ to sit at the right hand of God, is to be in the next place to God the Father in dignity and honor.—WATSON.

2. Says John Newton: "Christ has taken our nature into heaven, to represent us, and has left us on earth, with his nature, to *represent Him.*"

3. CONTRASTS IN THE CONDITION OF CHRIST.—When he was on earth, he lay in a manger; now he sits on a throne. Then he was hated and scorned of men; now he is adored of angels. Then his name was reproached; now "God hath given him a name which is above every name." Then he came in the form of a servant, and as a servant stood with his basin and towel, and washed his disciples' feet; now he is clad in his princely robes, and the kings of the earth cast their crowns before him. On earth he was the Man of Sorrow; now he is anointed with the oil of gladness. On earth was his crucifixion; now, his coronation. Then his Father frowned upon him in desertion; now he hath set him at his own right hand.—WATSON.

Of the Application of Redemption.—The Agent by whom applied.

Q. 29. HOW ARE WE MADE PARTAKERS OF THE REDEMPTION PURCHASED BY CHRIST?

We are made partakers of the redemption purchased by Christ, by the effectual application of it to us by his Holy Spirit.

What Truths are embraced in this Answer?

1. *Redemption has been purchased for his people by Christ.*—Heb. ix. 12. By his own blood, he entered in once into the holy place, having obtained eternal redemption for us.

OF THE APPLICATION OF REDEMPTION. 81

2. *Redemption must be applied to believers.*—*John*, i. 12. As many as received him, to them gave he power to become the sons of God, even to them that believe on his name.

3. *Redemption is effectually applied to believers by the Holy Spirit.*—*Ezek.* xxxvi. 27. I will put my Spirit within you, and cause you to walk in my statutes, and ye shall keep my judgments, and do them.

What Lessons do you derive from the above Doctrines?

I learn (1.) That Christ has bought redemption (or deliverance) from sin and suffering, by his blood. (2.) That all men are not sharers in it. (3.) That it is the office of the Holy Spirit to put me in possession of it. (4.) That the labors and sufferings of Christ for the benefit of my soul will be of no avail, unless I allow, and earnestly desire and supplicate, the Holy Spirit, to bring me to a proper state of mind and heart, corresponding to the salvation which Christ sought to confer upon me. (5.) That I should greatly honor, love, and obey, the Holy Spirit; and I learn, moreover, the great sin, and the dangerous consequence, of rejecting his teachings, or of resisting his operations in my soul.

What Illustrations are given?

1. Said *Bunyan:* "In my preaching I could not be satisfied, unless some fruits did appear in my work." "I would think it a greater happiness," saith *Matthew Henry*, "to gain one soul to Christ, than mountains of silver and gold to myself. If I do not gain souls, I shall enjoy all my other gains with very little satisfaction; and I would rather beg my bread from door to door than undertake this great work." *Doddridge*, writing to a friend, remarked: "I long for the conversion of souls more sensibly than for anything besides. Methinks I could not only labor but die for it with pleasure." Similar is the

death-bed testimony of the sainted *Brown*, of Haddington: "Now, after near forty years preaching of Christ, I think I would rather beg my bread all the laboring days of the week, for an opportunity of publishing the gospel on the Sabbath, than, without such a privilege, to enjoy the richest possessions on earth. Oh! labor, labor," said he to his sons, "*to win souls to Christ.*"

2. The *Rev. Pliny Fisk*, in his diary, thus writes: "There is nothing I desire so much for myself and my friends, as the influence of the Holy Ghost. I am clearly convinced that my sins will prevail, and my lusts increase their strength, in spite of all my efforts, unless the Holy Spirit purify and elevate my affections. I am persuaded that He can give me humility, repentance, benevolence, faith, love, and every grace. Blessed agent in the work of salvation, it is thine to sanctify; O let thy purifying influences come into my soul, and make me holy!"

How Redemption is applied.

Q. 30. How doth the Spirit apply to us the redemption purchased by Christ?

The Spirit applieth to us the redemption purchased by Christ, by working faith in us, and thereby uniting us to Christ, in our effectual calling.

What Truths are embraced in this Answer?

1. *Redemption is applied to God's people through faith.*—*Gal.* iii. 14. That we might receive the promise of the Spirit through faith.

2. *Faith in the believer is altogether the work of God.*—*Eph.* ii. 8. By grace are ye saved, through faith; and that not of yourselves: it is the gift of God.

3. *Believers are united to Christ in one mystical body.*—1 *Cor.* xii. 27. Now ye are the body of Christ, and members in particular.

4. *The union of Christ and the believer is formed by the operations of faith.*—*Eph.* iii. 17. That Christ may dwell in your hearts by faith.

5. *The believer is united to Christ in his effectual calling.*—1 *Cor.* i. 9. God is faithful, by whom ye were called unto the fellowship of his Son Jesus Christ our Lord.

What Lessons do you derive from the above Doctrines?

I learn, That the Holy Spirit secures to me the benefits of Christ's sufferings, when he brings me to an humble and exclusive trust in Christ (which act is called *Faith*); and hence arises a certain spiritual connection between me and Christ, by a process which is termed *Effectual Calling*.

What Illustrations may be given?

HARLAN PAGE.—This active and useful Christian is said to have been habitually impressed with the *necessity to every man of being born again*. As soon as any person came into his presence, it seemed to be the first question of his mind, "Is this a friend or an enemy of God?" The next thing was, if impenitent, to do something for his conversion; or, if a Christian, to encourage him in duty. Whatever else he saw in an individual, he felt that it availed him nothing unless he had received Christ into his heart by a living faith. This he felt and urged to be the sinner's first, great, and only duty in which he could be acceptable to God."—*Memoir*, p 196.

The Application of Redemption in Effectual Calling.

Q. 31. WHAT IS EFFECTUAL CALLING?

Effectual calling is the work of God's Spirit, whereby convincing us of our sin and misery, enlightening our minds in the knowledge of Christ, and renewing our wills, he doth persuade, and enable us to embrace Jesus Christ, freely offered to us in the gospel.

What Truths are embraced in this Answer?

1. *Effectual calling, is the work of the Holy Spirit.—John*, xvi. 14. He shall receive of mine, and shall show it unto you.

2. *In effectual calling, the Spirit convinces of sin.—John*, xvi. 8. He will reprove (or convince) the world of sin.

3. *In effectual calling, the Spirit convinces of misery.—Rom.* vii. 10. The commandment which was ordained to life, I found to be unto death.

4. *In effectual calling, the mind is enlightened in the knowledge of Christ.*—1 *Pet.* ii. 9. Who hath called you out of darkness into his marvellous light.

5. *In effectual calling, our wills are renewed.—Ezek.* xxxvi. 26. A new heart also will I give you, and a new spirit will I put within you.

6. *In effectual calling, we are persuaded to embrace Jesus Christ.—John*, vi. 44. No man can come to me, except the Father which hath sent me draw him.

7. *In effectual calling, we are enabled to embrace Jesus Christ.—Ezek.* xxxvi. 27. I will put my Spirit within you, and cause you to walk in my statutes, and ye shall keep my judgments, and do them.

8. *Jesus Christ is freely offered to all men in the gospel.—Rev.* xxii. 17. Whosoever will, let him take the water of life freely.

What Lessons do you derive from the above Doctrines?

I learn (1.) That Effectual Calling is the work of God's Spirit; that it consists in making me feel that I am a sinner, and therefore exposed to great misery; in giving me a proper acquaintance with Christ; and in so affecting or changing my natural state of mind, that I shall be inclined and enabled to accept, with my whole heart, the offer of salvation, which rests upon what Christ has done and suffered for me. (2.) That if Christ had not been made known to me as a Saviour, adapted to my sinful and perilous condition, I must have continued a sinner, and been lost. (3.) That a work of the Spirit is necessary in my heart, to bring it to a proper state, and to dispose it to accept and obey Christ, *in all his offices*, in order to salvation. (4.) If I have chosen Christ, and thereby obtained pardon, I am indebted to the Holy Spirit, and should be for ever thankful to him, and should honor him as the kind Author of my change of heart and of character. (5.) If I have not thus chosen Christ, I am guilty of offering ungrateful and wicked resistance to the agency of the Holy Spirit, whose office it is to convince of sin, and to lead to Christ.

What Illustrations can you relate?

1. WILLIAM KELLY.—To show the *necessity of an entire change of heart*, he was accustomed to mention a saying of Bishop Taylor: "If there be a crack in a bell, there is no possible way of repairing it; it must be cast *anew*."

2. Says the REV. THOMAS DOOLITTLE: "When I catechise my children or my servants, I ask them, *What is Effectual Calling?* and they answer me according to what is written in their book. But now I am retired to catechise myself, must I not be careful to answer according to what is written in my heart? O, my soul, what a difference is there betwixt answering this question by the words of the book, and from the experience of my own heart."

3. A person once said, in the presence of DR. NETTLETON, that to inculcate upon sinners their dependence on God for a new heart, is suited to discourage effort, and to lead them to sit down in despair. He replied, "The very reverse of this is true. Suppose a number of men are locked up in a room, playing cards. Some person informs them that the roof of the building is on fire, and that they must make their escape, or they will perish in the flames.

Says one of them, 'We need not be in haste, we shall have time to finish the game.' 'But,' says the person who gave the alarm, 'your door is locked.' 'No matter for that,' he replies, 'I have the key in my pocket, and can open it at any moment.' 'But I tell you that the key will not open the door.' 'Won't it?' he exclaims, and, rising from the table, flies to the door, and exerts himself to the utmost to open it. So sinners, while they believe there is no difficulty in securing their salvation at any moment, quiet their consciences, and silence their fears. But when they are taught that such is the wickedness of their hearts, that they will never repent unless God interposes by his regenerating grace, they are alarmed, and begin to inquire, in deep distress, 'What they shall do to be saved?'"

Benefits of Redemption in this Life.

Q. 32. WHAT BENEFITS DO THEY THAT ARE EFFECTUALLY CALLED, PARTAKE OF IN THIS LIFE?

They who are effectually called, do in this life partake of justification, adoption, and sanctification, and the several benefits which, in this life, do either accompany or flow from them.

What Truths are embraced in this Answer?

1. *Believers receive justification.*—Rom. viii. 30. Whom he called, them he also justified.
2. *Believers are adopted into the family of God.*—Rom. viii. 15. Ye have received the Spirit of adoption, whereby we cry, Abba Father.
3. *Believers partake of sanctification.*—Heb. x. 10. By the which will we are sanctified.
4. *All necessary blessings in this life are made over to the believer.*—1 Cor. iii. 22. All things are yours.

BENEFITS OF REDEMPTION IN THIS LIFE. 87

What Lesson do you derive from the above Doctrines?

I learn, The great folly and stupidity of those who neglect the invitations and blessings of the Gospel.

What Illustrations do you offer?

1. WHO KNOWS BEST?—Said John Newton to a gay friend, "I need not turn Deist to enjoy the best and the most that this life can afford." Newton had a *right* to say this, and so he believed. He had, as he says, "experienced the good and the evil on both sides." He had been a man of pleasure and of impiety, and knew how to estimate them. Thus he says to his friend, "If you were to send me an inventory of your pleasures, how charmingly your time runs on, and how dexterously it is divided between the coffee-house, play-house, the card-table, and tavern, with intervals of balls, concerts, &c., I could answer, that most of these I have tried, and tried again, and know the utmost they can yield, and have seen enough of the rest most heartily to despise them all. You know all that a life of pleasure can give, and I know it likewise." So far they were equal. But Newton had another experience found "in the pardon of his sins—communion with God, calm reliance on the Divine Providence, the cheering prospect of a better life, with foretastes of heaven in his soul." Supposing that such pleasures would be despised, he adds· 'But here lies the difference, my dear friend, *you condemn that which you have never tried."* An all-sufficient answer is this, to every one who questions the superiority of religion.

2. On her death-bed, a pious English woman, who had for months suffered great bodily pain, observed, respecting the state of her soul: "All is sweet peace again—solid peace. *I am as certain of heaven as if I were already there.* Not that I have merited heaven—no: I have **no** works, no worthiness,

'Nothing in my hand I bring,
   Simply to thy cross I cling.'

I have lain awake, night after night, examining the foundation of my hope, but I cannot find a single flaw. *I depend entirely upon the sacrifice of Christ for acceptance with God, and not at all upon my own works.* I have not a doubt or a fear. The fear and sting of death are both taken away; the fear, because Christ died for sinners; the sting, because he fulfilled and magnified the law."

Of Justification.

Q. 33. WHAT IS JUSTIFICATION?

Justification is an act of God's free grace, wherein he pardoneth all our sins, and accepteth us as righteous in his sight, only for the righteousness of Christ imputed to us, and received by faith alone.

What Truths are embraced in this Answer?

1. *Justification is an act of free and unmerited grace.*—Rom. iii. 24. Being justified freely by his grace.
2. *All our sins are pardoned in Justification.*—Psal. ciii. 3. Who forgiveth all thine iniquities.
3. *The perfect righteousness of Christ is imputed to the believer in Justification.*—2 Cor. v. 21. He hath made him to be sin for us, who knew no sin; that we might be made the righteousness of God in him.
4. *The believer is accepted as righteous by God, only by the imputation of Christ's righteousness.*—Rom. v. 19. As by one man's disobedience many were made sinners, so by the obedience of one shall many be made righteous.
5. *The benefit of Christ's imputed righteousness is received by faith.*—Rom. iii. 22. The righteousness of God, which is by faith of Jesus Christ unto all, and upon all them that believe.

OF JUSTIFICATION.

What Lessons do you derive from the above Doctrines?

I learn (1.) To praise the grace, or undeserved favor of God. (2.) That his favor is to be acquired only through what Christ has done and suffered. (3) That by trust in Christ, and in him alone, I may escape the punishment due for sins, and may be treated with all the divine kindness and love to be expected only by an innocent and holy being. (4.) That without this trust I cannot please God, but must for ever remain under condemnation, and suffer the wrath of God, as expressed in the penalty of the law—which is everlasting death.

> In vain we seek for peace with God
> By methods of our own.
> Blest Saviour! nothing but thy blood
> Can bring us near the throne!

What Illustrations are given?

1. THE OLD MAN IN PARIS —An old man, a seller of blacking, at his stand in Paris, was often observed to be occupied with some old book. Tracts, from time to time, were given him by a certain person, and with these he was much gratified. Upon his request, a New Testament was then given him, and this made him anxious for the whole Bible. When he received it, he stood over it in ecstasy, "Where shall I begin in this world of wonders?" he exclaimed; "I want to know it all at once." After standing in the street till late in the evening, to obtain a few pence by his blacking, this poor man devoted many hours every night to studying and reading the sacred volume to his wife, by the light of a glimmering lamp, till one or two in the morning. In a few months, at more than seventy years of age, he had made great advances in the knowledge of divine truth. When he discovered the doctrine of *Justification by Faith*, he was overwhelmed

with it, and he could not believe that any one had discovered it before, or, at least, so clearly as himself.

2. But few men have been more active, devoted, and useful Christians, than the late HARLAN PAGE, and yet, on his death-bed, when an allusion was made to his great usefulness, he replied, "O brother Hallock, I am nothing, and have done nothing. I am nothing but a poor sinner. I am a blank, and less than a blank. I hang on the mere merits of Christ. I have come short in everything. I have done wrong, and felt wrong, and cast myself alone on the blood and righteousness of Christ."

3. When DR. WATTS was almost worn out and broken down by his infirmities, he observed, in conversation with a friend, "I remember an aged minister used to say, that the most learned and knowing Christians, when they come to die, have only the same plain promises of the gospel for their support as the common and unlearned; and so," said he, "I find it. The plain promises of the Gospel are my support; and I bless God they are plain promises, that do not require much labor and pains to understand them; for I can do nothing now but look into my Bible for some promise to support me, and live upon that."

4. This was likewise the case with the pious and excellent MR. HERVEY He writes, about two months before his death: "I now spend almost my whole time in reading and praying over the Bible." And again, near the same time to another friend: "I am now reduced to a state of infant weakness, and given over by my physician. *My grand consolation is to meditate on Christ;* and I am hourly repeating those heart-reviving lines of Dr. Young:

> ' *This*—only this--subdues the force of death,
> And what is this? Survey the wondrous cure
> And at *each step* let higher wonder rise!
> 1. Pardon for infinite offence! 2. And pardon
> Through means that speak its value infinite!
> 3. A pardon bought with blood! 4. With blood divine;

5. With blood divine of Him I made my foe!
6. Persisted to provoke!—7. Though woo'd and aw'd,
Bless'd and chastised, a flagrant rebel still!—
8. A rebel 'midst the thunders of His throne!
9. Nor I alone! 10. A rebel universe!
11. My species up in arms! 12. Not one exempt!
13. Yet for the foulest of the foul He dies!
14. Most joy'd for the redeem'd from deepest gulf!
15. As if our race were held of highest rank,
And Godhead dearer, as more kind to man.'"

Of Adoption.

Q. 34. WHAT IS ADOPTION?

Adoption is an act of God's free grace, whereby we are received into the number, and have a right to all the privileges of the sons of God.

What Truths are embraced in this Answer?

1. *Adoption is an act of God's free grace.*—1 *John*, iii. 1. Behold what manner of love the Father hath bestowed upon us, that we should be called the sons of God.
2. *In adoption, the believer is received into the number of God's children.*—*Eph.* i. 5. Having predestinated us unto the adoption of children.
3. *In adoption, we receive a right to all the privileges of God's children.*—*Rom.* viii. 17. If children, then heirs: heirs of God, and joint heirs with Christ.

What Lessons do you derive from the above Doctrines?

I learn (1.) That Adoption is an undeserved kindness, whereby God receives certain persons into his family, who, before, were strangers and in a most wretched condition, and had nothing to recommend them to his liberality. He treats them thenceforth as his own redeemed and spiritual children, and bestows upon them, as such, the richest blessings, as though they had a just claim to them. (2.) That by nature I do not belong to God's family, and, in a religious sense, am not a child of God.

(3.) To ask God to adopt, or put me into his religious family, and to be my Father, and to bless me, as he does his regenerate children. (4.) That it is a great honor and happiness to look up to God, and, without presumption, to be able to address him as *my* Father in heaven.

What Illustrations can you relate?

1. MOSES was adopted as the son of Pharaoh's daughter, and ESTHER was the adopted child of her uncle Mordecai. Thus God adopts us into the family of heaven, and in adopting us, doth two things: when he makes sons, he doth not only give a new name, but a new nature. He works such a change as if another soul did dwell in the same body.— *Watson.*

2. Mrs. SUSAN HUNTINGTON, upon the loss of her mother, writes: "*O to be adopted, taken into God's Family—to have him exercise over us the endearing, the watchful attention and care of our omniscient and Almighty Parent!* But he promises to be the Father of those only, who, disclaiming all other dependence, fly to him, through Jesus Christ, as their best, their only portion; who feel the vanity of all human helpers; who love him with a filial and holy love, and who manifest their attachment by a hatred of sin which he hates, by a pursuit of the holiness which he enjoins, by a life of universal obedience to his law."

3. Says JOHN NEWTON: "I feel like a man who has no money in his pocket, but is allowed to draw, for all his wants, upon one infinitely rich; I am, therefore, at once a beggar and a rich man."

Sanctification.

Q. 35. WHAT IS SANCTIFICATION?

Sanctification is the work of God's free grace,

OF SANCTIFICATION. 93

whereby we are renewed in the whole man after the image of God, and are enabled more and more to die unto sin and live unto righteousness.

What Truths are embraced in this Answer?

1. *Sanctification is the work of God—Phil.* ii. 13. For it is God which worketh in you, both to will and to do of his good pleasure.

2. *Sanctification is a work carried on by degrees.—*2. *Cor.* iii. 18. But we all, with open face, beholding as in a glass, the glory of the Lord, are changed into the same image from glory to glory, even as by the Spirit of the Lord.

3. *Sanctification is a work of free undeserved mercy.—Tit.* iii. 4, 5. But after that the kindness and love of God our Saviour toward man appeared, not by works of righteousness which we have done, but according to his mercy he saved us, by the washing of regeneration, and renewing of the Holy Ghost.

4. *In sanctification there is a renewing of the sinner's mind.* —*Rom.* xii. 2. And be not conformed to this world; but be ye transformed by the renewing of your mind, that ye may prove what is that good, and acceptable, and perfect will of God.

5. *In sanctification, the renewal, though gradual, is complete.—Ezek.* xxxvi. 26. A new heart also will I give you, and a new spirit will I put within you: and I will take away the stony heart out of your flesh, and I will give you an heart of flesh.

6. *In sanctification, the sinner is renewed after the image, or likeness of God.—Eph.* iv. 24. And that ye put on the new man, which after God is created in righteousness and true holiness.

7. *In the progress of sanctification the sinner is enabled to die unto sin.—Rom.* vi. 6. Knowing this, that our old man is crucified with him, that the body of sin might be destroyed, that henceforth we should not serve sin.

8. *In the progress of sanctification the sinner is enabled to live unto righteousness.—Rom.* vi. 22. But now being made free from sin, and become servants to God, ye have your fruit unto holiness, and the end everlasting life.

9. *Dying to sin, and living to righteousness, is a constant and daily work.*—2 *Cor.* iv. 16. For which cause we faint not; but though our outward man perish, yet the inward man is renewed day by day.

What Lessons do you derive from the above Doctrines?

I learn (1.) That I must labor constantly after a higher degree of obedience to God, from day to day. (2.) That the work of self-control and self-improvement must be carried on, as long as I live. (3.) That I must conduct it with an humble and full reliance upon the Holy Spirit, to accomplish it in my soul. (4.) That I am not left alone in working out my salvation, but am encouraged to make vigorous efforts to overcome my sinful desires and habits, because the Almighty Spirit of God is ready, on account of Christ, to help me, and to make me successful in those efforts. (5.) It would save much useless debate, if the distinction which Dr. Nevins makes between *conversion* and *sanctification* were observed: that the former is instantaneous, while the latter is progressive; in other words, that religion is progressive, but the first step in that progression is instantaneous.

What Illustrations are furnished?

1. Dying Words of Wilberforce Richmond.—"Come, and sit near me; let me lean on you," said young Wilberforce to his sister, a few minutes before his death. Afterward, putting his arms around her, he said, "God bless you, my dear." He became agitated somewhat, and then ceased speaking. Presently, however, he said, "I must leave you; we shall walk no further through this world together; but I hope we shall meet in heaven. Let us talk of heaven. Do not weep for me, dear F——, do not weep; for I am very happy; but think of me, and let the thought make you press forward. I never knew happi-

ness till I found Christ as a Saviour. Read the Bible—read the Bible! Let no religious book take its place. Books about religion may be useful enough, but they will not do instead of the simple truth of the Bible." He afterwards spoke of the regret of parting with his friends. "Nothing," said he, "convinces me more of the reality of the change within me, than the feelings with which I can contemplate a separation from my family. I now feel so weaned from earth, my affections so much in heaven, that I can leave you all without a regret; yet I do not love you less, but God more."

2. JOHN NEWTON'S CONFESSION.—John Newton, in his old age, when his sight had become so dim as to be unable to read, hearing this Scripture repeated, "By the grace of God I am what I am," paused for some moments, and then offered this affecting soliloquy: "I am not what I *ought* to be. Ah! how imperfect and deficient! I am not what I *wish* to be. I abhor that which is evil, and I would cleave to that which is good. I am not what I *hope* to be. Soon, soon, shall I put off mortality, and with mortality all sin and imperfection. Though I am not what I *ought* to be, what I *wish* to be, and what I *hope* to be, yet I can truly say, I am not what I once was, a slave to sin and Satan; I can heartily join with the apostle, and acknowledge, '*By the grace of God I am what I am.*'"

3. MRS HANNAH MORE, on a bed of sickness, when conversing about the joys of heaven, remarked: "The meeting with dear friends will, I should think, constitute a part of our felicity, but a very subordinate one. Like Whitefield, I think, we shall be apt to say, 'Stand back, and keep me not from the sight of my Saviour.' Important as doctrines are," she observed, "yet except the leading ones, for which we ought to be ready to be led to the stake, they yield much with me to the purifying of the hidden man of the heart. *Conformity to God, and walking*

in his steps, spiritual-mindedness, and subduing of the old Adam within us,—here is the grand difficulty, and the acceptable offering to God!"

4. THREE WONDERS IN HEAVEN.—"If I ever reach heaven," said the eminently pious DR. WATTS, "I expect to find three wonders there. (1.) To meet some I had not thought to see there. (2.) To miss some whom I expected to meet there; but (3.) The greatest wonder of all will be to find *myself* there." If such were the views and feelings of such a man as Dr. Watts, who lived so near the verge of heaven, and breathed its holy atmosphere, even on earth, so as to be able to say with the most cheerful confidence, "I bless God I lie down at night unsolicitous whether I awake in this world, or another," how much greater will be the wonder, in the case of many careless and almost prayerless Christians, to find themselves in heaven at last?—*N. Y. Evang.*

5. An old divine well said: "Let us die to sin that lives in us; and live to Christ who died for us."

Benefits of Redemption in this life.

Q. 36. WHAT ARE THE BENEFITS WHICH, IN THIS LIFE, DO ACCOMPANY OR FLOW FROM JUSTIFICATION, ADOPTION AND SANCTIFICATION?

The benefits which, in this life, do accompany or flow from justification, adoption, and sanctification, are, assurance of God's love, peace of conscience, joy in the Holy Ghost, increase of grace, and perseverance therein to the end.

What Truths are embraced in this Answer?

1. *The believer has the assurance of God's love.*—*Rom.* v. 5. The love of God is shed abroad in our hearts by the Holy Ghost which is given unto us.

2. *The believer enjoys peace of conscience.—Rom.* v. 1. Being justified by faith, we have peace with God, through our Lord Jesus Christ.

3. *The believer possesses joy in the Holy Ghost.*—1 *Pet.* i. 8. In whom, though now ye see him not, yet believing, ye rejoice with joy unspeakable, and full of glory.

4. *The believer increases in grace.—Prov.* iv. 18. The path of the just is as the shining light, that shineth more and more unto the perfect day.

5. *The believer is enabled to persevere in grace.—Jer.* xxxii. 40. I will put my fear in their hearts, that they shall not depart from me.

What Lessons do you derive from the above Doctrines?

I learn the several advantages enjoyed by the true Christian in the present life. (1.) He is thereby made sure of the special love of God to himself. (2.) He is no longer troubled with a condemning conscience, or with the fears of God's future displeasure. (3.) The Holy Spirit communicates great joy in view of his new relations to God—to his law and gospel. (4.) Through the influence of the Spirit he becomes more and more averse to sin, and more strongly inclined to perform every good and pious act; he seeks to become more useful to the cause of Christ, and to do more good to his suffering and wicked fellow-men. (5.) He is secured from falling back into a careless, worldly, and sinful course of life;—he is made sure of heaven. (6.) To use all the care, diligence, and effort which may be required to secure those blessings for myself, in all their fulness and variety. (7.) That every Christian should, in this life, be growing better and happier every day.

What Illustrations can you give?

1. An eminently pious man thus writes of himself:— "When I shall be on my dying bed, what joy will it be

to think I am going to see my Father. I am going home to my Father's house; within a day or two I shall be with my Father."

2. The Rev. Samuel Pierce, towards the close of his last, and very painful sickness, writes to Dr. Ryland:—"Now I see the value of the religion of the cross. *It is a religion for a dying sinner.* It is all that the most guilty the most wretched, can desire. Yes, I taste its sweetness and enjoy its fulness with all the gloom of a dying bed before me. * * * * * I was delighted the other day, in re-perusing the 'Pilgrim's Progress,' to observe that, when *Christian* came to the top of hill *Difficulty*, he was put to sleep in a chamber called *Peace*. 'Why, how good is the Lord of the way to me,' said I. I have not yet reached the summit of the hill yet, but, notwithstanding, he puts me to sleep in the chamber of Peace every night. * * * * True, it is often a chamber of pain, but let pain be as formidable as it may, it has never yet been able to expel that peace which the great Guardian of Israel has appointed to keep my heart and mind through Christ Jesus."

3. Dr. Nettleton once fell in company with two men who were disputing on the Doctrine of the Saints' Perseverance. As he came into their presence, one of them said, "I believe this doctrine has been the means of filling hell with Christians." "Sir," said Dr. N., "do you believe that God knows all things?" "Certainly I do," said he. "How then do you interpret this text—'I never knew you?'" said Dr. N. After reflecting a moment, he replied, "The meaning must be, I never knew you as Christians." "Is that the meaning?" said Dr. N. "Yes, it must be," he replied, "for certainly God knows all things." "Well," said Dr. N., " I presume you are right Now, this is what our Saviour will say to those who, at the last day, shall say to him, 'Lord, Lord, have we not

eaten,' &c. Now, when Saul, and Judas, and Hymeneus, and Philetus, and Demas, and all who, you suppose, are fallen from grace, shall say to Christ, Lord, Lord,— he shall say to them, I never knew you—I NEVER *knew you as Christians.* Where, then, are the Christians that are going to hell?"

Benefits of Redemption at Death.

Q. 37. WHAT BENEFITS DO BELIEVERS RECEIVE FROM CHRIST AT DEATH?

The souls of believers are at their death made perfect in holiness, and do immediately pass into glory; and their bodies being still united to Christ, do rest in their graves till the resurrection.

What Truths are embraced in this Answer?

1. *The souls of believers are at death made perfect in holiness.*—*Heb.* xii. 23. To the spirits of just men made perfect.
2. *After death, the souls of believers pass immediately into glory.*—*Luke,* xxiii. 43. Jesus saith unto him, Verily I say unto thee, To-day shalt thou be with me in Paradise.
3. *The bodies of believers, while in their graves, remain united to Christ*—1 *Thess.* iv. 14. Them also which sleep in Jesus will God bring with him.
4. *The bodies of believers do rest in their graves.*—*Isa.* lvii. 2. They shall rest in their beds, each one walking in his uprightness.
5. *The bodies of believers shall be raised from their graves at the last day.*—1 *Thess.* iv. 16. The dead in Christ shall rise first.

What Lessons do you derive from the above Doctrines?

I learn (1.) That at death the souls of those who have

truly believed in Christ are entirely set free from all sinful desires and tendencies; they are restored altogether to the moral likeness of God; they pass at once into a glorious state of existence—a state of holiness—of larger capacities of enjoyment—a state of high dignity, excellence, blessedness, and permanency. In the meantime, their bodies, laid in the grave, are so related to Christ, and so regarded as members of his own body (1 *Cor.* vi. 15), that he will guard them until the day of resurrection;— their resurrection shall be provided for. (2.) That true Christians have no reason for regret, on their own account, when death comes. (3.) When our Christian friends are taken from us, there is ground for rich consolation. (4.) That my daily prayer should be, "Let my death be that of the righteous; let my last end be his; let me die 'in the Lord,' and not be driven away, with the wicked, in his wickedness." (5.) That I owe everlasting gratitude to God, for the provisions of his grace for encountering death, and for the grand event of the promised resurrection. (6.) That those are in error who have fancied either that the Christian's soul, at death, goes to any place inferior to heaven, or that it is in an unconscious state till the resurrection.

What Illustrations can you give?

1. "What a satisfying thought it is," writes the late Rev. SAMUEL PIERCE, "that God appoints those means of dissolution, whereby he gets most glory to himself. Of all the ways of dying, that which I most dreaded was by a consumption; but, oh! my dear Lord, if by this death I can most glorify thee, I prefer it to all others, and thank thee that by this means thou art hastening my further enjoyment of Thee in a purer world. A *sinless* state! 'Oh, 'tis a heaven worth dying for!' I cannot realize anything about heaven, but the presence of Christ, and

BENEFITS OF REDEMPTION AT DEATH.

his people, and a perfect deliverance from sin; and I want no more,—I am sick of sinning,—soon I shall be beyond its power.

> 'O joyful hour! O blest abode
> I shall be near and like my God!'"

2. When HARLAN PAGE was near death, he said to a clergyman who came in to see him: "Do look out some hymns that express a great deal of heaven. Many of the hymns seem tame. They are pretty poetry, but do not present the joys of redemption and the glory of Christ. When I have a clear view of Christ, my fears vanish, and I can trust myself wholly in his hands."

3. A few days before the REV. DR. PAYSON closed his earthly career, he dictated a remarkable letter to a sister, in which he says: "Were I to adopt the figurative language of Bunyan, I might date this letter from the land of Beulah, of which I have been for some weeks a happy inhabitant. The celestial city is full in my view. Its glories beam upon me, its breezes fan me, its odors are wafted to me, its sounds strike upon my ears, and its spirit is breathed into my heart. Nothing separates me from it but the river of death, which now appears but as an insignificant rill, that may be crossed at a single step, whenever God shall give permission. The Sun of Righteousness has been gradually drawing nearer and nearer, appearing larger and brighter as he approaches, and now he fills the whole hemisphere, pouring forth a flood of glory, in which I seem to float like an insect in the beams of the sun, exulting, yet almost trembling, while I gaze on this excessive brightness, and wondering, with unutterable wonder, why God should deign thus to shine upon a sinful worm. A single heart and a single tongue seem altogether inadequate to my wants; I want a whole heart for every separate emotion, and a whole tongue to express that emotion."

Benefits of Redemption at the Resurrection.

Q. 38. WHAT BENEFITS DO BELIEVERS RECEIVE FROM CHRIST AT THE RESURRECTION?

At the resurrection, believers being raised up in glory, shall be openly acknowledged and acquitted in the day of judgment, and made perfectly blessed, in the full enjoying of God to all eternity.

What Truths are embraced in this Answer?

1. *Believers shall, at the last day, be raised up in glory.*—1 *Cor.* xv. 43. It is sown in dishonor, it is raised in glory.

2. *Believers shall be openly acknowledged by Christ at the day of judgment.*—*Luke*, xii. 8. Whosoever shall confess me before men, him shall the Son of man also confess before the angels of God.

3. *Believers shall be acquitted by Christ in the judgment.* —1 *Pet.* i. 7. That the trial of your faith, being much more precious than of gold that perisheth, though it be tried with fire, might be found unto praise, and honor, and glory, at the appearing of Jesus Christ.

4. *Believers shall be made perfectly blessed in the enjoyment of God.*—1 *Cor.* ii. 9. Eye hath not seen, nor ear heard, neither have entered into the heart of man, the things which God hath prepared for them that love him.

5. *Believers shall enjoy God through all eternity.*—1 *Thess.* iv. 17. So shall we ever be with the Lord.

What Lessons do you derive from the above Doctrines?

I learn, that at the Day of Resurrection true Christians are greatly favored in these respects. (1.) Their bodies are brought up from the grave in a form and structure of great beauty, and splendor, and incorruptibleness, like unto Christ's honored body (*Phil.* iii. 21.) (2.) In the subsequent day, when God shall decide upon the everlasting states of men, true Christians shall be discharged from all the consequences of sin, and, before the whole world, shall be owned by God, and received as his children; they shall be introduced into a state of endless honor and happiness, with Christ and his holy angels; they shall there be blessed in an everlasting freedom from sin and suffering; in the noblest exercise of all those affections which render the soul like to God, and in the delightful consciousness that God is present with them to communicate a joy unspeakable in degree, and endless in duration. (2.) To bless God for taking away from his people the gloom of the grave. (3.) To commit the bodies of Christian friends who have died, to the care of their faithful and kind Redeemer. (4.) To trust his boundless power and faithfulness to re-form them out of a state of dust into a likeness to his own perfect body. (5.) To prepare myself for the judgment, by trusting in Christ now, and by serving him in all fidelity and cheerfulness. (6.) At the hour of death, to commit my soul and body to his keeping, that the one may rest safely its appointed time, in the grave, and that the other may be conducted at once to his heavenly presence.

> " And a trump shall be blown, and the dead shall awake
> From their long silent sleep that no morning could break;
> From their long silent sleep of a million of years—
> The righteous with hope, and the wicked with fears.
>
> "And their Judge shall descend on his chariot—the cloud;
> And the awe shall be deep, and the wail shall be loud;
> And the race of mankind shall with justice be given
> To the terrors of hell, or the glories of heaven."—KNOX.

What Illustrations are given?

1. A WORD FITLY SPOKEN.—A man of desperate opinions, travelling in a stage coach, who had indulged in a strain which betrayed licentiousness and infidelity, seemed hurt that no one either agreed or disputed with him. "Well," he exclaimed as a funeral procession slowly passed the coach, "there is the end of all." "No!" replied the voice

of a person directly opposite to him, "no! *for after death is the judgment.*" The words produced a good end at the time, for they silenced the speaker; and perhaps they were, by God's grace, ingrafted in his heart.

2. Lord Henry Otho, a follower of John Huss, having received sentence of condemnation from his Popish judges, said: "Kill my body, disperse my members whither you please, yet do I believe that my Saviour will gather them together again, and clothe them with skin; so that with these eyes I shall see him; with these ears I shall hear him; with this tongue I shall praise him, and rejoice with this heart forever." As he was going to the scaffold, he said to the minister, "I am sure that Christ Jesus will meet my soul with his angels; this death, I know, shall not separate me from him." After he had prayed silently, he said: "Into thy hands, O Lord, I commend my spirit; have pity on me through Jesus Christ, and let me see thy glory," and so he received the stroke of the sword.

3. Rev. Charles Simeon says: "I was waiting in Horsley-Down church yard for a corpse which I was engaged to bury, and for my amusement was reading the epitaphs upon the tomb-stones. Having read very many which would have been as suitable for Jews or heathens, as for the persons concerning whom they were written I at last came to one that characterized a Christian:

'When from the dust of death I rise,
To claim my mansion in the skies,
Even then shall this be all my plea:
'Jesus hath lived and died for me.'"

4. The Resurrection.—A free-thinker once said to R. Gahita, "Ye fools who believe in a resurrection! See you not that the living die? How then can ye believe that the dead shall live?" "Silly man," replied Gahita, "thou believest in creation. Well, then, if what never before existed now exists, why may not that which once existed exist again?"

PART II.

THE DUTY WHICH GOD REQUIRES OF MAN.

Nature of Man's Duty in general.

Q. 39. WHAT IS THE DUTY WHICH GOD REQUIRES OF MAN?

The duty which God requireth of man, is obedience to his revealed will.

What Truths are embraced in this Answer?

1. *There are certain duties required by God from man.*—Deut. x. 12. And now, Israel, what doth the Lord thy God require of thee but to fear the Lord thy God, to walk in all his ways and to love him, and to serve the Lord thy God with all thy heart and with all thy soul.

2. *The sum of man's duty to God is obedience.*—1 Sam. xv. 22. Behold, to obey is better than sacrifice, and to hearken than the fat of rams.

3. *The extent of the obedience required by God is a universal obedience.*—James, ii. 10. Whosoever shall keep the whole law, and yet offend in one point, he is guilty of all.

4. *The quality of obedience required from man is a perfect and perpetual obedience.*—Mat. xxii. 37. Thou shalt love the Lord thy God with all thy heart, and with all thy soul, and with all thy mind.

5. *The only rule of man's obedience is the revealed will of God.*—Micah, vi. 8. He hath showed thee, O man, what is good; and what doth the Lord require of thee, but to do justly, and to love mercy, and to walk humbly with thy God.

What Lessons do you derive from the above Doctrines?

I learn (1.) That I am not at liberty to do what I may feel inclined to do, irrespective of what God requires or forbids. (2.) I owe him a fearful debt (of penal suffering) for having done so much that He has forbidden, and neglected so much that he has enjoined. (3.) That I should earnestly study the Scriptures, with a view to act as they inculcate, both in the way of obedience to precept and of obtaining deliverance from the punishment which my past disobedience has merited.

What Illustrations do you give?

1. THE NEWGATE PRISONER.—Dr. F., the chaplain of Newgate, relates the incident, that when a reprieve arrived for one under sentence of death, he returned a Bible and Prayer-book, which the doctor had given him, with his thanks, observing that *he had no further need of them now!* So much is it beyond the power or disposition of unassisted nature to attend any longer to the requisitions of God than while the terrors of the law and the dread of wrath are impending; and so little is this state of feeling worth, if that be all.

2. THE BURMAN CONVERT.—As Mrs. Judson, one day, was reading with him Christ's Sermon on the Mount, he was deeply impressed, and unusually solemn. "These words," said he, "take hold of my very heart; they make me tremble. Here God commands us to do everything that is good in secret, not to be seen of men. How unlike our religion is this! When Burmans make offerings to the Pagodas, they make a great noise with drums and musical instruments, that others may see how good they are. But this religion makes the mind fear God; it makes it, of its own accord, fear sin."

3. DUTIES.—Mr. Dyer has well observed: "Take up all

duties in point of performance, and lay them down in point of dependence. Duty can never have too much of our diligence, nor too little of our confidence."

Of the Moral Law.

Q. 40. WHAT DID GOD AT FIRST REVEAL TO MAN FOR THE RULE OF HIS OBEDIENCE?

The rule which God at first revealed to man for his obedience, was the moral law.

What Truths are embraced in this Answer?

1. *There was a first rule of obedience given to man in the constitution of his nature.—Rom.* ii. 15. Which show the work of the law written in their hearts.

2. *There was a second rule of obedience given by God to his church in the ceremonial law.—Gal.* iii. 19. Wherefore then serveth the law? It was added because of transgressions, till the seed should come to whom the promise was made.

3. *The second, or ceremonial law, was but temporary, and instituted for a special purpose.—Gal.* iii. 24. The law was our schoolmaster to bring us unto Christ.

4. *The second, or ceremonial law, is now set aside.—Heb.* vii. 18. There is verily a disannuling of the commandment going before, for the weakness and unprofitableness thereof.

5. *The first rule of obedience given to man in the constitution of his nature, was the moral law.—Gen.* i. 27. God created man in his own image.

6. *The moral law is universal and unchangeable.—Mat.* v. 18. Verily, I say unto you, Till heaven and earth pass, one jot or one tittle shall in no wise pass from the law, till all be fulfilled.

What Lessons do you derive from the above Doctrines?

I learn (1.) That I am bound to act at all times according to the moral rule which God has laid down. (2.) This implies that I am a moral and accountable being.

What Illustrations can you give?

1. A TENDER CONSCIENCE.—Some men's consciences are like the stomach of the ostrich, that digests iron; they can swallow and concoct the most notorious sins (swearing, drunkenness, &c.) without regret. But a good conscience is the most tender thing in the whole world; it feels the touch of known sin, and grieves at the grieving of God's good Spirit.—*Gibbon.*

2. A GOOD SORT OF COWARDICE.—To be such a coward as not to dare to break any one of God's commandments, is to be the most valiant person in the world; for such an one will choose the greatest evil of suffering before the least of sinning; and, however the jeering Ishmaels of the world may be ready to reproach and to laugh one to scorn for "this niceness and scrupulosity," as they term it, yet the choice is a very wise one.—*Gibbon.*

3. BE JUST.—While Athens was governed by the thirty tyrants, Socrates was summoned to the Senate House, and ordered to go, with some other persons, whom they named, to seize one Leon, a man of rank and fortune, whom they determined to put out of the way, that they might enjoy his estate. This commission Socrates positively refused. "I will not, willingly," said he, "assist in an unjust act." Chericles sharply replied, "Dost thou think, Socrates, to talk in this high tone, and not to suffer." "Far from it," he replied, "I expect to suffer a thousand ills, but none so great as to do unjustly." A noble sentiment for those whose minds were only enlightened by philosophy and natural religion.—*Christian Treasury.*

Of the Summary of the Moral Law.

Q. 41. WHEREIN IS THE MORAL LAW SUMMARILY COMPREHENDED?

The moral law is summarily comprehended in the ten commandments.

What Truths are embraced in this Answer?

1. *The moral law is fully contained in the Scriptures.*—2 Tim. iii. 16, 17. All Scripture is given by inspiration of God, and is profitable for doctrine, for reproof, for correction, for instruction in righteousness; that the man of God may be perfect, thoroughly furnished unto all good works.
2. *There are summaries of the moral law.*—Rom. xiii. 3. If there be any other commandment, it is briefly comprehended in this saying, Thou shalt love thy neighbor as thyself.
3. *The sum of the moral law is contained in the ten commandments.*—Deut. x. 4. He wrote on the tables, according to the first writing, the ten commandments; which the Lord spake unto you in the mount.

What Lessons do you derive from the above Doctrines?

I learn (1.) To admire the wisdom of God that has embodied in so few words all the duties which we owe to God and to man. (2.) That it cannot be difficult to find out what God would have me to do. (3.) That ignorance of the law will form no just excuse for sinning against God. (4.) That the glorious majesty of God, who gave the Ten Commandments, is a reason for earnest and constant care to comply with his demands.

What Illustrations can you relate?

1. JONATHAN EDWARDS, when about twenty years of age, drew up seventy resolutions, setting forth his intentions and purposes relating to his future conduct, so far as God should give him grace to perform them. Among the rest are the following: "Resolved to do whatever I think to be my duty, and most for the good and advantage of mankind in general. Resolved so to do, whatever difficulties I meet with, how many soever, and how great soever..

2. Rowland Hill and the Antinomian.—An Antinomian one day called on Rowland Hill, to bring him to an account for preaching what he regarded as a severe and legal gospel. "Do you, sir," asked Rowland, "hold the ten commandments to be a *rule of life* to Christians?" "Certainly not," replied the visitor. The minister rang the bell, and, on the servant making his appearance, he quietly added, "John, show that man the door, and keep your eye on him until he is beyond the reach of every article of wearing apparel, or other property in the hall."

Sum of the Ten Commandments.

Q. 42. What is the sum of the ten commandments?

The sum of the ten commandments is, To love the Lord our God with all our heart, with all our soul, with all our strength, and with all our mind, and our neighbor as ourselves.

What Truths are embraced in this Answer?

1. *The sum of the moral law and the ten commandments are comprehended in two commandments.*—*Mat.* xxii. 40. On these two commandments hang all the law and the prophets.
2. *Love to God is the first and principal subject of the ten commandments.*—*Mat.* xxii. 37, 38. Thou shalt love the Lord thy God with all thy heart, and with all thy soul, and with all thy mind. This is the first and great commandment.
3. *Our duty to our neighbor, is the second subject of the ten commandments.*—*Mat.* xxii. 39. The second is like unto it, Thou shalt love thy neighbor as thyself.

What Lessons do you derive from the above Doctrines?

I learn (1.) That my whole duty is embraced in the proper exercise of love. (2) That God, being possessed of infinite excellence and the chief source of all good, deserves, and must have, all the love I am capable of feeling; I cannot love God too much. (3.) That I may love myself and promote my own interest. (4.) That in so doing, I am to regard the commands and will of God. (5.) That the law of God requires me to feel an interest in the welfare of my neighbor, as well as in my own: and this is obviously right; for, like myself, he is an intelligent and immortal being; his happiness is of equal value with my own; his rights are worth as much to him, as mine to me; in the dispensation of providence I should therefore be as willing that God should consult my neighbor's rights and happiness, as that he should consult mine, and I should rejoice in all the real good of my neighbor, as in my own. (6.) I am bound to love all men, in this sense, and to promote their happiness, whether they are good or bad, rich or poor, friend or enemy;—all to whom I can make myself useful.

What Illustrations follow?

1. DR. RICHARDS.—The late Rev. Dr. Richards, of Auburn, cherished the most abasing views of his own character. He was once asked, "Do you suppose that you have ever, for a moment, loved God as much as you ought?" and his immediate answer was, "No, NOT A THOUSANDTH PART;" *and burst into tears.—Gridley's Memoir.*

2. THE BOY THAT DID GOOD.—There once lived a boy in Chester, named William Tyrrel. He was a rosy-cheeked, stout, brave, little fellow, and a great favorite with all the neighbors. At school, no one was oftener at the head of his class, and no one brought home more tickets. One night, as the family were all sitting round a bright sparkling fire, Mr. Tyrrel said, "Children, what makes you most happy?" Some answered one thing, and

some another, but William looked up and said: "Father, I think I am happiest when I can make other people happy." "Right, right, my son," said Mr. Tyrrel, "stick to that all your life, and you will be a happy man. Remember the words of the Lord Jesus, how he said, '*It is more blessed to give than to receive.*'"

3. THE LITTLE GIRL THAT EVERYBODY LOVED.—Dr. Doddridge one day asked his little girl why it was that everybody loved her. "I know not," she replied, "except that I love everybody." This is the true secret of being loved. "He that hath (or would have) friends," saith Solomon, "must show himself friendly." Love begets love. If nobody loves you, it is your own fault.

4. THE MORAVIAN COTTAGER.—During a war in Germany, a captain of cavalry was ordered out on a party for getting provisions. He marched with his party, into a solitary and wooded valley. In the middle of it stood a little cottage; on perceiving it, he rode up and knocked at the door. Out comes an ancient Hernhutter, with a beard silvered by age. "Father," says the officer, "show me a field where I can set my troopers to work to get grain." "Presently," replied the Hernhutter. The good old man walked before, and conducted them out of the valley. After a quarter of an hour's march they found a field of barley. "There is the very thing that we want," says the captain. "Have patience for a few minutes," replied the guide, "and you shall be satisfied." They went on, and about the distance of a quarter of a league further, they arrived at another field of barley. The troop immediately dismounted, cut down the grain, trussed it up, and re-mounted. The officer, upon this, says to his conductor, "Father, you have given yourself and us unnecessary trouble; the first field was much better than this." "Very true, sir," replied the good old man, "BUT IT WAS NOT MINE." Here we have a beautiful *practical*

exhibition of *love to our neighbor*, and of calm resignation to the providential dispensations of God. How few professed Christians have been found acting in this manner! And yet, I doubt not, that this good man would experience more true satisfaction in the temper and conduct he displayed, than if he had either offered resistance, practised dissimulation, or set the troop to plunder his neighbor's field.—*Dick's Philosophy of Religion.*

5. *Love thy Neighbor as Thyself.*—The Rev. John Howe, one of the chaplains of Cromwell, was applied to by men of all parties, for protection, nor did he refuse his influence to any on account of difference in religious opinions. One day the Protector said to him: "Mr. Howe, you have asked favors for every one besides yourself; pray, when does your turn come?" He replied: "My turn, my Lord Protector, is always come, WHEN I CAN SERVE ANOTHER."

6. THE GOLDEN RULE.—"One of my great principles," said Robert Owen to Mr. Wilberforce, "is, that persons ought to place themselves in the situation of others, and act as they would wish themselves to be treated." "Is that quite a *new* principle, Mr. Owen?" was his answer, with a look of suppressed humor; "I think I have read something very like it in a book called the New Testament."

Preface to the Ten Commandments.

Q. 43. WHAT IS THE PREFACE TO THE TEN COMMANDMENTS?

The preface to the ten commandments is in these words, "I am the Lord thy God, which have brought thee out of the land of Egypt, out of the house of bondage."

Q. 44. WHAT DOTH THE PREFACE TO THE TEN COMMANDMENTS TEACH US?

The preface to the ten commandments teacheth us, That because God is the Lord, and our God, and Redeemer, therefore we are bound to keep all his commandments.

What Truths are embraced in this Answer?

1. *God is the Lord of all.*—1 *Tim.* vi. 15. The blessed and only Potentate, the King of kings, and Lord of lords.
2. *God is our God.*—*Psal.* xlviii. 14. This God is our God for ever and ever.
3. *God is our Redeemer.*—*Isa.* lxiii. 16. Thou, O Lord, art our Father, our Redeemer.
4. *Because God is the Lord, therefore we should keep his commandments.*—*Psal.* xlv. 11. He is thy Lord; and worship thou him.
5. *Because God is our God, therefore we should keep his commandments.*—*Josh.* xxiv. 18. Therefore will we also serve the Lord; for he is our God.
6. *Because God is our Redeemer, therefore we should keep his commandments.*—1 *Cor.* vi. 20. Ye are bought with a price: therefore glorify God in your body, and in your spirit, which are God's.

What Lessons do you derive from the above Doctrines?

I learn (1.) That the Israelites, when in Egypt, were slaves. (2.) That their relation to God as his chosen nation, and their remarkable deliverance, by the power of God, laid them under special obligations to obey and love him. (3.) I am reminded of my own natural state —a state of slavery to sin, to Satan, and to the world. (4.) I am reminded of the great deliverance which Jesus, by his death, has purchased for me, from sin, from Satan, and from hell. (5.) I am bound, therefore, by the high authority, as well as by the infinite mercy of God, to keep all those commandments which he designed not only for the Israelites but for the rest of mankind, and which are briefly condensed into the Ten now to be considered. (6.) I notice that the Preface, and each of the following commands, are adapted to men, not as masses, but as individuals, and hence I am taught to feel my own personal obligations to obedience.

What Illustrations are there?

1. THE WIDOW of a pious Scottish minister was sitting by her lonely fire-side, the morning after the death of her valued husband, lamenting her forlorn and destitute condition, when her little son, but five years of age, entered the room. Seeing the deep distress of his mother, he stole softly to her side, looked wistfully into her face, and said: "Mother, mother, *is God dead?*" Soft as the gentle whispers of an angel did the simple accent of the dear boy fall upon the ear of the disconsolate mother. A heavenly radiance lighted up her pale features. Then pressing her little boy fondly to her bosom, she exclaimed: "No, no, my son, God is not dead; *he lives*, and has promised to be a father to the fatherless—a husband to the widow. His promises are sure and steadfast, and upon them I will firmly and implicitly rely." Her tears were dried, and her murmurings forever hushed. The event proved that her confidence was not misplaced.

2. THE BIBLE SAYS SO.—CHILDREN should be early taught that the Bible is the great authority; and that when it speaks upon any point, the question is settled forever. They should be taught to go directly to the Scripture, to find what is good and what is bad, what is true, and what is false. Thus, with the blessing of God, they will acquire the habit of constantly subordinating their own notions and inclinations to the plain declarations of Scripture. It is a good sign to have a child often use the expression, "*The Bible says so.*"

DUTIES WHICH WE OWE TO GOD.

THE FIRST COMMANDMENT.

Q. 45. WHICH IS THE FIRST COMMANDMENT?

The first commandment is, Thou shalt have no other gods before me.

Duties Required.

Q. 46. WHAT IS REQUIRED IN THE FIRST COMMANDMENT?

The first commandment requireth us to know and acknowledge God to be the only true God, and our God; and to worship and glorify him accordingly.

What Truths are embraced in this Answer?

1. *We are required to know God.*—*Job*, xxii. 21. Acquaint now thyself with him.
2. *We are required to know God as the only true God.*—*Hosea*, xiii. 4. Thou shalt know no God but me.
3. *We are required to know God as our God.*—*Jer.* xxiv. 7. I will give them an heart to know me, that I am the Lord: and they shall be my people, and I will be their God.
4. *We are required to acknowledge God as the only true God.*—2 *Kings*, xix. 15. Thou art the God, even thou alone.
5. *We are required to acknowledge God to be our God.*—*Psal.* xlviii. 14. This God is our God for ever and ever.
6. *We are required to worship God as the only true God,*—*Mat.* iv. 10. Thou shalt worship the Lord thy God, and him only shalt thou serve.

7. *We are required to worship God as our God.—Psal.* xcv. 6, 7. O come, let us worship and bow down: let us kneel before the Lord our Maker. For he is our God; and we are the people of his pasture.

8. *We are required to glorify God as the only true God.—* 1 *Chron.* xvi. 25, 26. Great is the Lord, and greatly to be praised: he also is to be feared above all Gods. For all the gods of the people are idols: but the Lord made the heavens.

9. *We are required to glorify God as our God.—Psal.* cxlv. 1. I will extol thee, my God, O King; and I will bless thy name for ever and ever.

What Lessons do you derive from the above Doctrines?

I learn (1.) That I must have a God. (2.) That I must have Jehovah the God of Israel, and none other as my God. (3.) In view of what He is—a being of infinite perfection, and of what He has done for me and for the universe, I must love, revere, obey, submit to, exalt, and praise Him, above all other beings, and to the utmost of my ability, or I cannot claim to have rendered to Him what I owe, nor fully to have honored him as my God. (4.) So far as I have failed to do this, I have transgressed this commandment, I have wronged God and my own soul. (5.) A proper regard to God will lead me to employ my best influence over my fellow men, to bring them to right views of God and to right feelings, and a proper course of conduct towards Him. (6.) It will thus lead me to promote, in all proper ways, the missionary cause, and revivals of pure religion.

What Illustrations can you relate?

1. A LITTLE BOY asked his mother how many gods there were. A younger brother answered, "Why, one to be sure." "But how do you know that?" inquired the other. "Because," answered the other, "God fills every place, so there is no room for any other."

2. COLLINS, the celebrated English infidel, once meeting a plain countryman, inquired where he was going. "To church, sir." "What to do there?" "To worship God." "Pray tell me, is your god a great or a little god?" "He is so great, sir, that the heavens cannot contain him, and so little that he can dwell in my heart." Collins afterwards declared that this simple but sublime answer had more effect on his sceptical mind than all the volumes he had ever read.

3. "Sir," said a lady to the Rev. *Wm. Romaine*, of London, "I like the doctrine you preach, and think I can give up everything but one." "What is that, madam?" "Cards, sir." "You think you could not be happy without them?" "No, sir, I could not." "Then, madam, *they are your God*, and to them you must look for salvation." This pointed and faithful reply is said to have led to her conversion.

4. To FEAR GOD, is to have such a holy care of God upon our hearts, that we dare not sin. The wicked sin and fear not: the godly fear and sin not: "how then can I do this wickedness and sin against God?" It is a saying of ANSELM, "If hell were on one side, and sin on the other, I would rather leap into hell than willingly sin against my God."

5. CITY HEATHEN.—An excellent but somewhat eccentric clergyman, one Sabbath, at the close of the services, gave notice to his congregation that in the course of the week he expected to go on a mission to the heathen. The members of his church were struck with alarm and sorrow at the sudden and unexpected loss of their beloved pastor, and one of the deacons, in great agitation, exclaimed, "What *shall* we do?" "Oh, brother C——," said the minister, with great apparent ease, "I do not expect to go out of town."

6. THE CITY CHRISTIAN.—A pious and intelligent female

member of Rev. Mr. James' church, in Birmingham, England, upon her death-bed, said to him, "What a mercy it is that the work is finished, and that, when in health, *I sought God with all my heart, in his own appointed way.* I cannot talk to-day, I feel so ill; but all is sweet peace within. I die resting simply on the righteousness of Christ." In the evening she said, "*My God, my Bible, and my Saviour, are increasing sources of happiness,* to which I can turn at any moment, without disappointment, and I find them more solid as other things fade away."

7. WORLDLY AMUSEMENTS.—If Christians join in what are called worldly amusements (says Jones), I ask nothing about their creed. They show their *taste;* that is enough. A mere creed, however correct, will save no man. The *influence* of the creed is the essential matter. He who cultivates a sound spiritual taste cannot relish frivolity. Most of what is said about amusements is said to no purpose. Taste, not logic, rules the world. A new nature —*a relish for, a delight in, the sublime and holy, the infinite and eternal:*—plant this in the soul of man, and he looks upon the world's amusements as mere cobwebs. He further says: "I reject many things which I do not account sinful in the abstract. I look to influence and consequences. A thing may be lawful, and yet not expedient. '*If the Lord be God, follow him;* but if Baal, follow him.' The people of the world should see what master we serve. They are consistent in their cause and course: Christians ought to be equally so in theirs."

Sins Forbidden.

Q. 47. WHAT IS FORBIDDEN IN THE FIRST COMMANDMENT?

The first commandment forbiddeth the denying, or not worshipping and glorifying the true God, as

God and our God; and the giving of that worship and glory to any other which is due to him alone.

What Truths are embraced in this Answer?

1. *We are not to deny God.—Psal.* xiv. 1. The fool hath said in his heart, There is no God.
2. *We are not to refuse or neglect to worship God.—Isa.* xliii. 22. Thou hast not called upon me, O Jacob; but thou hast been weary of me, O Israel.
3. *We are not to refuse or neglect to glorify God.—Dan.* v. 23. The God in whose hand thy breath is, and whose are all thy ways, hast thou not glorified.
4. *We are not improperly to worship God, as if he were not the only true God.—Mat.* xv. 8. This people draweth nigh unto me with their mouth, and honoreth me with their lips; but their heart is far from me.
5. *We are not to worship God, as if he were not our God.— Ezek.* xliv. 9. Thus saith the Lord God; No stranger, uncircumcised in heart, nor uncircumcised in flesh, shall enter into my sanctuary.
6. *We are not to worship anything else besides God.—Rom.* i. 25. Who changed the truth of God into a lie, and worshipped and served the creature more than the Creator, who is blessed for ever. *Amen.*
7. *We are not to give that glory to any other which is due only to God.—Psal.* xcvii. 7. Confounded be all they that serve graven images, that boast themselves of idols; worship him, all ye Gods.

What Lessons do you derive from the above Doctrines?

I learn (1.) That this command is most grossly violated by those who have not acknowledged or worshipped any God at all: these are called *Atheists.* (2.) It is violated by those who acknowledge and adore many gods: such are *Polytheists,* or *Idolaters.* (3.) Even by such as profess to acknowledge and worship but one God it is violated, if they do not, with all their hearts, reverence and love him as the most wise and powerful, the most just and holy, the most good and gracious Being; if they do not trust and hope in him as the Fountain of all their good; if they do not diligently worship and praise him; if they do not humbly submit to his will and obey his laws. (4.) I shall violate this law if I frame in my fancy an idea untrue, or unworthy, of that One most excellent Being, and to such a creation of my own fancy yield my highest respect and affection. (5.) If also, upon any creature (myself, or any other person or thing) I bestow my chief esteem and affection, or employ my most earnest care and endeavor, or chiefly rely upon or delight in it, thus making that person or thing a god to myself. Hence (6.) whoever chiefly regards, seeks and pursues, confides and delights in wealth, or honor, or power, or pleasure; wit, wisdom, strength, or beauty; arts, science, literature; himself, friends, or any other creature, he hath another God, contrary to the design and meaning of this holy law.—[Dr. Barrow's Exposition.]

Q. 48. WHAT ARE WE SPECIALLY TAUGHT BY THESE WORDS [*before me*] IN THE FIRST COMMANDMENT?

These words [before me] in the first commandment teach us, that God who seeth all things, taketh notice of, and is much displeased with the sin of having any other god.

What Truths are embraced in this Answer?

1. *God seeth all things.*—*Heb.* iv. 13. Neither is there any creature that is not manifest in his sight: but all things are naked and opened unto the eyes of him with whom we have to do.

2. *God will take special notice of the sin of having another god.*—*Psal.* xliv. 20, 21. If we have stretched out our hands to a strange god, shall not God search this out?

3. *God is much displeased with the sin of having any other god.*—*Deut.* xxxii. 16. They provoked him to jealousy with strange gods.

What Lessons do you derive from the above Doctrines?

I learn (1.) That the great evil of Idolatry, both external and internal, consists in the manifest preference which it shows for the object of it, in comparison with God, who is ever present to observe that preference, and to feel the base affront which is thus put upon his infinite excellencies, and high relations to us and to the universe. (2.) That I can commit no sin without God's knowledge and high displeasure.

What Illustrations are given?

1. A CHILD CONSECRATED TO IDOLATRY.—A missionary was once standing near the temple of a very celebrated and cruel idol, when a father approached the shrine of the goddess. He led by the hand an interesting little boy, his son, probably his first-born, and it may be his only son. The little fellow was very much alarmed; for there was a great crowd of worshippers; and the musicians were beating their shrill drums, and sounding their hoarse trumpets, and crying aloud in honor of the goddess, and they were bowing frantically before the altar. The blood of goats and other animals was flowing near him, which had just been sacrificed to the goddess. Amidst all this confusion the little fellow was afraid; and he clung fast to his father, now looking round at the people, and then at the goddess, and then at the father, as much as to say, "Do, father, save me from these cruel people!" But no. His father had brought him to consecrate him to the service of the goddess; and to do this, he put into the poor boy's hand a piece of silver. This the boy handed to the priest; and then the father handed to the priest two sharp-pointed pieces of iron, which the priest sprinkled with the sacred water of the river Ganges, and returned to the parent. They were then handed to a cruel man, who (while the poor boy was gazing in wonder and horror

around) plunged one, if not both, into his naked side! The boy shrieked, and clung to his father. The musicians beat their drums and sounded their trumpets; the priests raised their voices to drown the crying of the boy; and he was borne away bleeding and terrified from the scene by his deluded but now happy father, who supposed that his son was consecrated to the goddess in that most cruel act. Verily, is it not true that the dark parts of the earth are full of the habitations of cruelty?

2. IDOL WORSHIP IN NEW YORK.—A gentleman in this city (says the *Evangelist*) while visiting in Cherry-street, for an Industrial School, went into a room where was a little company of Chinese offering sacrifice to an idol. A Chinaman was kneeling in front of the idol, burning some sweet-smelling substance in a little cup floating in water. The gentleman apologized for the intrusion, but they did not seem much troubled by it.

3. To a young man, who professed to be an Atheist, said Dr. NETTLETON, "You are not so sure as you pretend to be, that there is no God. You dare not go alone, and kneel down, and, in a solemn manner, offer a prayer. If there is no God you will incur no danger by so doing; and yet you dare not do it. This shows that *you are afraid that there is a God*, who cannot be deceived, and who will not be mocked."

4. REV. DR. WITHERSPOON, formerly President of Princeton College, N. J., was once on board a packet ship, where, among other passengers, was a professed Atheist. This unhappy man was very fond of troubling every one with his peculiar belief, and of broaching the subject as often as he could get any one to listen to him. He did not believe in a God and a future state; not he! By-and-by there came on a terrible storm, and the prospect was that all would be drowned. There was much consternation on board, but *no one was so greatly frightened as the pro-*

fessed Atheist. In this extremity, he sought out the clergyman, and found him in the cabin, calm and collected, in the midst of danger, and thus addressed him: "O Dr. Witherspoon! Dr. Witherspoon! we're all going; we have but a short time to stay. O how the vessel rocks! we're all going; don't you think we are, doctor?" The doctor turned to him with a solemn look, and replied in broad Scotch, "Nae doubt, nae doubt man; we're a'ganging; but *you and I dinna gang the same way.*" The poor man was speechless; and the worthy Doctor, who had not said much before, then took the opportunity of setting before him the guilt and folly of his conduct.

5. When CARDINAL WOLSEY, for some time the prime minister of Henry VIII., under whose displeasure and selfishness he was deprived of immense wealth and of all places of power and honor, was lying upon his death-bed, he called to him Kingston, the lieutenant of the Tower, and said, under a bitter sense of the base ingratitude of his royal master: "Had I but served my God as diligently as I have served the king, he would not have given me over in my gray hairs; but I receive a just reward for my indulgent labor and care, not regarding my service to God, but only to my king."

6. REV. DR. CHARLES HALL, when in Europe, visited Blenheim, the famous country-seat bestowed by Queen Anne on the first Duke of Marlborough, and after a most graphic account of it, adds: "As I wandered through these grounds, and opened my heart to these forms of beauty, I could feel the rivers of delight rolling in upon my soul. I forgot the Duke of Marlborough; I had no appreciation for his military glory, or for his royal mistress. *I thought only of God, who made this majesty and loveliness.* I felt that he intended and adapted the world —its creatures—its lakes, its forests—its landscapes, to speak of Him, to lead up our hearts to Him. I felt tha';

there is no mistake as to the *oneness of the Godhead in revelation and in nature.* And *my heart praised Him;* I cried out for holiness—that there with such beauty of the natural world, there might be nothing but moral consanguinity in my soul." In the valley of Oberhasli, in Switzerland, he says:—"My soul has been lifted up amid the grandeur of these everlasting hills. I have felt the *grandeur of God;* I have felt *my own littleness;* I have felt that it was an inexpressible condescension for Christ, having built this mighty earth, to die for the sinful creatures who creep on its surface." And at Chamouny he writes: "Here, amid the sublimest of God's works, I have communed with him, and have endeavored to re-consecrate myself to him. O Lord, who by thy power settest fast the mountains, exert that power to make this poor, vile heart *all thine own."—Dr. Smith's Discourse.*

THE SECOND COMMANDMENT.

Q. 49. WHAT IS THE SECOND COMMANDMENT.

The second commandment is, Thou shalt not make unto thee any graven image, or any likeness of anything that is in heaven above, or that is in the earth beneath, or that is in the water under the earth. Thou shalt not bow down thyself to them, nor serve them; for I the Lord thy God am a jealous God, visiting the iniquity of the fathers upon the children unto the third and fourth generation of them that hate me; and showing mercy unto thousands of them that love me, and keep my commandments.

SECOND COMMANDMENT.

What Lessons do you derive from the above Doctrines?

(1.) I learn that while the First command forbids the worshipping of a false God, the Second forbids the worshipping of the true God in a false manner. (2.) That the Second command requires me to render to the true God *that kind of worship* which is suited to his spiritual nature and unlimited perfections; that he alone knows what kind of worship is proper, and that he alone can prescribe it. (3.) That it is impossible, absurd, and wicked to make any outward, visible representation, by sculpture or painting, of that God who fills immensity with a *spiritual*, invisible presence and energy. (4.) That this command does not forbid the use of sculpture or painting for other purposes, as some have absurdly imagined; though statuary and painting have been shamefully abused as means of withdrawing men's regard from God. (5.) That I am not allowed to frame, even in my mind, any image or conception of God as possessing form, but when I attempt to worship him must fix my thoughts upon him simply as a Being possessing the sublime and incomprehensible attributes, and sustaining the supreme relations, ascribed to him in the Bible. (6) That the Papists commit a daring sin in blotting out the second command, or, in some cases, a large portion of it, from their Catechisms, and an unreasonable act in dividing the Tenth into two, for the sake of completing the original number. The reason is, that they make use of images and paintings in their worship, and that this command condemns their practice. (7.) That their pretence that they do not worship the image but only make use of it as a medium by which to worship God, is in the face of this Second Command; for God declares that he will *not* be *thus* worshipped. And, further, the same argument which the Papists use for their practice, may be employed with equal justness by the Pagans, in defence of their system of idol-worship; that they look upon the image as the symbol only, or residence of their divinities. It is also to be remembered, that God most severely punished the Israelites for the worship of the golden calf, though it was intended and used merely as a symbol, or remembrancer of the true God. (*Exod.* xxxii. 5.) (8.) That God is peculiarly indignant at this false, and to him degrading mode of worship, his indignation being expressed by the term *jealous*, to show the strength of his opposition to image-worship. (9.) That the effects of his displeasure are experienced even by the descendants of transgressors; while, on the other hand, the benefits of obedience are not confined to the obedient themselves, but reach to their descendants, and that, for a longer period, or to a greater extent, than the effects of transgression in the former case.

What Illustrations may be given?

1. A nobleman rebels against his prince; he loses his coronet, and his family suffers for centuries afterwards.. A father, through gambling, loses all his property; and his children and his children's children suffer. A parent becomes a drunkard and a debauchee, wastes his health and injures his constitution; and his offspring are diseased to the third and fourth generation. Now, what is all this, but *the sins of the fathers visited upon the children* in the arrangements of a Providence we can see, and in occurrences of daily life. Moreover, when God states that he visits the iniquities of the fathers upon the children, he does not refer to their *after* existence. This is referred to in *Ezek.* xviii. 19.—*Dr. Cumming.*

2. THE SECOND COMMANDMENT *versus* POPERY.—The Rev. *Dr. Nevins* has set forth this matter to the life. He says: "An examination, preparatory to confession, is recom-

mended to the devout Catholic, on the ten commandments, that he may see, before he goes to the priest to get forgiveness, wherein he has transgressed any of them. Now, he is not directed to examine himself on the second, but *twice over* on the tenth, so as to make out the full number. Now, I acknowledge it would have been awkward to have set the person to examine himself in reference to the second commandment. It might have led to a conviction of sins not recognized by the confessor. If he had asked himself, 'is there any graven image, or likeness of anything in heaven above, or in the earth beneath, to which I bow down?' himself would have been apt to answer, 'Why, yes, there is that image of Christ I kneel before; and there is that likeness of the Blessed Virgin I bow down to and adore;—I am afraid I have broken the second commandment.' If, then, he had gone to the priest with his scruples, you see it would have made work and trouble. It is true, the priest could have said to him, 'O, my child, you don't mean anything by it. You only use the image as a help to devotion. Your worship of it is only *relative*. Besides, you don't *adore* the image—you only *venerate* it—and you only give "*due* honor and veneration" to images—nothing more than that.' * * * * This explanation is not original with the modern Christian idolater. It is as old as Jewish and Pagan idolatry. The worshippers of the golden calf worshipped something *beyond* the calf. The calf was only a help to devotion, and they only paid 'due honor and veneration' to it. Nevertheless they 'sinned a great sin,' and 'the Lord plagued the people' on account of it. 'There fell of the people that day about 3,000.' I suppose it would have been just the same had they made ever so many explanations. But their explanations were not waited for. What signify all their explanations and distinctions to the great mass of the Catholic laity? They do not even understand them; and it seems that if they both understood and regarded them, it would not help the matter. It is this very explained and qualified worship which the commandment forbids."—*Thoughts on Popery.*

3. Amid the mummeries at Rome, the late Rev. Dr. HALL, in his journal, wrote: "I feel, as I see the disgusting pretence of this formal worship, this *fresco piety*, that God must be offended with formalism; and I am more put on my guard to deal honestly and truly with heaven in my devotions."

4. VIRGIN-MARYISM.—The man who knows Christianity best will deny to the Papist, who adheres to all the dogmas of his creed, the very name of Christian. At Rome, in particular, the Pope and all the people, from the cardinal chamberlain downwards, glory in the worship of the Virgin Mary; and their religion is not that of the New Testament, but a new and perfectly different creed, which may be named Virgin-Maryism, but certainly is not the religion of Jesus. The day begins with the Ave-Maria. Her image, and its attendant lustres, often kept constantly burning, glare at the corner of nearly every street. The most splendid churches in Rome are dedicated to her. Painting and poetry are called into her service; and we sometimes find, below these images, this invitation to passers-by: "Stop, traveller; bow the head to the mother of God—the Queen of heaven." When men recover from sickness, their cure is ascribed mainly to her, and votive offerings are hung up in her churches, as in the temples of Pagan idols in ancient Rome. Indeed, it seems obvious to the most superficial observer, that she has here supplanted the worship of the Redeemer, and that Satan has completely travestied Christianity in that city, to which he still with great subtilty points men as the metropolis of Christianity.—*Rev. W. K. Tweedie.*

5. Philip Henry made this shrewd and discriminating observation:—"I am too much a Catholic to be a *Roman* Catholic."

What is Required?

Q. 50. What is required in the second commandment?

The second commandment requireth the receiving, observing, and keeping pure and entire, all such religious worship and ordinances as God hath appointed in his word.

What Truths are embraced in this Answer?

1. *Religious worship is to be paid to God.*—*Psal.* xlv. 11. He is thy Lord; and worship thou him.
2. *God hath appointed certain religious ordinances to be observed in his worship.*—*Lev.* xviii. 4. Ye shall do my judgments, and keep mine ordinances, to walk therein: I am the Lord your God.
3. *We are required to accept of and esteem the worship and ordinances of God.*—*Psal.* cxix. 103. How sweet are thy words unto my taste! yea, sweeter than honey to my mouth.
4. *We are required to observe God's worship and ordinances.*—*Matt.* xxviii. 20. Teaching them to observe all things whatsoever I have commanded you.
5. *We are required to keep God's worship and ordinances pure.*—*Deut.* xii. 32. What thing soever I command you, observe to do it; thou shalt not add thereto, nor diminish from it.
6. *We are to keep God's worship and ordinances entire.*—*Luke,* i. 6. They were both righteous before God, walking in all the commandments and ordinances of the Lord blameless.

What Lessons do you derive from the above Doctrines?

I learn (1.) That the Scriptures alone are to guide me as to the manner and means of worshipping God, and that I am not to follow the inventions of men. (2.) That I have reason to admire the noble heroism of the Covenanters of Scotland, in the 17th century, who, at the sacrifice of home and property, and, in many cases, even at the sacrifice of life, resolved to worship God according to the simple methods which they learned from the Word of God, and not according to the forms imposed upon them by the tyrannical government of England. (3.) To place a high value upon all those scriptural methods and services by which I may approach God, and render to Him appropriate respect and homage.

What Illustrations are offered?

1. THE MASS.—"KIRWAN," in his Letters to Archbishop Hughes, thus relates his escape from early prejudices:— "Some book or tract, now forgotten, gave rise to some inquiries as to the Mass. I asked, What does it mean? I could not tell, though for years a regular attendant on it Why does the priest dress so? What book does he read from, when carried now to his right, now to his left? What mean those candles burning at noon-day? Why do I say prayers in Latin, which I understand not? Should I not know what I am saying when addressing my Maker? Why bow down and strike my breast when the little bell rings? What does it all mean? The darkness of Egypt rested upon these questions. I thus reasoned with myself: God is a spiritual and intelligent Being, and he requires an intelligent worship. What worship I render him in the Mass, I know not. My intelligent worship only is acceptable to him, and is beneficial to me. I am a rational being, and I degrade my nature, and insult my Maker, by offering to him a worship in which neither my reason, nor *His* intelligence is consulted. Having come to this conclusion, I gave up

the Mass as a form of worship well enough fitted for an idol, but unfitted to be rendered by a rational being to the infinitely intelligent Jehovah."

2. THE CONFESSIONAL.—"KIRWAN," in the same Letters, says: "Must I go to confession? My prejudices said, Yes. My reason said, No. And my logic was simply as follows: If I truly repent of my sins, God will forgive me; if I do not, the priest cannot absolve me. And I spurned as unreasonable, and as an insult to my common sense, your terrible doctrine, that 'Every Christian is bound, *under pain of damnation*, to confess to a priest all his mortal sins, which, after diligent examination, he can possibly remember yea, even his most secret sins—his very thoughts; yea, and all the circumstances of them which are of any moment.' I ask you, sir, if this dogma of the Council of Trent is not a horrible dogma? It suspends upon confessing to a priest what the Bible suspends on believing in Christ."

3. NO MEAT ON FRIDAYS.—"From my youth up," says "KIRWAN" (Rev. Dr. N. Murray), "I was taught to abstain from all meats on Fridays and Saturdays. Why on these days more than any other I was never told. And if by mistake I was involved in the violation of this law, I felt a burden upon my conscience, of which confession only could relieve me. Circumstances led me to inquire into this matter. I saw good Papists eating eggs, and fish, and getting drunk on these days; but this was no violation of the law of the Church! Yet if these persons should eat meat of any kind, or use gravy in any way, their consciences were troubled, and they must perform penance! This led me to ask, Is this reasonable? If I may eat meat on Thursday, why not on Friday? Can God, in things of this kind, make that to be a sin at one time which is not on another? I saw also persons, for whose moral worth I had the highest regard, eating meats on those days, and without any injury! And I came to

the conclusion that your regulations upon this matter were unreasonable, and rejected them. And, as far as I now remember, this was my first step towards light and freedom."—*Letters to Archbishop Hughes.*

Sins Forbidden.

Q. 51. WHAT IS FORBIDDEN IN THE SECOND COMMANDMENT?

The second commandment forbiddeth the worshipping of God by images, or any other way not appointed in his word.

What Truths are embraced in this Answer?

1. *We are not to worship God by images.*—*Deut.* iv. 15, 16. Take ye, therefore, good heed unto yourselves; (for ye saw no manner of similitude on the day that the Lord spake unto you in Horeb,) lest ye corrupt yourselves, and make you a graven image.

2. *We are not to worship God in any way not appointed in his word.*—*Deut.* iv. 2. Ye shall not add unto the word which I command you, neither shall ye diminish aught from it, that ye may keep the commandments of the Lord your God which I command you.

What Lessons do you derive from the above Doctrines?

I learn (1.) That as I am not to have any visible image of God before me in my worship, I must cultivate spirituality of mind, and fervency of devotion, and a simple realizing belief in the Scripture account of the Being whom I worship. (2.) That I am not allowed to figure Him to myself, even in my mind, as possessing form, though I may think of, and adore God incarnate in the person of the glorified Jesus. (3.) That all superstitious rules and ceremonies (those which God has not sanctioned) are to be avoided, and the service of God is to be made as spiritual and scriptural as possible. (4.) That I have no authority for calling in, as the Papists do, the aid of dead saints, in rendering worship to God, nor for honoring them by outward representation in statuary, and by forms of worship. (5.) That the second command, in its spirit and true intent, forbids men to neglect, despise, hinder, and oppose any of the proper methods of rendering worship to Jehovah. (6.) To pray that God will preserve pure religious ordinances, and powerful preaching in the land; for, as Watson, the Puritan, remarks: "*Idolatry came in at first for the want of good preaching—* the people began to have golden images when they had wooden priests."

What Illustrations are furnished?

1. POPERY REFUTED BY COMMON SENSE.—Some of the Roman Catholic Irish are so far enlightened by Sunday schools and Bible classes, that they can and do exercise their reason in resisting the abominations of Popery. One of them being asked by a priest, a curate, why he did not come to confession, said, "Please your Reverence, do *you* ever confess?" "Yes, I do—to the Rector." "And do you pay?" "Yes." "And to whom does the Rector confess?" "To the Bishop." "And does he pay him?" "Yes." "And to whom does the Bishop confess?" "To the Vicar-General." "And pays him?" "Yes." "And to whom does he confess?" "To the Pope." "And pays?" "Yes." "And to whom does the Pope confess?" "To Jesus Christ." "And does he pay anything?" "No." "Then, please your Reverence," said the man, "as I am very poor, I think I shall go to Jesus Christ at once."

2. OBSTRUCTIONS RAISED BY POPERY BETWEEN US AND GOD —"KIRWAN" observes to Archbishop Hughes, "My Bible, that hated book by pope, prelate, priest, and papal

peasant, teaches me that if any man sin he has an advocate with the Father—Jesus Christ. It everywhere teaches me that I may have free access to God through Jesus Christ; that if I sin, I may go for pardon directly to the throne of God, through the mediation of his Son. And this is a precious privilege—a privilege which may be enjoyed by all, '*without money and without price.*' Now, what do you ask of me to do, in order to receive the forgiveness of sin, and to be restored to the favor of God? You send me to Peter, or Paul, or some other saint on the catalogue, who may have never known me; and who may never hear me if I pray to them. Or you send me to Mary, whom you blasphemously call the Mother of God, to ask her to intercede for me. Nor will this suffice. I must go to your Confessional, and tell you *all* my sins; incurring the fearful penalty of refusal of pardon if I withhold one. Thus you take from me the privilege of going to God for myself, a privilege purchased for me by the death of Christ. You tell me I must go to the priest, and from the priest to the saint, or to the Virgin, and the saint or Virgin will go for me to the Saviour, and he will go for me to the Father. And then, when pardon is granted, it goes from the Father to the Son; from him to the saint or Virgin; from him or her to the priest; and when in the hands of the priest, he will give me absolution, *if I pay for it.* Why compel me to speak to my heavenly Father by proxy? * * * * Where has my Saviour taught me that I can only address him through a priestly attorney, whom I, however poor, must fee for his services?"—*Kirwan's Letters.*

Reasons Annexed.

Q. 52. WHAT ARE THE REASONS ANNEXED TO THE SECOND COMMANDMENT?

The reasons annexed to the second commandment are, God's sovereignty over us, his propriety in us, and the zeal he hath to his own worship.

What Truths are embraced in this Answer?

1. *God is our Lord and Sovereign.*—*Isa.* xxxiii. 22. The Lord is our judge, the Lord is our lawgiver, the Lord is our king; he will save us.

2. *We are the property of God.*—*Psal.* xcv. 7. He is our God; and we are the people of his pasture, and the sheep of his hand.

3. *God is very zealous for the purity of his worship.*—*Exod.* xxxiv. 14. For thou shalt worship no other God: for the Lord, whose name is Jealous, is a jealous God.

What Lessons do you derive from the above Doctrines?

I learn (1.) That there are good and substantial reasons for worshipping God in a scriptural and spiritual manner, and for avoiding all superstition and idolatry. (2.) That God is determined to punish those who give to another the honor and service which He so justly claims for himself. (3.) That parents have a special reason for rendering due worship to God, in the good or bad effect of their practice upon those most dear to them. (4.) That children have no right to imitate the conduct of idolatrous or superstitious parents, but are bound to avoid such methods of worship, and so to worship God as to counteract the judgments which He has appointed for all the transgressors of His holy law.

What Illustrations can you give?

1. A BRAHMAN, for the purpose of showing *the folly of rejecting Hinduism and embracing the Roman Catholic religion,* instituted the following comparison between the two systems:—' Has the Feringhi cheap pardons? So have we. Can the Romanist, by the mass, rescue his ancestors from purgatory? We, by ceremonies at Gaya, can do the same for ours. Can the priest change the bread and wine into flesh and blood? Our Muntras

can impart divine attributes to images. Who are the Romish monks but the counterparts of our Semyasses? Do the Catholics count their beads? So do we our Malas. Do they pray to Mother Mary? So do we to Gunga-mai. Do their priests eschew marriages? So do our Gosalies. Have they nuns? So have we our nach-girls, dedicated to the service of the temple. Do they boast their antiquity? Compare eighteen hundred years, the period they claim as the age of their church, with the four Jugs, (immense periods) of Hinduism."

2. FORCIBLE REPLICATION.—An intelligent Catholic lady recently said to a clergyman, "Why are you Protestants continually attacking us?" "I beg your pardon, madam," said the clergyman, "the case is *precisely the reverse.* Our name might teach you so. We believe that no one has a right to stand between us and our Father in heaven, but the only divinely-appointed Mediator, Jesus Christ. You attack us for this belief, and place in his stead the Virgin Mary. We believe that no one has a right to stand between us and the Bible; but you attack us by substituting the Pope. These two articles of our faith are vital and fundamental; we could more easily give up life than relinquish them." "Well," said she, "if you think and feel so, you should be allowed to hold your opinion." "That is just the third grand principle," said the clergyman, "of Protestant faith, *liberty of conscience.* In holding and defending it for ourselves, we maintain it in behalf of the rest of the world, Catholic as well as others. It is the Catholics that occupy the aggressive position, not the Protestants. They stand on the *defensive.*"

THE THIRD COMMANDMENT.

Q. 53. WHAT IS THE THIRD COMMANDMENT?

The third commandment is, Thou shalt not take

the name of the Lord thy God in vain; for the Lord will not hold him guiltless that taketh his name in vain.

Q. 54. WHAT IS REQUIRED IN THE THIRD COMMANDMENT?

The third commandment requireth the holy and reverend use of God's names, titles, attributes, ordinances, word and works.

What Truths are embraced in this Answer?

1. *God's name is to be used with holy reverence.—Psal.* xxix. 2. Give unto the Lord the glory due into his name.

2. *God's titles are to be used with holy reverence.—Rev.* xv. 3, 4. Great and marvellous are thy works, Lord God Almighty; just and true are thy ways, thou King of saints. Who shall not fear thee, O Lord, and glorify thy name.

3. *God's attributes are to be used with holy reverence.— Rev.* iv. 8. Holy, holy, holy, Lord God Almighty, which was, and is, and is to come.

4. *God's ordinances are to be used with holy reverence.— Eccl.* v. 1. Keep thy foot when thou goest to the house of God, and be more ready to hear, than to give the sacrifice of fools.

5. *God's word is to be used with holy reverence.—Prov.* xiii. 13. Whoso despiseth the word shall be destroyed: but he that feareth the commandment shall be rewarded.

6. *God's works are to be used and contemplated with holy reverence.—Job,* xxxvi. 24. Remember that thou magnify His work, which men behold.

What Lessons do you derive from the above Doctrines?

I learn (1.) To regard with the greatest reverence all that relates to the Most High God, and to speak or write of him in a solemn and thoughtful manner. (2.) By his *names* are intended such as "Lord," "God," "Jehovah,"

"Father," "Son," and "Holy Ghost;" by his *titles*, such as "God of Nature," "God of Grace," "Lord of Hosts," "Creator," "King of Nations," "Holy One of Israel," &c.; by *attributes* are intended his eternity, omniscience, omnipresence, wisdom, holiness, mercy, justice, &c.; by *ordinances* are meant, prayer and thanksgiving; praise; the sacraments; reading, preaching, and hearing of the Word of God; oaths, religion, fasting; by his *works* are designed those of creation, those of providence, but especially that of redemption. Hence (3.) I learn that this command requires a cautious, respectful, and adoring mention or thought of all the names and expressions by which God is made known; and of all the properties or excellencies ascribed to Him; that it also requires a reverential use of those outward modes or ceremonies of worship which he has prescribed, together with a devout attention and obedience to all that the Bible teaches and enjoins upon me; and further, it requires a devout study and contemplation of God, and submission to him, as he is manifested in the works of creation, and in all his providential dealings.

What Illustrations may be related?

1. THE YOUNG SWEARER REBUKED.—A MINISTER sailing up the Hudson river in a sloop, some forty-five years since, was pained by the profaneness of a young man. Seeking a favorable opportunity, he told him he had wounded his feelings by speaking against his best Friend—the Saviour. The young man showed no relentings, and at one of the landings left the boat. The minister was pained, and feared his labors were in vain. Seven years after, as this minister went to the General Assembly, at Philadelphia, a young man accosted him saying, he thought he remembered his countenance, and asked him if he was not on board a sloop on the Hudson river seven

years before, with a profane young man. At length the circumstances were called to mind. "I," said he, "am that young man. After I had left the sloop, I thought I had injured both you and your Saviour. I was led to him for mercy, and felt that I must preach his love to others I am now in the ministry, and have come as a representative to this Assembly."

2. THE SAVOYARD, THE PRIEST, AND THE BIBLE.—A young Savoyard, a poor little chimney-sweep, purchased one day a Testament, for which he paid ten sous, and set himself immediately to read it. Delighted to possess the Word of God, he ran to the priest in his simplicity, to show him the good bargain he had made with his savings. The priest took the book, and told the young Savoyard that it came from the hands of heretics, and that it was *a book forbidden to be read.* The peasant replied that "everything he had read in the book told him about Christ; and, besides," said he, "it is so beautiful!" "You shall see how beautiful it is," said the priest, seizing it and casting it into the fire. The young Savoyard went away weeping.—*Cheever.*

Sins Forbidden.

Q. 55. WHAT IS FORBIDDEN IN THE THIRD COMMANDMENT?

The third commandment forbiddeth all profaning or abusing of anything whereby God maketh himself known.

What Truths are embraced in this Answer?

1. *We are not to profane anything by which God maketh himself known.*—Lev. xviii. 21. Neither shalt thou profane the name of thy God: I am the Lord.

2. *We are not to abuse anything by which God maketh him-*

THIRD COMMANDMENT. 141

self known.—Mat. xxiii. 14. Wo unto you, Scribes and Pharisees, hypocrites! for ye devour widows' houses, and for a pretence make long prayers.

What Lessons do you derive from the above Doctrines?

I Learn (1.) That the third commandment forbids all irreverent and disrespectful thought, speech, writing, or conduct in relation to God, or to anything by which he makes himself known to me; that it forbids all perversion of sacred scripture, all trifling with its doctrines and sacred precepts; that it forbids a wrong use of anything which God has made for our benefit, and also of his dealings with us, either in the form of prosperity or adversity. (2.) The great need of habitual seriousness and caution, lest I offend against this broad precept; the need also of being constantly under the influence of God's Holy Spirit, so as to keep my soul in a proper state of regard for God and all that relates to Him. (3.) The great evil of perjury, or false swearing under oath, when a man calls the all-knowing Jehovah to witness that he is speaking truth, and that only, when he is conscious that he is speaking that which is not true, but the reverse This is supposed to be the prominent sin condemned by the Third Commandment (4.) That profane swearing is a monstrous sin; and that there is cause for deep sorrow and concern that it prevails so extensively, and even among children and youth. I learn, also, my solemn duty to endeavor to arrest this sin when I can, and to promote a deep reverence for God, and for all the means and modes of worship which he has been pleased to appoint.

What Illustrations are offered?

1. GIVE ME THE AXE.—It is related of the venerable *Dr. Matthews*, late President of Hanover College, that on one occasion, as he was walking near the college, with

his slow and noiseless step, a youth who had not observed his approach, while engaged in cutting wood, began to swear profanely in his vexation. The Doctor stepped up and said, "Give me the axe;" and then quietly chopped the stick of wood up himself. Returning the axe to the young man, he said in his peculiar manner, "You see now the wood may be cut without swearing." The reproof was effectual, and led to an entire abandonment of the impious habit.

2. QUIET REBUKE.—Rev. JOHN HOWE, hearing a gentleman speaking highly of some one in a large party, and at the same time mixing many horrid oaths with his discourse, mildly, but decidedly, said to him, that he had omitted one great excellence in the character of that individual. "What is it, sir?" said the other with eagerness; "what is it?" "It is this," said Mr. Howe, "*that he never was heard to swear an oath in common conversation.*"

3. WASHINGTON'S TESTIMONY.—Within the first month after the Declaration of Independence, Washington gave a noble testimony against profaneness, by declaring in his public orders that "he hopes the officers will, by example as well as influence, endeavor to check it, and that both they and the men will reflect that we can have little hope of the blessing of heaven on our arms, if we insult it by our impiety and folly: added to this, it is a vice so mean and low, without any temptation, that every man of sense and character despises it."

Reasons Annexed.

Q. 56. WHAT IS THE REASON ANNEXED TO THE THIRD COMMANDMENT?

The reason annexed to the third commandment is, That however the breakers of this commandment may escape punishment from men, yet the Lord our God will not suffer them to escape his righteous judgment.

What Truths are embraced in this Answer?

The sin of taking God's name in vain will be especially punished by God.—*Deut.* xxviii. 58, 59. If thou wilt not observe to do all the words of this law that are written in this book, that thou mayest fear this glorious and fearful name, "THE LORD THY GOD;" then the Lord will make thy plagues wonderful.

What Lessons do you derive from the above Doctrines?

I learn (1.) That human government is far less rigid than the Divine Government, which is perfect; that the former takes no notice of many sins for which God will hereafter call men to a strict account. (2.) That a man may be a good citizen in view of human laws; and yet a bad citizen as viewed by the laws of the higher government of God. (3.) That an escape from punishment in this life is no proof of not being liable to punishment in a future and endless state of existence. (4.) That I must regard the claims of both human and divine laws, and conduct myself rightly in view of both.

What Illustrations are presented?

A GENTLEMAN (?) much addicted to profane swearing, accompanied a pious miner to see one of the mines in Cornwall. During his visit to the pit he distressed his companion by many profane and abominable expressions; and as they ascended together, finding it a long way, he flippantly said, "As it is so far down to your work, how far do you suppose it is to hell?" The miner promptly replied: "I do not know how far it is to hell, sir; but I believe that if the rope by which we are drawn up should break, you would be there in one minute."

THE FOURTH COMMANDMENT.

Q. 57. WHICH IS THE FOURTH COMMANDMENT?

The fourth commandment is, Remember the Sabbath day, to keep it holy. Six days shalt thou labor, and do all thy work; but the seventh day is the Sabbath of the Lord thy God: in it thou shalt not do any work, thou, nor thy son, nor thy daughter, thy man-servant, nor thy maid-servant, nor thy cattle, nor thy stranger that is within thy gates. For in six days the Lord made heaven and earth, the sea, and all that in them is, and rested the seventh day: wherefore the Lord blessed the Sabbath day, and hallowed it.

What Lessons do you derive from the above Answer?

I learn (1.) That men are apt to forget the sacred character and uses of the Sabbath-day; and that a broad distinction must be made between the employments of that day, and those of the other days of the week. (2.) That God, and not man, has set apart the Sabbath-day, as one of abstinence from worldly business and recreations, and of devotion to religious purposes. (3.) That I am, therefore, under the strongest obligations to observe it in the manner now to be explained. (4.) That it is the duty of parents, of masters, and of heads of families, to see that their children, their servants, and inmates of their families, observe the Sabbath-day. (5.) By the "set times" are meant chiefly the Sabbath, and days of fasting and thanksgiving. Under the Jewish economy there were other set times and modes of worship, which were abolished when the Christian economy was introduced. Since then no *holidays* (holy days) but the Sabbath, are of divine authority or obligation, though it is equally our duty and our profit to attend meetings for the worship of God and religious improvement during the week also. Also (6.) That it is as much my duty to labor six days, as to avoid labor every seventh day. "A Christian must not only mind heaven, but his calling."

What Illustration is given?

No Sabbath.—In a "Prize Essay on the Sabbath," written by a journeyman printer in Scotland, there occurs the following admirable passage:—"Yoke-fellow! think how the abstraction of the Sabbath would hopelessly enslave the working-classes, with whom we are identified. Think of labor thus going on in one monotonous and continuous and eternal cycle—limbs for ever on the rack, the fingers for ever playing, the eyeballs for ever straining, the brow for ever sweating, the feet for ever plodding, the brain for ever drooping, the loins for ever aching, and the restless mind for ever scheming. Think of the beauty it would extinguish, of the giant strength that it would tame; of the sickness it would breed; of the groans it would extort; and of the cheerless graves that it would prematurely dig! See them, toiling and moiling, sweating and fretting, grinding and hewing, weaving and spinning, sowing and gathering, mowing and reaping, razing and building, digging and planting, unloading and storing, struggling—in the garden and in the field, in the granary and in the barn, in the factory and in the mill, in the warehouse and in the shop, on the mountain and in the ditch, on the roadside and in the wood, in the city and in the country, on the sea and on the shore, on the earth, and in the earth; in days of brightness and of gloom. What a sad picture would the earth present if we had no Sabbath."

Duties Required.

Q. 58. WHAT IS REQUIRED IN THE FOURTH COMMANDMENT?

The fourth commandment requireth the keeping holy to God such set times as he hath appointed in his word; expressly one whole day in seven, to be a holy Sabbath to himself.

What Truths are embraced in this Answer?

1. *God in his worship hath appointed set times for his worship.—Lev.* xix. 30. Ye shall keep my Sabbaths, and reverence my sanctuary: I am the Lord.
2. *God requires one day in seven for himself.—Deut.* v. 14. The seventh day is the Sabbath of the Lord thy God.
3. *The Sabbath is the day appointed for the worship of God.—Exod.* xxxv. 2. On the seventh day there shall be to you a holy day, a Sabbath of rest to the Lord.
4. *The whole of the Sabbath is God's, and must be used in his service.—Exod.* xxxi. 15. Whosoever doeth any work in the Sabbath day, he shall surely be put to death.
5. *The Sabbath is to be kept holy to God.—Deut.* v. 12. Keep the Sabbath day to sanctify it, as the Lord thy God hath commanded thee.

What Lessons do you derive from the above Doctrines?

I learn that from twelve on Saturday night to twelve on Sabbath night, is a period sacred to God and separated from worldly uses, and that any one part of this period is as sacred as any other part of it, and to be observed accordingly.

What Illustration is given?

The late Rev. Charles Hall, of New York, presents, in his own practice, a striking and a rare instance of strict conformity to the law of the Sabbath. The Rev. Dr. Smith says of him in this respect: "Neither by labor, by recreation, nor by travel, under whatever urgency of temptation, would he desecrate the blessed day of God. After a week's toil in a narrow room in the crowded city, he would resolutely decline walking in his garden on that day, however solicited by the early flowers, the spring birds and the balmy air. He would avoid the very appearance of evil; he would not even seem to saunter away the holy hours. On his return from his tour in Europe, the ship that bore him arrived at the wharf in this city on Sabbath morning. His family were at Newark; a little more than half an hour's ride in the cars would have taken him there. His affectionate heart yearned to greet them; but it was the Lord's day, and his eye was still 'single.' So he tarried in the city until Monday, 'and rested the Sabbath day, according to the commandment.'"

Change of the Sabbath.

Q. 59. WHICH DAY OF THE SEVEN HATH GOD APPOINTED TO BE THE WEEKLY SABBATH?

From the beginning of the world to the resurrection of Christ, God appointed the seventh day of the week to be the weekly Sabbath; and the first day of the week, ever since, to continue to the end of the world, which is the Christian Sabbath.

What Truths are embraced in this Answer?

1. *The seventh day of the week was at first appointed by God as the weekly Sabbath.*—Deut. v. 14. The seventh day is the Sabbath of the Lord thy God.

2. *The change of the Sabbath took place immediately after the resurrection of Christ.—John,* xx. 19. (*Compared with ver.* 26.) Then the same day at evening, being the first day of the week, when the doors were shut where the disciples were assembled for fear of the Jews, came Jesus and stood in the midst.

3. *The first day of the week is the Christian Sabbath, or Lord's day.—Acts,* xx. 7. Upon the first day of the week, when the disciples came together to break bread, Paul preached unto them.

4. *The first day of the week shall continue to be the Lord's day, without change, till the end of the world.—Rev.* xxii. 19. If any man should take away from the words of the book of this prophecy, God shall take away his part out of the book of life.

What Lessons do you derive from the above Doctrines?

I learn (1.) That the event of the resurrection of Christ is evidently regarded by God as of greater moment than that of the creation of the world; for the Sabbath which, for four thousand years, had been the appointed memorial of the latter, ceased to be such when the former event occurred, of which thenceforth the Sabbath changed in consequence, to the first day of the week, became the perpetual memorial. (2.) That when the first day of the week dawns upon me, the first and happiest of my thoughts should be of Christ and of his glorious ascent from the grave, in confirmation of his claims and success as a Redeemer. (3.) That the early Christians had good reason to call this the "Lord's day;" not only for that just assigned, but Christ had besides probably authorized the title, either personally or by his apostles, under the inspiration of the Holy Ghost.

What Illustrations are given?

1. IGNATIUS, one of the early fathers, who lived at the same period with the apostle John, thus commends the

religious observance of the first day of the week: "Let every one that loveth Christ, keep holy the first day of the week, the Lord's day."

2. Says the Rev. *Thomas Watson*: "The reason why God did institute the old Sabbath was, because God would have it kept as a memorial of the creation; but the Lord hath now brought the first day of the week in the room of it in memory of a more glorious work than creation, and that is redemption. It cost more to redeem us than to create us. In the creation there was but speaking a word; in the redeeming of us there was the shedding of blood. In the creation God gave us ourselves; in the redemption he gave us Himself. By creation we have a life in Adam; by redemption we have a life in Christ. By creation we had a right to an earthly Paradise; by redemption we have a title to a heavenly kingdom."

3. THE FIRST, THE BEST DAY OF THE WEEK.—God hath made all the days, but he hath *blessed* this. As Jacob got the blessing from his brother, so the Sabbath got the blessing from all the other days of the week. *The Sabbath is the cream of time.* The other days of the week are most employed about earth; this day about heaven. Now Christ takes the soul into the mount, and gives it transfiguring sights of glory. The Apostle John was in the Spirit on the Lord's day,—he was carried up in divine raptures towards heaven. *Christ wrought most of his miracles on the Sabbath:* so he doeth now; the dead soul is raised, the heart of stone is made flesh. *God hath anointed this day with the oil of gladness above its fellows.—Thomas Watson.*

Sanctification of the Sabbath.

Q. 60. HOW IS THE SABBATH TO BE SANCTIFIED?

The Sabbath is to be sanctified by a holy resting

all that day, even from such worldly employments and recreations as are lawful on other days; and spending the whole time in the public and private exercises of God's worship, except so much as is to be taken up in the works of necessity and mercy.

What Truths are embraced in this Answer?

1. *The Sabbath is to be kept by every one individually as a day of rest for himself.*—*Exod.* xxxi. 15. Whosoever doeth any work in the Sabbath day, he shall surely be put to to death.

2. *The rest of the Sabbath is to be kept by every family, and is to extend to our servants and cattle.*—*Deut.* v. 14. That thy man servant and thy maid servant may rest as well as thou.

3. *The Sabbath is to be kept by communities as a day of rest.*—*Lev.* xxiii. 3. Six days shall work be done: but the seventh day is the Sabbath of rest, a holy convocation: ye shall do no work therein.

4. *We are, on Sabbath, to abstain from all worldly employments.*—*Jer.* xvii. 21. Thus saith the Lord, Take heed to yourselves, and bear no burden on the Sabbath day.

5. *We are, on Sabbath, to abstain from such secular acts as can be postponed to another day.*—*Luke,* xxiii. 56. And they returned, and prepared spices and ointments; and rested the Sabbath day, according to the commandment.

6. *We are, on Sabbath, to abstain from recreations and pastimes, though lawful on other days.*—*Isa.* lviii. 13. If thou turn away thy foot from the Sabbath, from doing thy pleasure on my holy day; and call the Sabbath a Delight, the Holy of the Lord, Honorable; and shalt honor him, not doing thine own ways, nor finding thine own pleasure, nor speaking thine own words.

7. *The Sabbath is to be employed in public exercises of God's worship.*—*Isa.* lxvi. 23. From one Sabbath to another, shall all flesh come to worship before me, saith the Lord.

8. *The Sabbath is to be employed in private acts of secret and social worship.*—*Lev.* xxiii. 3. It is the Sabbath of the Lord in all your dwellings.

9. *Works of necessity are lawful on the Sabbath day.*—*Mat.* xii. 1. Jesus went on the Sabbath day through the corn, and his disciples were an hungered, and began to pluck the ears of corn, and to eat.

10. *Works of mercy are lawful on the Sabbath day.*—*Luke,* xiii. 16. Ought not this woman, being a daughter of Abraham, whom Satan hath bound, lo, these eighteen years, be loosed from this bond on the Sabbath day?

What Lessons do you derive from the above Doctrines?

I learn (1.) That I must abstain on the Sabbath from all kinds of business, done for gain or livelihood, which, by prudent management, might have been done previously, or may be left undone till after the Sabbath; that I must abstain from the reading of newspapers and books that are not religious; from studying the arts and sciences; from writing letters upon worldly topics and interests; from making up accounts and posting books; from unnecessary travelling; from walking and riding for pleasure; from conversing about the general news of the time, trade, politics, &c.; from feasting and visiting of friends and neighbors; from unnecessary preparation of food and other manual labors. (2.) That great sin is committed on the Sabbath by multitudes who think that they pay a proper respect to the day; and much more by others, who do what they please on that day. (3.) That it is not enough to abstain from the things mentioned above, if I do not also give my attention to religious worship and improvement. (4.) That the right or wrong use of every seventh day cannot fail to exert a decided influence, good or bad, upon my character and happiness, in this life and in the next.

What Illustrations are given?

1. On the morning of his last Sabbath on earth, as the

day was breaking, a friend who had been sitting with him, said, to the late Rev. Dr. CHARLES HALL, "Dear brother, it is the Sabbath's dawn. May the Sun of righteousness arise, with healing on his wings." He replied, "The Sabbath—the Sabbath—the sweet, blessed Sabbath!" His friend then repeated the lines:

> "Welcome, delightful morn,
> Thou day of sacred rest!"

He added—

> "Lord, make these moments blest."

As the sun was lighting up the East, the chair in which, from difficulty of breathing, he was obliged to sit, was drawn toward the window, that he might look out once more upon the loved face of nature. It was one of those serene and beautiful Sabbaths, that had often called from his lips the exclamation—

> "Sweet day, so cool, so calm, so bright,
> The bridal of the earth and sky!"

A member of his family not being aware of what had passed, said to him, "It is the Sabbath." "Yes," replied he, "It is *a smile of the Lord.*"

2. "Who can believe," says *Dr. Belfrage,* "that *one whole day in seven is too much* to be observed to the Lord, who believes that a whole eternity shall be occupied, and occupied most delightfully, in his service?"

3. A CONCLUSIVE OBJECTION.—A motion was once made in Parliament to drill the militia on Sunday, for the sake of saving time, and was likely to pass, when an old member rose and said, "I have one objection to this,— *I believe in an old book called the Bible.*" The members looked at one another, and the motion was dropped.

4. THE HOUSE OF GOD.—When men attend *public worship but once on the Sabbath,* and assign as a reason, that

they were reading the Bible, I expect that they could not have been reading the 95th Psalm, nor the 25th verse of the 11th chapter of Hebrews.—*Rev. Dr. Nevins.*

5. It is good to rest on the Sabbath day from the works of our calling; but if we rest from labor and *do no more*, the ox and the ass keep the Sabbath as well as we, for they rest from labor. *We must dedicate the day to God;* we must not only "keep a Sabbath," but "sanctify a Sabbath."—*Thomas Watson.*

6. Two Extremes.—Among Christians, there has been a difference of opinion respecting *the degree of strictness* with which the Sabbath is to be observed. Some are for retaining all the rigor of the Jewish law, while others insist that now its severity is relaxed. It is possible so to overstrain the duties of the day, as to make men think that they can hardly speak, or move, or look around them, without violating its sanctity; and thus to give the Sabbath a gloomy and forbidding aspect. It is possible to grant such liberty, that it shall resemble a human festival rather than a season of devotion—a day of idleness, gossiping, and amusement, mixed up with some religious offices.—*Dick's Lectures.*

Sins Forbidden.

Q. 61. What is forbidden in the fourth commandment?

The fourth commandment forbiddeth the omission or careless performance of the duties required, and the profaning the day by idleness, or doing that which is in itself sinful, or by unnecessary thoughts, words, or works, about our worldly employments or recreations.

What Truths are embraced in this Answer?

1. *We are not to omit any of the duties required from us on the Sabbath.—Ezek.* xxii. 26. Her priests have violated my law, and have profaned mine holy things; they have put no difference between the holy and profane, neither have they showed difference between the unclean and the clean, and have hid their eyes from my Sabbaths, and I am profaned among them.

2. *The duties of the Sabbath are not to be performed carelessly.—Deut.* x. 12. Serve the Lord thy God with all thy heart, and with all thy soul.

3. *The Sabbath is not to be profaned by idleness.—Exod.* xx. 8. Remember the Sabbath day, to keep it holy.

4. *Sinful acts are aggravated by being committed on the Sabbath—Ezek* xxiii. 38. They have defiled my sanctuary in the same day, and have profaned my Sabbaths.

5. *Unnecessary thoughts about our worldly concerns are forbidden on the Sabbath.—Amos,* viii. 5. When will the new moon be gone, that we may sell corn? and the Sabbath, that we may set forth wheat?

6. *Unnecessary conversation about our worldly affairs is forbidden on the Sabbath.—Isa.* lviii. 13. Not doing thine own ways, nor finding thine own pleasure, nor speaking thine own words.

7. *Unnecessary works for forwarding our worldly concerns are forbidden on the Sabbath.—Jer.* xvii. 21. Thus saith the Lord; Take heed to yourselves, and bear no burden on the Sabbath day.

What Truths are embraced in this Answer?

I learn (1.) That I must prepare for the Sabbath, by having as little labor of a worldly sort as possible to be attended to on that day. (2.) That I must make the "works of necessity" as few as may be. (3.) That I must relieve the destitute, the sick, and other suffering persons, as far as practicable during the six days, so that the Sabbath may be the more unreservedly devoted to pursuits strictly religious.

What Illustrations are given?

1. BE AT CHURCH IN TIME.—Mrs. CHAPONE was asked why she always came so early to church! "Because," said she, "it is part of my religion never to disturb the religion of others."

2. THE WOOD-CUTTER.—In one of the central counties of New Jersey, a poor mechanic, eminent for his pious zeal and consistency, was very much tried by the conduct of an ungodly neighbor, who was in the habit of cutting his wood for the week on the Lord's day, and the sound of whose axe continually disturbed the old Christian's meditation. Father H., as he was called, often remonstrated earnestly and kindly with his neighbor, but with no effect. At length he adopted a different course. On Saturday afternoon his neighbor found the old man very busy at his wood pile, and inquired in astonishment what he was doing. "Why," replied Father H., "you will persist in cutting your wood on God's holy day, and it grieves me so much that I mean to do it for you this afternoon, so that you will have no temptation to do it to-morrow." The man was at once overcome, and exclaimed, "No, you shall not; I will do it myself; nor will you ever, after this, have reason to complain of me for chopping wood on the Lord's day." And he was as good as his word.— *Am. Messenger.*

3. *Safe Reasoning.*—"If you are not afraid of God, I am afraid of you," said a stranger as he passed a counting room on the Sabbath, and saw it open. He next day refused to sell his produce to the Sabbath-breaker on any credit whatever. He acted wisely. In three months the Sabbath-breaker was a bankrupt

4. THE LITTLE BOY'S REBUKE.--One Sunday a lady called to her little boy, who was tossing marbles on the side-walk, to come into the house. "Don't you know you shouldn't

be out there, my son? Go into the back yard, if you want to play marbles—it is Sunday." "Well, yes. But *ain't it Sunday in the back yard*, mother?"

Reasons Annexed.

Q. 62. WHAT ARE THE REASONS ANNEXED TO THE FOURTH COMMANDMENT?

The reasons annexed to the fourth commandment are, God's allowing us six days of the week for our own employments, his challenging a special propriety in the seventh, his own example, and his blessing the Sabbath day.

What Truths are embraced in this Answer?

1. *God having allowed us six days for our own employment, claims the seventh for himself.—Exod.* xxxi. 15, 16. Six days may work be done, but in the seventh is the Sabbath of rest.—Wherefore the children of Israel shall keep the Sabbath.
2. *God claiming the Sabbath as his own property, requires us to keep it.—Lev.* xxiii. 3. Ye shall do no work therein: it is the Sabbath of the Lord.
3. *God having set us the example of resting on the Sabbath requires us to follow it.—Exod.* xxxi. 17. It is a sign between me and the children of Israel for ever: for in six days the Lord made heaven and earth, and on the seventh day he rested and was refreshed.
4. *God requires the Sabbath to be observed by us because he himself blessed and sanctified it.—Gen.* ii. 3. God blessed the seventh day, and sanctified it.

What Lessons do you derive from the above Doctrines?

I learn (1.) That there are strong and sufficient reasons why I should strictly observe the Sabbath—reasons that apply also to all other persons. (2.) That it is base and ungrateful to grudge the devoting of only a seventh part of my time to God, while he has given me six-sevenths for attending to my worldly affairs and recreations. (3.) I may suppose that as God could have created the world by an immediate act, he was pleased to employ six days in making it, followed by one of rest, thus to prepare the way, by his own high example, for his intelligent creatures to observe *a similar order in their own employments;* in other words, to prompt them to act in accordance with the Fourth Command. (4.) As God on the Seventh day looked with delight upon the world of beauty and of life which his operations had completed on the preceding six days, so he designs that on each seventh day of our lives we should employ ourselves in reflecting upon his varied works of Creation, of Providence, and of Redemption. (5.) Another strong reason for observing the Sabbath, in the way prescribed, is, that *Sabbath-breaking has been the most common beginning and cause of a life of crime and infamy,* while, on the other hand, the observance of the Sabbath is the best preparation for a life of virtue and respectability.

What Illustrations are given ?

1. SCOTCH SABBATHS.—"I have heard" (says one) "many curious stories illustrative of that *veneration with which the Sabbath is regarded in Scotland.* Let me mention one. A geologist, while in the country, and having his pocket hammer with him, took it out and was chipping the rock on the way-side, for examination. His proceedings did not escape the quiet eye and ready tongue of an old Scotch woman. ' What are you doing there, man ?' 'Don't you see? I'm breaking a stone.' 'Y'are doing mair than that: y'are breaking the Sabbath.' "

2. WILBERFORCE AND THE SABBATH.—This celebrated man ascribes his continuance for so long a time, under

such a pressure of cares and labors, in no small degree to the conscientious and habitual observance of the Sabbath. "Oh what a blessed day," he says, " is the Sabbath, which allows us a precious interval wherein to pause—to come out from the thickets of worldly concerns, and give ourselves up to heavenly and spiritual objects! *It is a blessed thing to have the Sabbath devoted to God.* There is nothing in which I would commend you to be more conscientious than in keeping the Sabbath day."

3. SETTLING ACCOUNTS.—A GENTLEMAN introduced an infidel friend to a minister, with the remark, "He never attends public worship." "Ah!" said the minister, "I am almost tempted to hope you are bearing false witness against your neighbor." "By no means," said the infidel, "for I always spend Sundays in settling my accounts." The minister immediately replied: "You will find, sir, that the day of judgment will be spent in the same manner."

4. YOU CAN TRUST HIM.—NICHOLAS BIDDLE, when President of the United States Bank, once dismissed a clerk because the latter refused to write for him on the Sabbath. The young man, dependent on his exertions, was thus thrown out of employment by what some would call an over-nice scruple of conscience. But, a few days after, Mr. Biddle being requested to nominate a cashier for another bank, recommended this very individual, and mentioned this incident as a proof of his trust-worthiness. "*You can trust him,*" said he "*for he would not work for me on Sunday.*"

5. THE DAY OF REST.—The rest of the Sabbath is necessary, after the engagement of the week, as is the night's rest after the work of the day. After six days of labor our strained muscles need a season to renew their elasticity—our irritable nerves to recover their moral

state—our fretted spirits to resume their equanimity. A simple change of necessary labor does a great deal; the entire cessation of all that is unnecessary does still more. The fitting devotional exercises of the day are calming and soothing, and productive of that healthy state of mind with which it is desirable to enter upon the duties of the succeeding days. The influence of the Sabbath on the week's tumultuous cares is like oil poured on a stormy sea.—*N. Y. Times.*

THE DUTIES WHICH WE OWE TO MAN,

CONTAINED IN THE LAST SIX COMMANDMENTS OF THE LAW.

THE FIFTH COMMANDMENT.

Q. 63. WHAT IS THE FIFTH COMMANDMENT?

The fifth commandment is, Honor thy father and thy mother; that thy days may be long upon the land which the Lord thy God giveth thee.

What Lessons do you derive from the above Answer?

I learn (1.) That I must love, obey, and provide for my father and mother. (2.) That God greatly cares for the comfort of my parents, or he would not have given this command so prominent a place, nor connected with obedience to it a special promise, such as no other of the ten commands furnishes. (3.) That disobedience to parents, and a neglect of their welfare, is a base and aggravated

What Illustrations are given?

1. The late Professor B. B. EDWARDS, for a long time after the decease of his mother, remained sad and melan-

choly. Those who saw the influence of his affliction, said, one to another: "Behold how he loved her!" He felt a pious joy in looking forward to his college vacations, when he might place some green sods upon her grave.—*Park's Memoirs.*

2. A FATHER'S PRAYER.—A boy disobeyed his father. His father, with a look of sorrow, retired to his room. The boy wished to know what his father was doing, or going to do, for he felt guilty. So, with the mean spirit of a disobedient boy, he looked through the key-hole. There he saw his father on his knees at prayer. He listened and heard his father praying for him. This struck him to the heart. He went away and prayed for himself. God heard the prayer of this pious father, and his son became a Christian indeed.—*N. Y. Observer.*

Duties Required.

Q. 64. WHAT IS REQUIRED IN THE FIFTH COMMANDMENT?

The fifth commandment requireth the preserving the honor, and performing the duties belonging to every one in their several places and relations, as superiors, inferiors, or equals.

What Truths are embraced in this Answer?

1. *The several stations in society are ordained by God.*—Rom. xiii. 1. The powers that be, are ordained of God.
2. *We must preserve the honor due to every one in their several stations.*—1 Pet. ii. 17. Honor all men.
3. *We must preserve the honor due to our superiors.*—Lev. xix. 32. Thou shalt rise up before the hoary head, and honor the face of the old man, and fear thy God: I am the Lord.
4. *We must preserve the honor due to our inferiors.*—Rom. xii. 16. Condescend to men of low estate.

5. *We must preserve the honor due to our equals.—Rom.* xii. 10. Be kindly affectioned one to another with brotherly love ; in honor preferring one another.

6. *We are faithfully to perform the duties which belong to every one in their several stations.—Rom.* xiii. 7. Render therefore to all their dues.

7. *We must perform the duties which we owe to our superiors.—Rom.* xiii. 1. Let every soul be subject unto the higher powers.

8. *We must perform the duties which we owe to our inferiors.—Eph.* vi. 9. And, ye masters, do the same things unto them, forbearing threatening: knowing that your Master also is in heaven.

9. *We must perform the duties which we owe to our equals—Eph.* v. 21. Submitting yourselves one to another in the fear of God.

10. *All our social duties must be performed with a due regard to the authority of God.—Eph.* vi. 7. With goodwill doing service, as to the Lord, and not to men.

What Lessons do you derive from the above Doctrines ?

I learn (1.) That all men do not stand on the same level, but that some are so situated as to hold a certain authority and command over others. (2.) That the present state of society being such by God's arrangement, I must regard it as wise and useful. (3.) Out of this state of things grows a large number of duties, the performance of which binds society most happily together. (4.) I ought to be content with the station in life which God has given, and attentive to its specific duties. (5.) The *superiors* to whom I owe respect and various duties, are such as the following :—not only my father and mother, but all others who are appointed over me in places of authority, whether in the family, or in the church of Christ, or in the State,—all who are above me in station, office, dignity, or gifts. (6.) By *inferiors* are meant, all who are under me in those respects. (7.) *Equals* are those of about equal age, gifts, or condition in the world.

FIFTH COMMANDMENT.

(8.) Among the *relations* existing, are those of husband and wife, parent and child, minister and people, master and servant, employer and apprentices, magistrate and private citizen, teacher and pupil, brothers and sisters, elder and younger. (9.) It becomes a duty to examine the Scriptures, and to employ deep reflection, to ascertain what course of conduct I owe to my fellow-men, according as they are related to me in any of the ways just pointed out; and then, conscientiously and carefully to pursue that course, *because God requires it.*

What Illustrations are given?

1. GENERAL HARRISON.—On his way to Washington, to enter upon the duties of the Presidential chair, General Harrison made a visit to his native place in Virginia, and here, for the last time, saw the home of his infancy. He passed through the house from room to room, until, upon arriving at a retired bed-chamber, he burst into tears, saying to a friend, who accompanied him, "*This is the spot where my mother used to pray with me.*" This was the hidden influence which had followed him through all the exciting scenes of his eventful life.—*Dr. Magie.*

2. THE POOR WIDOW.—"Uncle Oliver," said the pastor of a country church, to an elderly farmer of his flock, "I wish you would carry a load of wood to old Mrs. W., the widow of our Christian brother, who lived so long just beyond you on the road to D." "I will try to do it," said the farmer; "but to whom shall I look for the pay?" Said the pastor, "Read, when you go home, the first three verses of the 41st Psalm; and then, if you want any better security for payment, call on me." It was but a few days after, the old gentleman met his pastor, and said, "I like that security you mentioned, and have no fear that it will fail me in the time of need—for my heart

so felt the assurance, when reading it, that I could scarce close my eyes that night."—*N. Y. Evang.*

3. I CANNOT PRAY FOR FATHER ANY MORE!—A CHILD knelt, at the accustomed hour, to thank God for the mercies of the day, and pray for care through the coming night; then, as usual, came the earnest, "God bless dear mother and"—but the prayer was stilled! the little hands unclasped, and a look of agony and wonder met the mother's eye as the words of hopeless sorrow burst from the lips of the kneeling child, "I cannot pray for *father any more!*" Since her little lips had been able to form the dear name she had prayed for a blessing upon it; it had followed close after *mother's* name, for *he* had said *that* must come first; and now say the familiar prayer, and leave her father *out!* No wonder that the new thought seemed too much for the childish mind to receive. I waited for some moments that she might conquer her emotion, and then urged her to go on. Her pleading eyes met mine, and, with a voice that faltered too much almost for utterance, she said, "O mother, I cannot leave him *all out;* let me say, 'thank God that I *had* a dear father *once!*' so I can still go on and keep him in my prayers." And so she always does, and my stricken heart learned a lesson from the loving ingenuity of my child. Remember to thank God for mercies *past*, as well as to ask blessings for the future.—*Presbyterian.*

Sins Forbidden.

Q. 65. WHAT IS FORBIDDEN IN THE FIFTH COMMANDMENT?

The fifth commandment forbiddeth the neglecting of, or doing anything against, the honor and duty which belongeth to every one in their several places and relations.

FIFTH COMMANDMENT.

What Truths are embraced in this Answer?

1. *We are not to neglect the honor due to every one.*—1 *Pet.* iii. 8. Love as brethren.—Be courteous.

2. *We are not to neglect the honor due to our superiors.*—*Rom.* xiii. 7. Render therefore to all their dues.—Honor to whom honor.

3. *We are not to neglect the honor due to our inferiors.*—*Gen.* xxiii. 7. Abraham stood up and bowed himself to the people of the land, even to the children of Heth.

4. *We are not to neglect the honor due to our equals.*—*Rom.* xii. 16. Be of the same mind one toward another.

5. *We are not to do anything against the honor belonging to every one.*—1 *Cor.* ix. 22. To the weak became I as weak, that I might gain the weak.

6. *We are not to do anything against the honor due to our superiors.*—*Eccl.* x. 20. Curse not the king, no, not in thy thought.

7. *We are not to do anything against the honor due to our inferiors.*—*Mat.* xxiii. 11. He that is greatest among you, shall be your servant.

8. *We are not to do anything against the honor due to our equals.*—*Phil.* ii. 3. Let each esteem other better than themselves.

9. *We are not to neglect the duties which are due to our fellow-men.*—*Rom.* xiii. 8. Owe no man anything, but to love one another.

10. *We are not to neglect the duties which are due to our superiors.*—*Tit.* iii. 1. Be subject to principalities and powers.—Obey magistrates.

11. *We are not to neglect the duties which are due to our inferiors.*—*Col.* iv. 1. Masters, give unto your servants that which is just and equal.

12. *We are not to neglect the duties which are due to our equals.*—*Gal.* v. 13. By love serve one another.

13. *We are not to do anything against the duties which we owe to our fellow-men.*—1 *Thes.* v. 15. Follow that which is good, both among yourselves and to all men.

14. *We are not to do anything against the duty which we owe to our superiors.*—1 *Pet.* iii. 6. Sarah obeyed Abraham, calling him lord.

15. *We are not to do anything against the duty which we*

owe to our inferiors.—Mat. xxiii. 4. They bind heavy burdens, and grievous to be borne, and lay them on men's shoulders.

16. *We are not to do anything against the duty which we owe to our equals.—Phil.* ii. 3. Let nothing be done through strife or vain glory.

What Lessons do you derive from the above Doctrines?

I learn (1.) That I am not allowed to be inattentive, much less to be opposed, to the rendering of due respect and kindness to all classes of my fellow-men, and to my various relatives. (2.) That there are many, beside myself, that have rights, and whose happiness must be honestly and faithfully consulted.

What Illustration is given?

1. *The words of Ali to his Sons.*—"My sons, never despise any person; consider your superior as your father, your equal as your brother, and your inferior as your son."

2. ANNE BOLEYN.—Queen Anne Boleyn is said to have been provided daily with a purse, the contents of which were entirely appropriated to the poor, when she casually met with proper objects—justly thinking no week well passed which did not afford her pleasure in the retrospect. Impressed with this conviction, the unfortunate Queen insisted that all her attendants should employ their leisure in making clothes for the poor, which she took care to see properly distributed.—*Percy Anecdotes.*

3. CHARITABLE PASTOR.—A Parisian, paying a visit to a curate in the middle of winter, remarked that he was living in a house with naked walls, and inquired why he had not got hangings to protect him from the rigor of the cold? The good pastor showed him two little children that he had taken care of, and replied, "I had rather clothe these poor children than my walls."—*Ibid.*

4. GEORGE THE THIRD.—An application was once made to the benevolent compassion of George III., out of the due order, by a person who was reduced, with a large family, to extreme distress. It succeeded far beyond his hopes. He was so overpowered by the graciousness and extent of the benefaction, as, upon receiving it, to fall on his knees, and, with a flood of grateful tears, to thank the donor for his goodness. "Rise," said the condescending sovereign; "go and thank God for having disposed my heart to relieve your necessities."—*Ibid.*

5. ISLE OF MAN.—It is a proverb among the hospitable inhabitants of the Isle of Man, that "When one poor man relieves another, God himself laughs for joy." Poor-rates, and most other parochial rates, are unknown; and there is not, in the whole island, either hospital, workhouse, or house of correction, though in every parish there is at least one charity school, and often a small library. A collection is made, as in Scotland, after the morning service of every Sunday, for the relief of such poor of the parish as are thought deserving of charity. The donation is optional, but it is usual for every one to give something.—*Ibid.*

6. HOW TO RUIN A SON.—1. Let him have his own way. 2. Allow him a free use of money. 3. Suffer him to roam where he pleases on the Sabbath. 4. Give him full access to wicked companions. 5. Call him to no account of his earnings. 6. Furnish him with no stated employment. 7. Do not discourage the use of intoxicating liquors.

Reasons Annexed.

Q. 66. WHAT IS THE REASON ANNEXED TO THE FIFTH COMMANDMENT?

The reason annexed to the fifth commandment

is, A promise of long life and prosperity (as far as it shall serve for God's glory and their own good) to all such as keep this commandment.

What Truths are embraced in this Answer?

1. *Long life is promised to those who honor their parents.*—*Eph.* vi. 2, 3. Honor thy father and mother, that—— thou mayest live long on the earth.
2. *Temporal prosperity is promised to those who honor their parents.*—*Eph.* vi. 2, 3. Honor thy father and mother, that it may be well with thee.
3. *Temporal prosperity and long life are always regulated by a regard to the glory of God.*—*John,* xi. 4. This sickness is not unto death, but for the glory of God.
4. *Temporal prosperity is always limited to what is best for the people of God.*—*Prov.* xxx. 8. Give me neither poverty nor riches; feed me with food convenient for me.

What Lessons do you derive from the above Doctrines?

I learn (1.) That I should desire to live, and to be prospered in my plans and undertakings, only so far as may promote my best interests—the interests of my soul— and my usefulness, and the glory of God. (2.) That the afflictions and early death of some who have been obedient to the Fifth Command, are to be explained consistently with the annexed promise, by supposing that those providential arrangements were occasioned by God's regard for their true interest, their eternal happiness, and his own glory. (3.) That eternal life, and my being instrumental in honoring God, are of more value than great length of days on earth; are to be more esteemed than great temporal possessions, or pleasures, or distinctions.

What Illustrations are presented?

1. The late PRESIDENT DWIGHT, of Yale College, says: "In conversing with the plain people of this country,

distinguished for their good sense, and careful observations of facts, I have found them to a great extent firmly persuaded of the verification of this promise (of temporal blessings) *in our own days;* and ready to produce a variety of proofs from cases in which they have seen the blessing realized. Their opinion on this subject is mine; and with their experience mine has coincided."—*Works*, vol. iii., p. 297.

2. The AMERICAN INDIANS, as a first lesson, inculcate upon their children obedience to parents, and respect for old age; and among no people is filial obedience more promptly or generally rendered. A father need only say, in presence of his children, "I want such a thing done; who is the *good* child that will do it?" and they vie with each other in their ready compliance with his wishes. When an old decrepit man or woman passes by, led by a child, the father calls the attention of his children to the scene, and remarks: "What a *good* child that must be, who pays such attention to the aged! That child looks forward to the time when it likewise will be old." Or, perhaps, he will say, "May the Great Spirit, who looks upon him, *grant this good child a long life.*"

3. DISOBEDIENCE TO PARENTS.—There is too little respect paid to parental authority at the present day. It is grievous to go into many families and hear the language daily used by the children. There is truth as well as rhyme in a couplet by Randolph:

> "Whoever makes his parent's heart to bleed
> Shall have a child that will revenge the deed."

One thing is certain, *an undutiful son and a disobedient daughter cannot long prosper.* For a season they may appear well to the eye of a stranger, but their self-will and stubbornness are soon discovered, and they are despised.

A child who disobeys his parents will not hesitate to abuse anybody. Neither age nor talents receive respect from him.—*N. Y. Obs.*

4. For Parents.—"To give children good instruction and a bad example," says Archbishop Tillotson, "is but BECKONING to them with one hand to show them the way to heaven, while we take them by the other and LEAD them to HELL."

THE SIXTH COMMANDMENT.

Q. 67. Which is the sixth commandment

The sixth commandment is, Thou shalt not kill.

What Lessons do you derive from the above Answer?

I learn (1.) That except God had expressly given permission, as he did to Noah, it would be unlawful to take the life of the lower animals; but he allows us to use for food those that are adapted to that purpose, and to destroy those that are hurtful or dangerous to us. (2.) That the precept is designed, therefore, to protect human life.

Duties Required.

Q. 68. What is required in the sixth commandment?

The sixth commandment requireth all lawful endeavors to preserve our own life and the life of others.

What Lessons do you derive from the above Answer?

1. *We must use all lawful endeavors to preserve our own lives.*—1 *Tim.* v. 23. Use a little wine for thy stomach's sake, and thine often infirmities.

2. *We are to use no unlawful endeavors for the preservation of our lives.*—*Mat.* xvi. 25. Whosoever will save his life, shall lose it.

3. *We must use all lawful endeavors to preserve the lives of others.*—*Prov.* xxiv. 11, 12. If thou forbear to deliver them that are drawn unto death, and those that are ready to be slain; if thou sayest, Behold, we knew it not; doth not he that pondereth the heart consider it?

4. *We are to use no unlawful endeavors to preserve the lives of others.*—*Num.* xxxv. 31. Ye shall take no satisfaction for the life of a murderer.

What Lessons do you derive from the above Doctrines?

I learn (1.) That I am required to use such means for prolonging my own life and the life of others, as the laws of God and of man allow. (2.) That I may, by force, defend life from violence, unless it be demanded by the laws of my country on account of crime. (3.) That my bodily health and that of others should be carefully provided for, in respect to food, medicine, clothing, and other needful accommodations. (4.) That my appetite and desires must not be gratified in such a measure or degree as tends to destroy or shorten life. (5.) That it is my duty to contribute to the relief of human want and disease.

What Illustrations can you relate?

1. "Never mind the Property—Save the Lives."—When the great book establishment of the Messrs Harper, in the City of New York, was on fire (Dec. 10, 1853), and in evident danger, with its immensely valuable contents, of soon being destroyed, Col. John Harper, one of the firm, when informed, in his counting-room, of this fact, and the inquiry was added, "What portion of the property shall we save first, sir?" promptly and nobly replied, "Never mind the property—save the lives." There were about six hundred persons engaged at the time in the various

buildings of the establishment, all of whom, through the most vigorous exertions of the firemen and others, were rescued from an impending and horrible death by fire. "This is a sad calamity, sir," said a friend to Mr. John Harper, alluding to the conflagration, "a large number of poor persons thrown out of employment." "Ah, yes," answered Mr. Harper, "God bless them, they must be seen to."

2. At a time of famine in the city of Rome, Pompey provided grain for their relief; and when the mariners were reluctant to sail thither in a tempest, said he, "It is not necessary that we should live, but it is necessary that Rome be relieved."

3. "DON'T STEP THERE."—A layer of snow was spread over the icy streets, and pedestrians walked carefully, shod with India-rubber, toward the churches, on a cold Sabbath morning in February. Walking somewhat hastily, for he was late, a gentleman noticed a bright-looking little lad, with his eyes fixed upon one spot on the side-walk; and, as he approached, the lad said, "Please don't step there, sir; I slipped there, and fell down." The gentleman thanked the philanthropic little fellow, and passed round the dangerous spot. Selfishness would hurry away from the place of a fall, muttering, "It is none of my business what becomes of those who follow." Pride would seek to hide his humiliation. Mischief and malignity would wait for a laugh or a sneer at the coming helpless traveller; but benevolence halts for a little to utter a kind warning, and to guard a fellow-being against a calamity.

Sins Forbidden.

Q. 69. WHAT IS FORBIDDEN IN THE SIXTH COMMANDMENT?

The sixth commandment forbiddeth the taking

away of our own life, or the life of our neighbor, unjustly, or whatsoever tendeth thereunto.

What Truths are embraced in this Answer?

1. *We are not to destroy our own lives.—Acts,* xvi. 28. Do thyself no harm.
2. *We are to avoid everything which would tend to take away our own lives.—Job,* xiv. 14. All the days of my appointed time will I wait, till my change come.
3. *We are not to take away the life of another person unjustly.—Lev.* xxiv. 17. He that killeth any man shall surely be put to death.
4. *We are to avoid everything which would tend to take away the life of another.—Deut.* xxiv. 6. No man shall take the nether or the upper millstone to pledge: for he taketh a man's life to pledge.

What Lessons do you derive from the above Doctrines?

I learn (1.) That human life, in some cases, may be *justly* taken away; as when it is necessary to my own defence, or that of others, from unlawful violence; also, when it is taken by a magistrate in due course of law, as the punishment of some flagrant crime; and also in lawful war, in defence of our country, or of civil and religious liberty. (2.) Hence, also, I learn, that it is wicked to form any designs against my own life or the life of others; it is contrary to this command, also, to indulge in envy, rage, malice, impatience, discontent, and immoderate grief, under trouble; to practice gluttony and drunkenness; to over-work myself or any in my employment, for the sake of gain; to expose my life or theirs to unnecessary dangers; or even to neglect proper means for preserving life. (3.) If the care of the life of the body is so guarded by the divine law, how much more worthy of care is the salvation of my own soul and of the souls of my fellow-men? If the short life on earth is of so much

SIXTH COMMANDMENT.

value, how incalculably more valuable is the life of everlasting ages? (4.) How great, therefore, is the crime of doing anything to hinder my own salvation or that of others?

What Illustrations are given?

1. How to dispose of an Injury.—In a school-room, in Boston, a little boy, about seven years of age, was sitting beside his sister, about five years old. George got angry with his sister about something, doubled up his fist, and struck her on the head. The little girl was just going to strike him back again, when the teacher, seeing it, said: "My dear Mary, you had better kiss your brother. See how angry and unhappy he looks!" Mary looked at her brother. He looked sullen and wretched. Her resentment was soon gone, and love for her brother returned to her heart. She threw both her arms around his neck, and kissed him. The poor boy was wholly unprepared for such a kind return for his blow. He could not stand before the generous affection of his sister. His feelings were touched, and he burst into tears. His gentle sister took the corner of her apron, and wiped away his tears, and sought to comfort him by saying: "Don't cry, George; you did not hurt me much." But he only wept the more.

2. The True Philosophy.—"What do you mean to do with K——?" said a friend of Theodore Hooke, alluding to a man who had grossly vilified him. "Do with him?" rejoined Hooke, "why I mean to let him alone *most severely.*"

3. Thomas Watson well remarks, that surfeiting shortens life; "more die of it than by the sword;" *many dig their graves with their teeth;* "the *cup* kills more than the *cannon.*"

4. Self-Murder may also be committed not only by an

act of violence or by poison, but by indulging envy, discontent, immoderate grief, and despondency.

5. PETER THE GREAT made a law, in 1722, that if any nobleman beat or ill-used his slaves, he should be looked upon as insane, and a guardian should be appointed to take care of his person and of his estate. The great monarch once struck his gardener, who, being a man of great sensibility, took to his bed, and died in a few days. Peter, hearing of this, exclaimed, with tears in his eyes, "Alas! I have civilized my own subjects; I have conquered other nations; yet I have not been able to civilize or to conquer myself."—*Percy Anecdotes.*

THE SEVENTH COMMANDMENT.

Q. 70. WHICH IS THE SEVENTH COMMANDMENT?

The seventh commandment is, Thou shalt not commit adultery.

Duties Required.

Q. 71. WHAT IS REQUIRED IN THE SEVENTH COMMANDMENT?

The seventh commandment requireth the preservation of our own and our neighbor's chastity, in heart, speech and behavior.

What Truths are embraced in this Answer?

1. *We are to preserve our own chastity.*—1 *Thes.* iv. 4. That every one of you should know how to possess his vessel in sanctification and honor.
2. *We are to avoid all occasions of temptation.*—*Prov.* v. 8. Remove thy way far from her, and come not nigh the door of her house.

3. *We are to be chaste in our thoughts*—2 *Tim.* ii. 22. Flee also youthful lusts.

4. *We are to be chaste in our words.*—*Eph.* v. 4. Neither filthiness, nor foolish talking.

5. *We are to be chaste in our actions.*—1 *Pet.* iii. 2. While they behold our chaste conversation coupled with fear.

6. *We are to endeavor to preserve our neighbor's chastity as well as our own.*—*Eph.* v. 11. Have no fellowship with the unfruitful works of darkness, but rather reprove them.

What Lesson do you derive from the above Doctrines ?

I learn that in mind as well as body I must guard myself against immodesty; and to help me to do this effectually, it will be well to call to mind the noble reply of Joseph, when tempted to a gross sin of this kind: "How can I do this great wickedness, and sin against God?"

What Illustrations are given?

1. WILLIAM KELLY, of the Isle of Man, was very earnest and affectionate in his exhortations to his young friends, and used often to repeat to them that passage in the 119th Psalm:

> How shall the young preserve their ways
> From *all* pollution free?
> By making still their course of life
> With thy commands agree.

And he would conclude by saying, "Remember the word *all*."

2. The pious *M'Cheyne*, of Scotland, remarks: "Eve, Achan, David, all fell through the 'lust of the eye.' I should make a covenant with mine, and pray, 'Turn away mine eyes from beholding vanity.' * * * * * * * Satan makes unconverted men like the deaf adder to the sound of the Gospel. I should pray to be made deaf by the Holy Spirit *to all that would tempt me to sin.* I ought to *meditate often on heaven as a*

world of holiness—where all are holy, where the joy is holy joy, the work holy work; so that without *personal holiness* I never can be there."—*Memoir*, p. 139

Sins Forbidden.

Q. 72. WHAT IS FORBIDDEN IN THE SEVENTH COMMANDMENT?

The seventh commandment forbiddeth all unchaste thoughts, words, and actions.

What Truths are embraced in this Answer?

1. *All unchaste thoughts are forbidden.*—*Mat.* v. 28. Whosoever looketh on a woman to lust after her, hath committed adultery with her already in his heart.
2. *All unchaste conversation is forbidden.*—*Eph.* iv. 29. Let no corrupt communication proceed out of your mouth.
3. *All unchaste actions are forbidden.*—*Eph.* v. 3. Fornication and uncleanness,—let it not once be named among you.

What Lessons do you derive from the above Doctrines?

I learn (1.) The danger from immodest pictures, songs, books, dress, gestures; danger from the theatre and ballroom, from intemperate eating and drinking; danger from idleness, pride, and vanity; and from all influences unfriendly to a pure heart and a pure life. (2.) The vast importance of always obeying the Holy Spirit, who kindly seeks to keep me from this as well as from all other sins.

What Illustrations are afforded?

The NURSE OF INFIDELITY is sensuality. Youth are sensual. The Bible stands in their way. It prohibits the indulgence of *the lust of the flesh, the lust of the eye, and the pride of life.* But the young mind loves these things; and therefore it hates the Bible, which prohibits them. It is prepared to say, "If any man will bring me arguments against the Bible, 1 will thank him; if not, I will invent them."—*Cecil.*

THE EIGHTH COMMANDMENT.

Q. 73. WHICH IS THE EIGHTH COMMANDMENT?

The eighth commandment is, Thou shalt not steal.

Q. 74. WHAT IS REQUIRED IN THE EIGHTH COMMANDMENT?

The eighth commandment requireth the lawful procuring and furthering the wealth and outward estate of ourselves and others.

What Truths are embraced in this Answer?

1. *Wealth is to be procured and retained only by lawful means.—Rom.* xii. 17. Provide things honest in the sight of all men.
2. *We are to endeavor to procure wealth.—Prov.* vi. 6. Go to the ant, thou sluggard; consider her ways, and be wise.
3. *We are to endeavor by lawful means to promote and further our outward estate.—Prov.* xxvii. 23. Be thou diligent to know the state of thy flocks, and look well to thy herds.
4. *We are to assist others in procuring the good things of life.—Gal.* vi. 10. As we have therefore opportunity, let us do good unto all men.
5. *We are to endeavor lawfully to further the wealth and outward estate of our neighbor.—Phil.* ii. 4. Look not every man on his own things, but every man also on the things of others.

What Lessons do you derive from the above Doctrines?

I learn (1.) That I may not take away, or retain, the property of another without his knowledge or against his consent. (2.) That I must respect the right of others to all that justly belongs to them, as I desire and insist that they shall respect my right to what justly belongs to me. (3.) That in seeking to gain property I must proceed in an honest and fair manner; and further, that I must encourage and assist my fellow-men to acquire property for themselves in the same manner. (4.) That God is an impartial guardian of the rights of property, in all cases where those rights are well founded. (5.) That even small thefts are criminal, since they are a transgression of one of the great laws of God's government. (6.) That I am bound to endeavor to prevent all loss or damage to property—my own or that of other men; I am to deal with them in a kind, honest, and benevolent manner, wishing their prosperity; I am to restore to them any lost property of theirs which I may have found; and I am to afford assistance when it is needed by the poor, in the prosecution of their lawful business.

What Illustration can you give?

1. Knud Iverson, a Norwegian lad, ten years old, residing in Chicago, was commanded by some vicious boys to go into a neighboring garden and steal some fruit for them. But his pious parents had taught him to keep the commands of God, and nobly did he, in this case, keep the command now to be considered. He refused to go and steal the fruit. The boys threatened to drown him if he did not comply with their wicked command. He still refused, and they put him into the water, and held him as long as they dared, and then raised him up and repeated their threat, but the boy preferred, even at the risk of losing his life, to obey God's command rather

than theirs. He was plunged again and again into the water, and there held until life was extinct. What a noble example of Christian firmness and piety does this Norwegian lad furnish; what strength of love for the commands of God—love stronger than that of life itself! So greatly have some good people in Chicago and elsewhere admired the conduct of this young martyr to the right, that they have recently (1853) contributed more than a thousand dollars for a marble monument with an inscription, declaring the fact that his life was sacrificed to duty; that he chose to be drowned rather than, by stealing, to disobey God, and his Christian parents.

2. THE ONE JOURNEY.—"When I was a young man," says *James Simpson*, "there lived in our neighborhood a Presbyterian, who was universally reported to be a very liberal man, and uncommonly liberal in his dealings. When he had any of the produce of his farm to dispose of, he made it an invariable rule to give good measure, over good, rather more than could be required of him. One of his friends, observing his frequently doing so, questioned him why he did it, told him he gave too much, and said it would not be to his own advantage. Now, my friends, mark the answer of this Presbyterian: "God Almighty has given me but one journey through the world, and when gone, I cannot return to rectify mistakes." Think of this friends—*but one journey through the world.*

3. BE PROMPT.—"How do you accomplish so much in so little space of time?" said a friend to *Sir Walter Raleigh*. "When I have anything to do I go and do it," was the reply.

Sins Forbidden.

Q. 75. WHAT IS FORBIDDEN IN THE EIGHTH COMMANDMENT?

The eighth commandment forbiddeth whatsoever

doth, or may, unjustly hinder our own or our neighbor's wealth or outward estate.

What Truths are embraced in this Answer ?

1. *Wealth is not to be procured or retained by unlawful means.*—1 *Tim.* vi 10. The love of money is the root of all evil: which while some coveted after, they have erred from the faith, and pierced themselves through with many sorrows.

2. *We are not to neglect lawful means for procuring wealth for ourselves and families.*—1 *Tim.* v. 8. If any provide not for his own, and specially for those of his own house, he hath denied the faith, and is worse than an infidel.

3. *We are not to do that which may hinder the increase of our wealth and outward estate.*—*Prov.* xxiii. 21. The drunkard and the glutton shall come to poverty; and drowsiness shall clothe a man with rags.

4. *We are not to neglect the relief of our neighbor, or the furtherance of his wealth when it is in our power.*—*Deut.* xv. 8. Thou shalt open thy hand wide unto him, and shalt surely lend him sufficient for his need, in that which he wanteth.

5. *We are not to do anything which may hinder the furtherance of our neighbor's wealth.*—*Zech.* viii. 17. Let none of you imagine evil in your hearts against his neighbor.

What Lessons do you derive from the above Doctrines ?

I learn (1.) That I must avoid every act which may wrongfully prevent the increase of my own worldly substance, or that of my fellow-men. And, hence (2.) That I must avoid idleness, carelessness, wastefulness, imprudence in lending money, or giving it to undeserving objects. (3.) That I must abstain from a niggardly economy, and also from all unlawful methods of making money, such as gambling, fraud, forgery, taking advantage of a man's ignorance or necessity in buying or selling, adulterating goods, refusing to pay debts at the time and way agreed upon, breach of trust, contracting debts when uncertain as to ability to pay, and especially with a design not to pay. (4.) I may not oppress, or even neglect, the poor, nor refuse to contribute to the support of the gospel at home and abroad, in a manner answerable to my means.

What Illustrations are given?

1. THE BEGGAR AND DR. SMOLLET.—A beggar, asking Dr. Smollet for alms, he gave him, through mistake, a guinea. The poor fellow perceiving it, hobbled after him to return it; whereupon Smollet returned it to him, with another guinea, as a reward of his honesty, exclaiming, at the same time: "What a lodging has honesty taken up with!"

2. THE FOUNDATION PRINCIPLE OF THIS COMMANDMENT.—It is founded on that never-failing rule for the direction of our practice (*Mat.* vii. 12), *that what I judge due to myself, were I in another man's condition, is certainly as due to him in his own.* This is a rule applicable to all affairs. Therefore, whatsoever thou hast to transact with thy neighbor, though thou mayest spy advantages upon him, and such as, if thou shouldst take, possibly he might never know or never be able to redress; yet then, take thy conscience aside, and seriously ask whether thou couldst be content, and think it honest and just to be so dealt with thyself; if not, whatsoever the temptation be, or how much soever thou mightest gain by hearkening unto it, reject it with scorn, as that which could induce thee to violate the first principle of common honesty among men, and contradicts all the laws both of nature and Scripture.—*Bp. Ezekiel Hopkins.*

THE NINTH COMMANDMENT.

Q. 76 WHICH IS THE NINTH COMMANDMENT?

The ninth commandment is, Thou shalt not bear false witness against thy neighbor.

NINTH COMMANDMENT.

Duties Required.

Q. 77 WHAT IS REQUIRED IN THE NINTH COMMANDMENT?

The ninth commandment requireth the maintaining and promoting of truth between man and man, and of our own and our neighbor's good name, especially in witness bearing.

What Truths are embraced in this Answer?

1. *We should at all times use our speech with caution.*—*Prov.* xvii. 27. He that hath knowledge spareth his words.
2. *We must at all times speak and maintain the truth.*—*Zech.* viii. 16. Speak ye every man the truth to his neighbor.
3. *We must endeavor to promote the truth.*—*Phil.* iv. 8. Whatsoever things are true——think on these things.
4. *We must endeavor to preserve our own good name.*—*Mat.* v. 16. Let your light so shine before men, that they may see your good works, and glorify your Father which is in heaven.
5. *We must endeavor to preserve our neighbor's good name.*—*Tit.* iii. 2. Speak evil of no man.
6. *We must be specially careful to speak truth in witness-bearing.*—*Prov.* xiv. 5. A faithful witness will not lie; but a false witness will utter lies.

What Lessons do you derive from the above Doctrines?

I learn (1.) That while falsehood is a crime, it is especially so when designed to operate to the disadvantage of my fellow-men. (2.) To put a high value upon my own reputation and that of my fellow-men, especially when called under oath to answer to questions put to me in a court of justice or elsewhere. (3.) The duty of so acting as to be worthy of respect, and of a good name. (4.)

That I should be candid and just in my opinions and conversation concerning others; that I should forbear harsh, censorious, and rash observations; that I should never speak evil of the absent, unless called so to do by obvious duty to others; that I should defend their character and doings when unjustly attacked, and discourage tale bearing.

What Illustrations are in point?

1. FENCES FOR THE TONGUE.—God hath set two fences to keep in the tongue—the teeth and the lips; and this commandment is a third fence set about it, that it should not break forth into evil.—*Watson.*

2. SLANDERING is to report things of others unjustly. Holiness itself is no shield from slander. You may smite another, and never touch him. *The wounds of the tongue* no physician can heal, and to pretend friendship to a man, and yet slander him, is most odious.—*Watson.*

3. PYTHAGORAS being asked what made men like God, answered, "When they speak the truth."—*Ib.*

4. It was a law of the Scythians that the man who told a lie in connection with an oath, should lose his head, because such an offence was adapted to take away all truth and mutual confidence from among men.

5. The CHURCH OF ROME violates this commandment, by allowing a lie or a false oath, if it be designed to promote the Catholic cause. But God's cause has no need of lies for its support or advancement; and it is an insult to the God of Truth to pretend to promote it by falsehood.

6. A MAN MAY BE KILLED IN NAME as well as in person. Some are loath to take away their neighbor's goods; conscience would fly in their face; but better take away their grain out of their field, their wares out of their shop, than take away their good name. This is a sin for which

reparation can never be made—a blot in a man's name being like a blot on white paper, which will never be got out.—*Watson.*

7. Philip Henry says: "We should be troubled as much at unjust praises as at unjust slanders."

8. The Rev. Samuel Pierce, of Birmingham, was a man of an excellent spirit. It was a rule with him to discourage all evil speaking; nor would he approve of *just* censure unless some good end was to be answered by it. Two of his friends being on a visit at his house, one of them, during the absence of the other, suggested something to his disadvantage. He put a stop to the conversation, by answering, "He is here; take him aside, and tell him of it by himself; you may do him good."

9. Be True.—How striking these words of old George Herbert, sung two centuries ago:

> Lie not, but let thy heart be true to God;
> Thy mouth to it, thy actions to them both.
>
> Dare to be true. Nothing can need a lie:
> A fault which needs it most, grows two thereby.

10. Asiatic Proverbs.—He who relates the faults of others to you, designs to relate yours to others. If you be reproved for your faults, do not be angry with him who does it; but turn your anger against the things for which he has reproved you.

Sins Forbidden.

Q. 78. What is forbidden in the ninth commandment?

The ninth commandment forbiddeth whatsoever is prejudicial to truth, or injurious to our own or our neighbor's good name.

NINTH COMMANDMENT.

What Truths are embraced in this Answer?

1. *We are never to be inattentive or careless as to what we speak.*—Prov. xxix. 11. A fool uttereth all his mind: but a wise man keepeth it in till afterwards.
2. *We are to do nothing which is prejudicial to truth.*—Eph. iv. 25. Putting away lying, speak every man truth with his neighbor.
3. *We are not to do anything which is injurious to our own good name.*—Job, xxvii. 6. My righteousness I hold fast, and will not let it go: my heart shall not reproach me so long as I live.
4. *We are not to do anything which will be injurious to our neighbor's good name.*—Exod. xxiii. 1. Thou shalt not raise a false report; put not thine hand with the wicked to be an unrighteous witness.

What Lessons do you derive from the above Doctrines?

I learn (1.) To avoid the utterance of what I know to be false, with the intention to deceive another; all lies for sport, for profit, for concealing some wrong action, for preventing danger, for mischief, or from mere habit or carelessness. (2.) That my own just reputation will be hurt by my thinking too highly or too low of myself, by an unnecessary exposure of my faults, by associating with low or vicious or unprofitable companions, or by attempting to fill a station for which I am not fitted. (3.) That the reputation of others will be hurt, when I judge them from a wrong standard, or point of view; when I decide unfavorably, without full evidence, on their motives; when I put a wrong construction upon their words or deeds; when I raise, spread, or receive false reports, to their disadvantage; when by encouragement or example, I draw them into what is sinful, to the injury of their character and standing in society. (4.) To forbear to use or to receive flattery, or undue praise, as unjust both to myself and others; also, as being false, adapted to deceive,.

and sometimes to ruin, both soul and body. (5.) The force of the Apostle James' language concerning the tongue—*Ep.*, chap. iii. 2-10.

What Illustrations are given?

1. DIOGENES used to say: "Of all wild beasts, a slanderer is the worst."

2. THE TONGUE.—A certain man sent a servant to market to bring him the *best* article which he could find there, and the servant returned with a *tongue;* being sent a second time, for the *worst* article in the market, he again brought back a *tongue.* "I hear," says William Kelly, "many complain of their having *bad teeth;* but I have never heard any one complain of his having a *bad tongue.* I don't read, however, in Scripture, of any threatenings against bad teeth; but I find dreadful judgments denounced against a bad tongue."

3. BISHOP BEVERIDGE says: "I resolve never to speak of a man's virtues to his face, nor of his vices behind his back."

4. AN ODD YOUNG LADY.—At the house of *Rev. B. Jacobs*, of Cambridgeport, some young ladies were one day talking about one of their female friends. As he entered the room, he heard the epithets, "odd," "singular," &c., applied. He asked, and was told the name of the young lady in question, and then said, very gravely, "Yes, she is an odd young lady; she is a *very* odd young lady; I consider her extremely singular." He then added, very impressively, "She was never heard to speak ill of any absent friends." The rebuke was not forgotten by those who heard it.

5. PETER THE GREAT, of Russia, had many good traits of character; among others, the following: When any

one, in his presence, was speaking to the disadvantage of an absent person, he at first listened attentively, and then was accustomed to ask, "Is there not a fair side also to the character of the person of whom you are speaking? Come, tell me what good qualities you have remarked about him."

THE TENTH COMMANDMENT.

Q. 79. WHICH IS THE TENTH COMMANDMENT?

The tenth commandment is, Thou shalt not covet thy neighbor's house, thou shalt not covet thy neighbor's wife, nor his man-servant, nor his maid-servant, nor his ox, nor his ass, nor anything that is thy neighbor's.

Duties Required.

Q. 80. WHAT IS REQUIRED IN THE TENTH COMMANDMENT?

The tenth commandment requireth full contentment with our own condition, with a right and charitable frame of spirit toward our neighbor, and and all that is his.

What Truths are embraced in this Answer?

1. *We must be contented with our condition in life.*—*Heb.* xiii. 5. Let your conversation be without covetousness; and be content with such things as ye have.
2. *We are to cultivate a right and charitable disposition towards the person of our neighbor.*—*Rom.* xii. 15. Rejoice with them that do rejoice, and weep with them that weep.

TENTH COMMANDMENT.

3. *We are to cultivate a right disposition towards the property of our neighbor.—Luke,* xii. 13. Take heed, and beware of covetousness.

What Lessons do you derive from the above Doctrines?

I learn (1.) That my *desires* are to be kept within just bounds, and that it is wrong for me not only to deprive my neighbor of anything that is his, but even to desire or wish to do it. (2.) On the other hand, that I should be pleased with what promotes the comfort or advantage of my neighbor; and should be so far satisfied with my own condition in life that I shall always exercise a kind and loving disposition towards my fellow-men, in respect to their retaining and enjoying what they lawfully possess. (3.) That this law comprehends and recapitulates all the rest concerning my neighbor, and provides the most effectual method for rendering obedience to them— the regulation of my desires. To *covet* is "to have an earnest desire for anything in the lawful possession of another, and which, at the same time, he may desire to retain." This command prohibits the violation (in wish and desire) of the Eighth Command, and also of the Seventh, and then universally; so that it may be viewed as a supplement to the other precepts of the Second Table, commanding us to observe them, not only in the letter, but in spirit.

What Illustrations can you relate?

1. AHAB AND NABOTH.—King Ahab desired the vineyard of Naboth, and, because the latter was unwilling to dispose of it, Ahab gave his consent to the murder of Naboth, that he might gain possession of the vineyard. The story is recorded at length in 1 *Kings,* xxi. 2–19.

2. THE TWO MERCHANTS.—Two merchants of the same city, being neighbors and jealous of each other, lived in

a scandalous enmity. One of them, entering into himself, submitted to the voice of religion, which condemned his resentments. He consulted a pious person, in whom he had great confidence, and inquired of him how he should manage to bring about a reconciliation. "The best means," answered he, "is this: Whenever any person shall enter your store, in order to purchase, and you have not what suits them, recommend to them to go over to your neighbor." He did so. The other merchant being informed of the person by whom these purchasers came to him, was so struck with the good offices of a man whom he considered his enemy, that he repaired immediately to his house to thank him for it, begged pardon, with tears in his eyes, for the hatred he had entertained against him, and besought him to admit him into the number of his best friends. His prayer was heard, and religion closely united those whom self-interest and jealousy had divided.—*Chris. Treasury.*

3. PHILIP HENRY.—In speaking of contentment, he used to say: "When the mind and the condition meet, there is contentment. Now, in order to that, either the condition must be brought up to the mind, and that is not only unreasonable, but impossible, for as the condition riseth, the mind riseth with it; or else the mind must be brought down to the condition, and that is both possible and reasonable." And he observed: "That no condition of life will of itself make a man content, without the grace of God; for we find Haman discontented in the court, Ahab discontented on the throne, Adam discontented in Paradise; nay, and higher we cannot go, the angels that fell were discontented even in heaven itself."

4. COVETOUSNESS.—Says Watson, "A man may be said to be given to covetousness, when his thoughts are wholly taken up about the world; when he takes more pains for

the getting of earth than for the getting of heaven; when all his discourse is about the world; when he doth so set his heart upon worldly things that for the sake of them he will part with the heavenly; when he overloads himself with worldly business; when his heart is so set upon the world, that to get it he cares not what unlawful indirect means he useth."

5. Men first break the Tenth Commandment by coveting, and then they break the Eighth by stealing. It was an excellent appeal that Samuel made to the Hebrew people: "Witness against me before the Lord, whose ox have I taken, or whose ass, or whom have I defrauded." And it was a brave speech of St. Paul, "I have coveted no man's silver, or gold, or apparel." Whence was this! It was from contentment: "I have learned, in whatever state I am, therewith to be content."—*Watson*.

Sins Forbidden.

Q. 81. WHAT IS FORBIDDEN IN THE TENTH COMMANDMENT?

The tenth commandment forbiddeth all discontentment with our own estate, envying or grieving at the good of our neighbor, and all inordinate motions and affections to anything that is his.

What Truths are embraced in this Answer?

1. *We are not to be discontented with our condition in life.*—1 *Cor.* x. 10. Neither murmur ye as some of them also murmured, and were destroyed of the destroyer.

2. *We are not to be envious at the good of others.*—*Gal.* v. 26. Let us not be desirous of vain glory,—envying one another.

3. *We are not to grieve at the good of others.*—*James*, v. 9. Grudge not one against another.

4. *We are not improperly to desire the possession of our*

neighbor's property.—Deut. v. 21.. Neither shalt thou desire————anything that is thy neighbor's.

5. *We are not to form any purpose in our mind, for unlawfully obtaining possession of our neighbor's property.*—*Psal.* l. 18. When thou sawest a thief, then thou consentedst with him.

What Lessons do you derive from the above Doctrines?

I learn (1.) That I must suppress or avoid all such uneasiness or fretfulness respecting my own circumstances as would lead me to hate others, or to be unhappy, in view of anything which they possess, and which I may be in want of. (2.) The sin of Envy—a sin destructive to peace of mind and amiableness of temper, and liable to be greatly injurious to those also concerning whom I shall indulge it. (3.) That while I am not allowed to be discontented with my condition, I am not therefore obligated not to seek to improve my condition—my habits—my character—my property—and various means of happiness. (4.) I am taught to love others as I love myself, and to promote their good estate as well as my own.

What Illustrations are at hand?

1. How to avoid Discontent.—Watson advises us (1.) To believe that condition best which God carves out to us by his providence. (2.) To consider that the less estate we have, the less account we shall have to give at the last day; the less riches, the less reckoning.

2. Explanation.—We may desire the house of our neighbor, but not if his yielding it to us is to be injurious either to his worldly prosperity or to his feelings. But among the Israelites it was otherwise, and the law most minutely provides for the preservation, in its entireness, of the property of each family and branch of a family (*Lev.* xxv. 23–31). We may desire to have the servant of our neighbor, if the welfare of that servant is

to be promoted by the change of situation; but the ancient people of God had, according to the law, and for the space of time it prescribed, a right of property in the labor of those who were with them in servitude. Hence, in the Tenth Commandment, they occupy a middle place between a man's family and his chattels; and to allure them from him was, in one sense, like depriving him of his wife or children; and, in another sense, like taking from him without his consent, or without just remuneration, his house or his field, his ox or his ass. Whatever our neighbor has, that he has a right to dispose of, we may desire, but not selfishly, and without a regard to his feelings and interests, nor so vehemently, but that we may be fully content without it.—*Maresi Sup. Don.*, p. 62.

3. THE TWO HEAPS.—"I see, in this world," said the Rev. JOHN NEWTON, "two heaps—one of human happiness, and one of misery. Now, if I can take but the smallest bit from the second heap, and add to the first, I carry a point. If, as I go home, a child has dropped a halfpenny, and if by giving it another, I can wipe away its tears, I feel that I have done something. I should be glad, indeed, to do great things, but I will not neglect such little ones as these."

4. DO AS YOU WOULD BE DONE BY.—What a great change the complete observance of this "Golden Rule," even for one single day, would produce among us! The effect of it would utterly astonish you! Strange sights would meet you on every side. You would see a great deal of property at once change hands, old debts would be paid off, whether outlawed or not outlawed, whether the papers were burned up, or not burned up. You would see lands and houses belonging to Mr. Gripe quickly and quietly pass over to Mr. Type; you would see "any quantity" of borrowed books, umbrellas, and the like, returned to their legitimate and patient owners.

You would see rum-selling and rum-buying, as the lawyers have it, "done away" at once. Gambling, and betting, and swearing, and cheating, and "shaving," and "puffing," would entirely cease. There would be no lies told. Not one. There would be no lampoons written. Not one syllable of slander, or of obloquy, or of abuse, or of ridicule, would be spoken; not an unkind look be given, not an unkind feeling entertained. All fretfulness and strife in families would cease; brothers and sisters would for one day live in harmony; husbands' and wives would forget their differences; the young would be kind to the old folks at home; the old would instruct with mild suavity the young. Friends long separated by misunderstanding would come together again; neighbors would greet each other kindly. Let this "Golden Rule" prevail, and the main current of conversation and behavior would be changed.—*Boston Traveller.*

CHAPTER II.

SPECIAL DUTIES WHICH GOD REQUIRES OF MAN UNDER THE GOSPEL DISPENSATION.

INTRODUCTION.—SHOWING MAN'S INABILITY TO KEEP THE MORAL LAW—THAT THERE ARE VARIOUS DEGREES OF GUILT IN BREAKING IT—AND THE DESERT OF EVERY TRANSGRESSION.

Q. 82. IS ANY MAN ABLE PERFECTLY TO KEEP THE COMMANDMENTS OF GOD?

No mere man since the fall is able, in this life, perfectly to keep the commandments of God, but doth daily break them in thought, word, and deed.

What Lessons do you derive from the above Answer?

1. *No mere man since the fall is able to keep the commandments of God perfectly.—Eccl.* vii. 20. There is not a just man upon earth, that doeth good and sinneth not.

2. *Adam, before the fall, was able to keep God's law perfectly.—Eccl.* vii. 29. God hath made man upright.

3. *Our Lord Jesus Christ, not being a mere man, did in this life perfectly keep the commandments of God.—Isa.* xlii. 21. The Lord is well pleased for his righteousness' sake; he will magnify the law, and make it honorable.

4. *All men, in this life, break the commandments of God daily.—Gen.* vi. 5. Every imagination of the thoughts of his heart was only evil continually.

5. *The saints, removed from this life to heaven, perfectly keep the commandments of God.—Isa.* lvii. 2. Each one walking in his uprightness.

6. *We all daily break the commandments of God in our thoughts.—Gen.* viii. 21. The imagination of man's heart is evil from his youth.

7. *We all daily break the commandments of God in our words and conversation.—James,* iii. 8. The tongue can no man tame; it is an unruly evil, full of deadly poison.

8. *We all daily break the commandments of God in our actions.--Rom.* vii. 19. The good that I would, I do not; but the evil which I would not, that I do.

What Lessons do you derive from the above Doctrines?

I learn (1.) That Jesus Christ was altogether distinguished from other men, inasmuch as he embodied, or showed forth, the law of God in its perfect excellence and widest range of precepts. (2.) That it is my duty to strive to imitate him, and, on the other hand, to avoid the imitation of the conduct and spirit of men generally. (3.) That I have cause for daily humiliation and sorrow over the corrupt tendencies of my mind and heart, and over my manifold acts of wrong-doing. (4.) That my hope of reform and of perfect obedience, must be in God's grace manifested through the Lord Jesus Christ. (5.)

Though I have no reason, from Scripture, or observation, or past experience, to hope to attain a complete and habitual conformity to the law of God in this life, yet not being therefore excused from obeying it, I am bound to make most vigorous and prayerful efforts to observe it in all respects and in its whole extent; for my inability has proceeded from a wrong and blameworthy state of feeling towards God and my fellow-men. (6.) To anticipate with pleasure that life to come, in which I shall, through God's grace, perfectly keep and honor the admirable law of my Creator and Redeemer. (7.) To limit the meaning of certain texts of Scripture which *seem* to support the doctrine that Christians may, and do attain, complete, absolute *perfection* of character and conduct *in this life*. "In some of those texts," as Dr. Woods remarks, "the language used is intended to set forth the *sincerity* or *uprightness* of believers, in distinction from hypocrites, and also their freedom from any such offences as would expose their public character to discredit, or their piety to suspicion. Job was *perfect* and *upright*— words doubtless of the same general import, denoting real *integrity* or *goodness*. (8.) In several instances the Psalmist uses the strong language of self-justification, and seems at first view to say he is not chargeable with any sin, when his meaning evidently is, that he is innocent of the crimes which his enemies laid to his charge. (9.) In some cases, pious men, under the former dispensation, are said to have *followed the Lord wholly*, when the obvious meaning is, that they kept themselves from idolatry, and adhered uniformly to the worship of the true God. (10.) When the New Testament writers speak of *perfection*, they often refer to a state of *maturity* or *manhood* in knowledge or in holiness, in distinction from a state of *childhood*—a state of *advancement* in piety, in distinction from the common state of *new converts;* and sometimes they refer to the purity and blessedness of heaven, which is the high object to which all Christians aspire. But in no case do the circumstances require that the language employed should be understood to denote *complete sanctification as actually attained in the present life.*

What Illustrations can you produce?

1. THE CHILD'S WISH.—A group of children were talking together, when the question was proposed, "What is the thing you wish for most?" Several of the children said they would like to have nice or pretty things. But when it came to the turn of a little boy, ten years old, to speak, he said, "I wish to live without sinning." These were not idle words, not mere profession; for the child showed by his conduct that he hated sin. How many of the dear children wish to live without sinning? How many *try* to live without sinning?—*Am. Messenger.*

2. Mrs. HAWKES, a pious English woman, in one of her letters, thus writes: "You want to know how I have been conquering *self.* Alas! I have been only fighting against self, but I am still very far from being a conqueror; and I am thankful to say, as you do, *Jesus shows me my strength is in him*; and my desire is, to be as a little child. When I want to act, I go to him for wisdom and strength. If I feel anger, I run to him, and show it to him. When I feel pride rising upon any occasion, I go to him and confess it. To him I take every sin as it arises, every want, every desponding thought. To him I go for every good thought, every good desire, every good word and work, crying,—Lord, help me in this—Lord, help me in the other. *It is thy grace alone that can produce anything good in me.* What else is meant by Christ's living in me, and I in him? It is by this simple faith that we must bring forth good fruits; and, to obtain it, we must plead

the promises. How are we to be transformed in the the spirit of our minds, and to be changed into his image, from glory to glory? Not by looking within, but by looking to Jesus."

Different Degrees of Guilt in Breaking the Law.

Q. 83 ARE ALL TRANSGRESSIONS OF THE LAW EQUALLY HEINOUS?

Some sins, in themselves, and by reason of several aggravations, are more heinous in the sight of God than others.

What Truths are embraced in this Answer?

1. *Some sins are in themselves more heinous in the sight of God than others.*—1 *John*, v. 16. There is a sin unto death: I do not say that ye shall pray for it.
2. *Aggravations make sins more heinous in the sight of God.*—*Mat.* xxiii. 14. Wo unto you, Scribes and Pharisees, hypocrites! for ye devour widows' houses, and for a pretence make long prayer; therefore ye shall receive the greater damnation.

What Lessons do you derive from the above Doctrines?

I learn (1.) Not only to regard some acts of transgression as more offensive to God than others, but to examine the circumstances that attend them, as rendering them more or less criminal. (2.) The value of those distinctions concerning this matter, which are presented in the Assembly's Larger Catechism, and the importance of frequently meditating upon them, so as to gain a holy dread of sin, and to guard myself especially against its more flagrant forms. Those distinctions are thus stated:

"*Sins Receive their Aggravations,*

1. "*From the persons offending:*—If they be of riper

age, greater experience, or grace; eminent for profession, gifts, place, office, guides to others, and whose example is likely to be followed by others.

2. "*From the parties offended:*—If immediately against God, his attributes and worship; against Christ, and his grace; the Holy Spirit, his witness and workings; against superiors, men of eminence, and such as we stand especially related and engaged unto; against any of the saints, particularly weak brethren, the souls of them, or any other; and the common good of all or of many.

3. "*From the nature and quality of the offence:*—If it be against the express letter of the law, if it break many commandments, contain in it many sins: If not only conceived in the heart, but breaks forth in words and actions, if it scandalize others, and admit of no reparation: If against means, mercies, judgments, light of nature, conviction of conscience, public or private admonition, censures of the church, civil punishments; and against our prayers, purposes, promises, vows, covenants and engagements to God or men: If done deliberately, wilfully, presumptuously, imprudently, boastingly, maliciously, frequently, obstinately, with delight, continuance, or relapsing after repentance.

4 "*From circumstances of time and place:*—If on the Lord's day, or other times of divine worship; or immediately before or after these, or other helps to prevent or remedy such miscarriages: If in public, or in the presence of others, who are thereby likely to be provoked or defiled."

I learn (3.) That while some sins are greater than others, none are to be regarded as little sins—as unworthy of anxious care—as matters of indifference, for it cannot be a trifle to violate the law of so great a God as Jehovah.

What Illustrations are given?

1. LITTLE SINS.—Respecting the danger of what some improperly call little sins, it has been said, "A small pen-knife will take away life, as well as a large sword."

2. Says *Pliny Fisk*: "Once I was blind to the evil of sin in general; and in particular to the number and aggravation of my own transgressions. Except for some overt transgression, I felt but little consciousness of guilt. But I have since realized that sin is an evil and bitter thing, and that my own sins are exceedingly numerous and aggravated. Many things which once appeared lawful, and even laudable, appear now exceedingly sinful and odious, and never more so, I think, than when all thought of punishment is out of mind. When I think of my sins as violations of God's reasonable and holy law, they appear inexcusable, and criminal, beyond description. When I consider them as committed against God, they look like a compound of the most presumptuous rebellion, the most wanton ingratitude, the most wicked irreverence. When I dwell on their tendency, as it respects my fellow-sinners, they seem to be unmixed malevolence."

3. PITHY SAYING.—He that makes light of small sins, is in the ready way to fall into great ones.

Desert of every Violation of the Law.

Q. 84. WHAT DOTH EVERY SIN DESERVE?

Every sin deserveth God's wrath and curse, both in this life, and that which is to come.

What Truths are embraced in this Answer?

1. *Every sin deserves the wrath and curse of God in this*

life.—*Gal.* iii. 10. Cursed is every one that continueth not in all things which are written in the book of the law to do them.

2. *Every sin deserves the wrath and curse of God for ever in the world to come.*—*Rom.* vi. 23. The wages of sin is death: but the gift of God is eternal life, through Jesus Christ our Lord.

What Lessons do you derive from the above Doctrines?

I learn (1.) That it involves no small danger to transgress, even once, the law of God; how much greater danger, then, to be guilty of numberless transgressions? (2.) That the sufferings of this life form but a small and inconsiderable part of what I deserve on account of my sins. (3.) It is wise to seek immediate deliverance from exposure to the infinitely greater—the everlasting sufferings of the life to come. (4.) If God should treat me according to simple justice I could not be happy, but must be utterly miserable, in time and in eternity. (5.) Whatever be my afflictions in the present life, I have no just reason to complain, for they are altogether trifling when compared with what it would be just for God to send upon me.

What Illustrations are given?

1. WAGES OF SIN.—The wages that sin *bargains* with the sinner to give, are life, pleasure, and profit; but the wages it *pays* him with are death, torment, and destruction. He that would understand the falsehood and deceit of sin must compare its promises and its payment together.—*South.*

2. THE MALIGNITY OF SIN.—The heinousness of any sin is not to be judged of by the magnitude of the object about which it is conversant, or the grossness of the outward action. When the Lord expressly says, " *Thou shalt*

not," and his rational creature says, "I WILL," whether the contest be about "an apple," or a kingdom, it is stubbornness and rebellion.—*Scott.*

Special Duties Required of Man under the Gospel Dispensation.

Q. 85. WHAT DOTH GOD REQUIRE OF US, THAT WE MAY ESCAPE HIS WRATH AND CURSE DUE TO US FOR SIN?

To escape the wrath and curse of God due to us for sin, God requireth of us faith in Jesus Christ, repentance unto life, with the diligent use of all the outward means whereby Christ communicateth to us the benefits of redemption.

What Truths are embraced in this Answer?

1. *God himself hath devised a way of escape from the effects of sin.*—*John,* iii. 16. God so loved the world, that he gave his only begotten Son, that whosoever believeth in him, should not perish, but have everlasting life.
2. *Faith in Christ is necessary for escaping the wrath and curse of God.*—*Acts,* xvi. 31. Believe on the Lord Jesus Christ, and thou shalt be saved.
3. *True repentance is necessary for escaping the wrath and curse of God.*—*Luke,* xiii. 3. Except ye repent, ye shall all likewise perish.
4. *A diligent use of the means of grace is required of all who would escape the wrath and curse of God.*—*Phil.* ii. 12, 13. Work out your own salvation with fear and trembling: for it is God which worketh in you both to will and to do of his good pleasure.
5. *The benefits of salvation are usually communicated to sinners by means of the ordinances.*—*Rom.* x. 14. How then shall they call on him in whom they have not believed? and how shall they believe in him of whom they have not heard? and how shall they hear without a preacher?

What Lessons do you derive from the above Doctrines?

I learn (1.) That, on account of sin, I am in great peril. (2.) That God has graciously appointed certain means of escape. (3.) That if I neglect the means appointed I must suffer the punishment which I deserve. (4.) That my deliverance from sin and its consequences should be one great business of my life on earth. (5.) It becomes me to warn, and otherwise to assist, my fellow-men to avoid, or get away from, the miseries which sin has created.

What Illustrations are given?

1. A QUESTION.—"MAMMA," said a little child, "my Sabbath-school teacher tells me that this world is only a place in which God lets us live awhile that we may prepare for a better world. But, mother, I do not see any body preparing. I see you preparing to go into the country, and Aunt Ellen is preparing to come here. But I do not see any one preparing to go there. *Why don't you try to get ready?* You scarce ever *speak* about going."—*Ch. Treasury.*

2. JOHN NEWTON wisely remarks: "Many have puzzled themselves about the origin of evil. I observe there is evil, and that there is A WAY TO ESCAPE IT, and with this I begin and end."

SECTION I.

OF FAITH IN JESUS CHRIST.

Q. 86. WHAT IS FAITH IN JESUS CHRIST?

Faith in Jesus Christ is a saving grace, whereby we receive and rest upon him alone for salvation, as he is offered to us in the gospel.

What Truths are embraced in this Answer?

1. *Faith in Jesus Christ is a saving grace.—John,* xx. 31. That believing ye might have life through his name.
2. *Jesus Christ is received as our Saviour, by faith.—John,* i. 12. As many as received him, to them gave he power to become the sons of God, even to them that believe on his name.
3. *By faith we depend upon Christ for salvation.—Acts,* xv. 11. We believe, that through the grace of the Lord Jesus, we shall be saved.
4. *By faith we depend on Christ alone for salvation.—Gal.* ii. 16. We have believed in Jesus Christ, that we might be justified by the faith of Christ, and not by the works of the law.
5. *By faith we receive Christ as offered in the Gospel.— Eph.* i. 13. In whom ye also trusted, after that ye heard the word of truth, the gospel of your salvation.

What Lessons do you derive from the above Truths

I learn (1.) That trust in Christ is essential to future happiness. (2.) That I must put no trust in any supposed goodness or in any efforts of mine own, as deserving of salvation, or as recommending me to Christ. (3.) That I am indebted to God, not only for the gift of his dear Son, as my Saviour, but for the disposition so to accept of that gift as to be profited by it, or to have an interest in it, and hence there is no merit in faith. (4.) That I must look to Christ daily and thankfully, not only for pardon, but for the destruction of all that is sinful in my heart and life, as preparatory to a residence with him in heaven.

How can you Illustrate this subject?

1. I was once called, says the excellent William Jay, of England, to attend the dying bed of a young female. In answer to my inquiries, she replied: "I have little to relate as to my own experience. I have been much tried and tempted, but this is my sheet-anchor. He hath said, 'Him that cometh unto me, I will in no wise cast out.' I

know I come to him, and I EXPECT HE WILL BE AS GOOD AS HIS WORD. Poor and unworthy as I am, he will not trifle with me, nor deceive me. It would be beneath his greatness as well as his goodness."

2. HOW TO GO TO CHRIST.—A MINISTER of the Gospel one day had gone into his cellar, which in winter was quite dark, and entered by a trap door. A little daughter, only three years old, was trying to find him, and came to the trap door; but, on looking down, all was dark, and she called: "Are you down cellar, papa?" "Yes, would you like to come, Mary?" "It is dark; I can't come down, papa." "Well, my daughter, I am right below you, and I can see you, though you cannot see me, and if you will drop yourself, I will catch you." "Oh, I should fall: I can't see you, papa." "I know it," he answered, "but I am really here, and you shall not hurt yourself. If you will jump, I will catch you safely." Little Mary strained her eyes to the utmost, but she could see no glimpse of her father; she hesitated, then advanced a little farther, then, summoning all her resolution, she threw herself forward, and was received safely in her father's arms. A few days after, she again discovered the cellar door open, and supposing her father to be there, she called: "Shall I come again, papa?" "Yes, my dear, in a minute," he replied, and had just time to reach his arms towards her, when, in her childish glee, she fell shouting into his arms; and clasping his neck, said: "I knew, dear papa, I should not fall." The above is a plain illustration of the manner in which a sinner, of any age, must put his trust in Christ alone, in his alleged power, and willingness, and offer to save, at once, *now*, whoever casts himself, like this little girl, into the open arms of his mercy; not waiting for any *fitness* for the act, nor doubting a happy result, as was found in the case above.

3. CHINESE CHILDREN.—Miss Grant, at Singapore, had a school for little Chinese girls. She was one day asking a class this question, "Were you sure of dying to-morrow, what would you do to-day?" One said, "She would be getting her grave ready"—which is a very important business among the Chinese; but another, with a resolute countenance, said, "I would believe *strongly* in Jesus."

4. HOW TO STRENGTHEN FAITH.—The sailor, by using his eyes in looking for land, acquires great keenness of sight. Use the eye of Faith in looking for your eternal haven, and you give it greater clearness of vision.

SECTION II.

OF REPENTANCE UNTO LIFE.

Q. 87. WHAT IS REPENTANCE UNTO LIFE?

Repentance unto life is a saving grace, whereby a sinner, out of a true sense of his sin and apprehension of the mercy of God in Christ, doth, with grief and hatred of his sin, turn from it unto God with full purpose of, and endeavor after, new obedience.

What Truths are embraced in this Answer?

1. *Repentance is a saving grace.*—2 Cor. vii. 10. Godly sorrow worketh repentance to salvation, not to be repented of.
2. *In repentance there must be a true sense of sin.*—Psal. li. 4. Against thee, thee only have I sinned, and done this evil in thy sight.
3. *In repentance there is an apprehension of mercy in God.*—Rom. ii. 4. The goodness of God leadeth thee to repentance.

4. *The mercy of God to the sinner is exhibited only in Christ.*—*Rom.* iii. 25. Whom God hath set forth to be a propitiation through faith in his blood, to declare his righteousness for the remission of sins that are past, through the forbearance of God.

5. *In true repentance there is a sincere grief for sin.*—*Jer.* xxxi. 19. I was ashamed, yea, even confounded, because I did bear the reproach of my youth.

6 *In true repentance there is a sincere hatred of sin.*—*Ezek.* xxxvi. 31. Then shall ye remember your own evil ways, and your doings that were not good, and shall loathe yourselves in your own sight for your iniquities, and for your abominations.

7. *In true repentance, the sinner turns from his sin.*—*Ezek.* xviii. 30. Repent, and turn yourselves from all your transgressions.

8. *In true repentance, the sinner returns back unto God.*—*Lam.* iii. 40. Let us search and try our ways, and turn again to the Lord.

9. *In repentance, there is a full purpose of future obedience to God*—*Psal.* cxix. 59. I thought on my ways, and turned my feet unto thy testimonies.

10. *In true repentance, there is an anxious endeavor to obey God.*—*Jer.* xxxi. 18. Turn thou me, and I shall be turned; for thou art the Lord my God.

11. *The obedience following true repentance, is a new obedience.*—*Rom.* vii. 6. That we should serve in newness of spirit, and not in the oldness of the letter.

What Lessons do you derive from the above Doctrines?

I learn (1.) That mere sorrow on account of sin does not amount to Repentance. (2.) That so long as sin is committed, repentance will be a pressing duty. (3.) That I should study the great wrong I have done in breaking God's law and opposing his revealed will, in days past. (4.) That I must look to God for the aid of his Holy Spirit to make me hate sin more deeply, and to turn from the practice of all sin, whether inward or outward, against God and against man, and against my own soul. (5.) That I should deeply adore, and earnestly *ap-*

prehend, or lay hold of, the mercy of God which is shown to repenting sinners, on account of what Christ has suffered in our behalf. (6.) That this repentance or change of heart does not merit everlasting life, for it is produced and maintained in the soul by the *gracious act* of God, and is simply a necessary preparation for the life of heaven. (7.) God would dishonor himself and his holy law should he pardon any sinner who does not condemn and hate himself for his transgression of that law, and does not sincerely purpose and endeavor to honor it, and thus to honor God in all his future conduct. (8.) Hence, I learn, that careless and impenitent sinners will derive no benefit from Christ's sufferings. (9.) That their guilt and sinfulness are fearfully increased by not regarding the mercy that is offered them through Christ, upon condition of their repentance.

How can you Illustrate this Subject?

1. WHAT IS PENITENCE?—Penitence is the tear that drops from the eye of faith, when that eye is fixed upon the cross.

2. REPENTANCE—NOT MERE SORROW.—Repentance is not mere sorrow for sin, or hell would be the most penitent world in the universe. Not a lost soul there but is sorry for the course which led to so fearful a termination.— *Ford.*

3. SECRET SIN.—It was an impressive saying of Bishop TAYLOR: "Though I could commit sin so secretly that no person living should ever hear of it, and though I were sure that God would never punish me for it, yet would I not commit sin, for the very filthiness of sin."

4. Mr. BOLTON said to his children, who stood around his dying bed, "See that none of you meet me in an unconverted state, at the Day of Judgment."

5. "I WILL RUN THE RISK."—At the close of a discourse of great pungency and plainness, a preacher made a

solemn appeal to his hearers, whether in view of the truths and warnings he had uttered, they would run the risk of delaying the work of repentance? At the close of the service, in passing down the aisle, a lady, deeply impressed with the appeal which had been made, said, in a low but earnest tone, to a gay young lady of her acquaintance, "Can you resist such an appeal as you have just heard? Will you venture to run the risk of your soul?" "O yes," she replied in a thoughtless tone, "I will run the risk." A few days after, the pastor who made this appeal was called to attend the funeral of a young lady, in a certain street, who had died suddenly. It proved to be the young lady who had ventured to run such a dreadful risk of losing her soul. Behind the curtain of eternity we may not penetrate or follow the soul to its last account.—*Zion's Herald.*

6. THE LAST QUESTION.—A little boy, on his death-bed, urging his father to repentance, said, "Father, I am going to heaven; what shall I tell Jesus is the reason why you won't love him?" Before the weeping father could answer, the child had fallen asleep in Jesus.

7. DISTRESS FOR SIN.—In a powerful revival, the Rev. DR. NETTLETON once said, "It may be new to some of you that there should be such distress for sin. But there was great distress on the day of Pentecost, when thousands were pricked in the heart, and cried out, 'Men and brethren, what shall we do?' Some of you may, perhaps, be ready to say, 'If this is religion, we wish to have nothing to do with it.' My friends, this is not religion. Religion does not cause its subjects to feel and act thus. These individuals are thus distressed, not because they have religion, but because they have no religion, and have found it out. It was so on the day of Pentecost. They had made the discovery that they were lost sinners, and that their souls were in jeopardy every hour."

SECTION III.

OF THE DILIGENT USE OF THE MEANS OF GRACE— VIZ., THE WORD OF GOD, THE SACRAMENTS AND PRAYER.

Q 88. WHAT ARE THE OUTWARD MEANS WHEREBY CHRIST COMMUNICATETH TO US THE BENEFITS OF REDEMPTION?

The outward and ordinary means whereby Christ communicateth to us the benefits of redemption, are his ordinances; especially the word, sacraments and prayer, all which are made effectual to the elect for salvation.

What Truths are embraced in this Answer?

1. *There are certain means of grace to be observed by the people of God.*—*Acts*, ii. 42. They continued steadfastly in the apostles' doctrine and fellowship, and in breaking of bread, and in prayers.

2. *The means of grace have been appointed by Christ.*— *Matt.* xxviii. 20. Teaching them to observe all things whatsoever I have commanded you.

3. *The benefits of redemption are communicated by the means of grace.*—*Eph.* iv. 11, 12. He gave some, apostles; and some, prophets; and some, evangelists; and some, pastors, and teachers; for the perfecting of the saints, for the work of the ministry, for the edifying of the body of Christ.

4. *The word of God is one special means of grace.*—*John*, xx. 31. These are written, that ye may believe that Jesus is the Christ, the Son of God; and that, believing, ye might have life through his name.

5. *The Sacraments are special means of grace.*—1 *Cor.* x. 16. The cup of blessing which we bless, is it not the communion of the blood of Christ? The bread which we break, is it not the communion of the body of Christ?

6. *Prayer is a special means of grace.*—*Mark*, xi. 24.

What things soever ye desire when ye pray, believe that ye receive them, and ye shall have them.

7. *The means of grace are, by the Spirit, rendered effectual to the salvation of God's people.*—1 *Thess.* i. 5. Our gospel came not unto you in word only, but also in power, and in the Holy Ghost, and in much assurance.

What Lessons do you derive from the above Doctrines?

I learn (1.) That the elect, or God's chosen people, will not be saved without the use of means, for they need the influence of means to change their dispositions and manner of life, bringing these into a correspondence with the heavenly state. (2.) That it is not wise, or respectful to God, to neglect the means of salvation; for God has commanded them to be used by all. (3.) I have no business to decline the use of these means so long as I am not assured that I am one of the elect; for God gives no one such assurance except as it may be gained from using the means of grace, and by the use of them being brought to that faith in Christ, and that repentance unto life, which have already been explained. (4.) I must daily thank God for these means of salvation, use them with humble dependence on God to make them avail to my preparation for heaven, and labor to give to all my fellow-men the same advantages for eternal life. (5.) My compassion should go forth daily to those in Christian lands who neglect or pervert and abuse the gospel of Christ and Christian rites, and also to the millions of mankind to whom Christ has never been held forth as an almighty and sufficient Saviour.

What Illustrations are given?

1. THE BIBLE WITHHELD BY ROMISH PRIESTS.—Says "Kirwan" to Archbishop Hughes: "God has commanded me to 'Search the Scriptures.' *Who has given you authority to forbid me?* What right have you to forbid me, more

THE DILIGENT USE OF THE MEANS OF GRACE. 211

than I have to forbid you? Produce your credentials! Where does God place his Revealed Will in the keeping of pope, prelate, or priest, to be doled out to his erring children in such ways and parcels as they may deem best? He has no more placed the Bible under your control, or that of your church, than he has the sun in heaven or the vital air."

2. PRAYING TO SAINTS.—"In looking over the Bible," says the Rev. Dr. Nevins, "the book which contains the religion of Protestants, and which, being older than the Roman Catholic religion, proves the seniority of Protestantism over Popery, I find no account of praying to saints. I do not read of Joshua praying to Moses, or of Elisha invoking Elijah. No! there is not a word of what constitutes so much of the doctrine of the Catholic in either Testament. We do not find anything in the Acts or Epistles about praying to the beloved Virgin, whom they call *our Lady*, in allusion to the phrase *our Lord*. * * * * * Catholic books are full of the blessed Virgin. The Bible is all about Christ. There is the difference."—*Thoughts on Popery*.

3. A CHILD'S REBUKE.—On a certain occasion when a minister was speaking of the neglect of family duties, of reading the Scriptures, and of family prayer, a little girl, who listened attentively, and perceived that the preacher was describing a neglect that she had herself noticed at home, whispered to her mother, "Ma, is the minister talking to you?" To the mother this simple question was more powerful than the sermon. She was immediately brought under deep convictions of sin, which resulted in her hopeful conversion to God.

ALEXANDER PATERSON.—"It was our *Communion* last Sabbath," he writes to his friend, Mr. Edie, "and I think I never felt my soul more drawn forth to Jesus, and away from myself and every creature. And oh, if communion on earth be so sweet, what must it be in heaven, where there is no wandering heart, and no tempting devil, and no ensnaring world. * * * * The marriage supper hastens. Oh, how little have we seen of Christ! There is enough in him to fill men and angels with new wonder to all eternity."

OF THE WORD OF GOD AS A MEANS OF GRACE.

Q. 89. HOW IS THE WORD MADE EFFECTUAL TO SALVATION?

The Spirit of God maketh the reading, but especially the preaching of the word, an effectual means of convincing and converting sinners, and of building them up in holiness and comfort, through faith, unto salvation.

What Truths are embraced in this Answer?

1. *The Holy Spirit alone makes the word effectual to salvation.*—1 *Pet.* i. 22. Ye have purified your souls in obeying the truth through the Spirit.
2. *The reading of the word is made an effectual means of convincing sinners.*—2 *Kings*, xxii. 10, 11. Shaphan read it before the king. And it came to pass, when the king had heard the words of the book of the law, that he rent his clothes.
3. *The reading of the word is made an effectual means of converting sinners.*—*Psal.* xix 7. The law of the Lord is perfect, converting the soul.
4. *The reading of the word is an effectual means of building up God's people in holiness.*—*Acts*, xx. 32. I commend you to God, and to the word of his grace, which is able to build you up, and to give you an inheritance among all them which are sanctified.
5. *The reading of the word is an effectual means of comforting God's people.*—*Rom.* xv. 4. Whatsoever things

were written aforetime, were written for our learning, that we, through patience and comfort of the Scriptures, might have hope.

6. *The reading of the word is made effectual to salvation through faith.*—2 *Tim.* iii. 15. From a child thou hast known the Holy Scriptures, which are able to make thee wise unto salvation, through faith which is in Christ Jesus.

7. *The preaching of the word is especially an effectual means of convincing sinners.*—*Acts*, ii. 37. When they heard this, they were pricked in their heart, and said unto Peter, and to the rest of the apostles, Men and brethren, what shall we do?

8. *The preaching of the word is especially an effectual means of converting sinners.*—*Acts*, xxvi. 17, 18. The Gentiles, unto whom now I send thee, to open their eyes, and to turn them from darkness to light, and from the power of Satan unto God.

9. *The preaching of the word is especially an effectual means of building up God's people in holiness.*—*Col.* i. 28. We preach, warning every man, and teaching every man in all wisdom; that we may present every man perfect in Christ Jesus.

10. *The preaching of the word is especially an effectual means of comforting God's people.*—1 *Thess.* iii. 2. And sent Timotheus—to establish you, and to comfort you concerning your faith.

11. *The preaching of the word is made effectual to salvation, only through faith.*—*Heb.* iv. 2. The word preached did not profit them, not being mixed with faith in them that heard it.

What Lessons do you derive from the above Doctrines?

I learn (1.) That the use of the means of religious instruction, improvement, comfort, and salvation, will not be availing except the energy of the Holy Spirit be exerted in connection with them. And (2.) That, to enjoy the aid of the Holy Spirit, I must rely wholly and constantly upon the merit, death, and intercession of the Son of God. (3.) That none can be saved who are not thus looking to Christ, however diligently they may read the Scriptures, attend upon public preaching, or abound in prayer. (4) That the only proper and profitable manner of performing these duties is to seek therein the promised favor of the Holy Spirit. (5.) That the whole credit of the spiritual peace, comfort, purity, and salvation of those who are finally saved, must be forever given to God the Spirit, through the mediation and worthiness of God the Son. (6.) That a merely outward and formal religion has no fitness or efficacy to prepare men for everlasting life.

What Illustrations can you give?

1. WHAT THE SPIRIT CAN DO.—The Spirit is an almighty Spirit. He can break the strongest bad habits, like tow before the fire. He can make the most difficult things easy, and the mightiest objections melt away like snow in spring. The Spirit can take a Roman Catholic monk, brought up in the midst of Romish superstition—trained from his infancy to believe false doctrine, and obey the Pope—steeped to the eyes in error—and make that man the clearest upholder of justification by faith the world ever saw. He has done so already. He did it with *Martin Luther.*—The Spirit can take an English tinker, without learning, patronage, or money—a man at one time notorious for nothing so much as blasphemy and swearing—and make that man write a religious book which shall stand unrivalled and unequalled in its way, by anything since the time of the apostles. He has done so already. He did it with *John Bunyan,* the author of the "Pilgrim's Progress."—The Spirit can take a sailor, drenched in worldliness and sin—a profligate captain of a slave ship—and make that man a most successful minister of the Gospel—a writer of letters, which are a storehouse of experimental religion; and of hymns, which

are known and sung wherever English is spoken. He has done it already. He did it with *John Newton.—Ryle.*

2. Dr. GRIFFIN showed his profound sense of the need of divine influence to give efficacy to preaching, by a remark which he dropped concerning a young man, a pupil of his, who had just commenced preaching. "He has," said he, "a very active mind and superior talents. The only question I have about him is, *whether he will pray down the Holy Spirit while he preaches?*"

Proper use of the Word of God.

Q. 90. HOW IS THE WORD TO BE READ AND HEARD, THAT IT MAY BECOME EFFECTUAL TO SALVATION?

That the word may become effectual to salvation, we must attend thereunto with diligence, preparation, and prayer, receive it with faith and love, lay it up in our hearts, and practice it in our lives.

What Truths are embraced in this Answer?

1. *The Word of God must be attended to, and understood.*—*Acts*, viii. 30. Understandest thou what thou readest?
2. *The Word of God must be attended to with diligence.*—*Acts*, xvii. 11. And searched the Scriptures daily, whether those things were so.
3. *The Word of God must be attended to with preparation.*—*James*, i. 21. Lay apart all filthiness and superfluity of naughtiness, and receive with meekness the ingrafted word, which is able to save your souls.
4. *The Word of God must be attended to in the exercise of prayer.*—*Psal.* cxix. 18. Open thou mine eyes, that I may behold wondrous things out of thy law.
5. *The Word of God must be received with faith.*—1 *Thess.* ii. 13. For this cause also thank we God without ceasing, because, when ye received the Word of God which ye

heard of us, ye received it not as the word of men, but (as it is in truth) the Word of God, which effectually worketh also in you that believe.

6. *The Word of God must be received with love.—Psal.* cxix. 97. O how love I thy law!

7. *The Word of God must be meditated upon.—Col.* iii. 16. Let the word of Christ dwell in you richly in all wisdom.

8. *The Word of God must be laid up in the heart.—Deut.* xi. 18. Ye shall lay up these my words in your heart, and in your soul.

9. *The truths of the Word must be reduced to practice in our lives.—James,* i. 22. Be ye doers of the Word, and not hearers only, deceiving your own selves.

What Lessons do you derive from the above Doctrines?

I learn (1.) That but few so read the Scriptures or attend upon Gospel preaching, as to make them effectual for salvation. (2.) That I must be more earnest, and prayerful, and laborious in effort, to gain salvation, as an attainable and most desirable result of attendance upon the preached gospel. (3.) That I must not be satisfied with any result short of this, either in my own case or that of others. (4.) That salvation is not to be expected without incessant effort.

What Illustrations are given?

1. A CONVERSATION ABOUT A REVIVAL.—"Mamma," said Lucy to her mother, "What is a Revival? I often see it stated in the papers that there has been a revival in such and such places. What does it mean?" "A revival," said her mother, "is a certain state of things in a community, produced by the presence and operation of the Holy Spirit on the minds and hearts of the people, leading them to believe and act more like rational, accountable beings, than they do at other times." "Why, mother, how do people feel and act in revivals?" "They

feel that they have souls which must be happy or miserable forever, and that much needs to be done to prepare them for happiness. Those who love the blessed Saviour feel very anxious that others should love him too. Parents are uncommonly desirous that their children should now turn from the ways of sin, and be engaged in serving the Lord and doing good; and ministers feel that their unconverted hearers are exposed to everlasting suffering, and that unless they soon repent and love God, and pray, they will lie down in everlasting sorrow. Many of those who are not Christians begin to feel that they have done very wrong in neglecting to receive the Lord Jesus as their Saviour, and living in disobedience to the commands of God. Those who have been in the practice of swearing, or breaking the Sabbath, or drinking, or gambling, or attending theatres, or neglecting the worship of God, feel very guilty for their past conduct, and often inquire of the minister, or some intelligent Christian, what they shall do to be saved. Those unconverted persons who have always been honest and moral, and who have been in the habit of attending religious meetings, sometimes are in great distress and perplexity, in view of their ingratitude to their Maker and Redeemer, and are ready to cry out, in the language of the humble publican, 'God be merciful to me a sinner!' And sometimes little children are seen weeping over their sins, and asking pious people to pray for them. And, as the result of the universal feeling and anxiety in the community, people desire to assemble together very often, for preaching, and exhortation, and prayer; and when at meeting, they find no difficulty in keeping awake. They hear with all their ears, and are ready to put in practice what they hear. There is a life, and zeal, and unction, in the exhortations, and prayers, and singing, that makes it manifest that the Holy Spirit is present. As the revival advances, those who were anxious about themselves, one after another, repent of their sins, submit to God, believe in the Lord Jesus Christ, and are filled with love, and joy, and peace, and comfort. Fathers, who had never prayed with their family before, now call them together, and read the Bible and pray with them. After those who have become Christians in this revival have waited long enough to try the evidences of their conversion, they offer themselves to the church to become members. They wish to obey the Saviour's command in regard to the Lord's Supper, 'This do in remembrance of me.'"—[*Selected.*]

2. A PRACTICAL PREACHER.—A New England clergyman, enforcing on his congregation the necessity of practical godliness, and contrasting the early Christians with those of the present generation, very properly remarked: "We have too many resolutions, and too little action. 'The *Acts* of the Apostles,' is the title of one of the books of the New Testament; their *resolutions* have not reached us.

OF THE SACRAMENTS AS MEANS OF GRACE.

Of the Efficacy of the Sacraments.

Q. 91. HOW DO THE SACRAMENTS BECOME EFFECTUAL MEANS OF SALVATION?

The sacraments become effectual means of salvation, not from any virtue in them, or in him that doth administer them; but only by the blessing of Christ, and the working of his Spirit in them that by faith receive them.

THE SACRAMENTS AS MEANS OF GRACE. 219

What Truths are embraced in this Answer?

1. *The sacraments possess no virtue in themselves.—Acts,* viii. 13, 23. Simon himself believed also, and was baptized. But Peter said unto him, I perceive that thou art in the gall of bitterness, and in the bond of iniquity.

2. *The sacraments are not rendered effectual by any virtue in the person administering them.—*1 *Cor.* iii. 7. Neither is he that planteth anything, neither he that watereth; but God that giveth the increase.

3. *The sacraments are rendered effectual by the blessing of Christ.—Matt.* iii. 11. He shall baptize you with the Holy Ghost, and with fire.

4. *The sacraments are made effectual by the operation of the Spirit of God.—John,* vi. 63. It is the Spirit that quickeneth; the flesh profiteth nothing.

5. *The sacraments become effectual to those only who receive them by faith.—Mark,* xvi. 16. He that believeth and is baptized, shall be saved.

What Lessons do you derive from the above Doctrines?

I learn (1.) Not to depend on the outward religious ceremony, but on the influences of the Holy Spirit in my heart, when I observe the ordinance of baptism in the Lord's Supper. (2.) The error of those who think they will be saved merely because they have been baptized or have partaken of the memorials of Christ's death. (3.) The error of the tenet of the Romish Church, that the efficacy of the sacrament depends upon the intention of the priest to bless, or otherwise, who administers them, thus wrongfully and arrogantly ascribing to him that power to withhold or bestow religious benefit which belongs alone to the Holy Spirit. (4.) The duty resting upon all who love Christ to profess the fact, and to observe the Lord's Supper in honor of his death.

What Illustration is given?

A RELIGION WITHOUT A HOLY SPIRIT.—"A gentleman of

intelligence, who was born of Catholic parents, and educated in the Catholic Church, but left it recently for Protestantism, said to his brother, who is still a Catholic: 'Why, brother, as long as I was a Catholic I never knew that there was a Holy Spirit.' And what (asks Dr. Nevins) do you think was the brother's reply? 'Well, I don't know that there is one now!' The narrative of what passed between these two men (adds Dr. N.) struck me with great force. A religion without a Holy Spirit! and this the religion, according to the computation of Bishop England, of *two hundred millions of mankind!* It made me sorry. My religion, thought I, would be very imperfect without a Holy Spirit. I want a sanctifier as well as a surety. I want one to act internally *upon* me as well as one to act externally *for* me. What should I do with my *title* to heaven, without a *fitness* for it? As a sinner, I am equally destitute of both. There can be no heaven without holiness. And whence has any man holiness but from the Holy Spirit? And is it likely he will act when he is not acknowledged? * * * *
* * * * These men knew not that there was a Holy Spirit. Why did they not know it? I will tell you. Because so little is said of the Holy Spirit among the Catholics,—there is so little need of any such agent, according to their system! They do not believe in the necessity of a change of heart. Why should there be a Holy Spirit? The priest does not want any such help to prepare a soul for heaven. *The Catholic system is complete without a Holy Spirit.* Therefore nothing is said of him in the pulpit, and the confession box; and the sinner is not directed to seek his influences or rely on his aid. * * * * This is one of the *capital* crimes of the Catholic Church. She does not speak *against* the Holy Ghost. No, she is *silent* about him."—*Thoughts on Popery.*

Of the Nature of the Sacraments.

Q. 92. WHAT IS A SACRAMENT?

A sacrament is a holy ordinance instituted by Christ, wherein by sensible signs, Christ and the benefits of the new covenant, are represented, sealed, and applied to believers.

What Truths are embraced in this Answer?

1. *The sacraments are holy ordinances.*—1. *Cor.* x. 21. Ye cannot drink the cup of the Lord, and the cup of devils; ye cannot be partakers of the Lord's table, and of the table of devils.
2. *The sacrament of baptism was instituted by Christ.*—*Matt.* xxviii. 19. Go ye therefore and teach all nations, baptizing them.
3. *The sacrament of the supper was instituted by Christ.*—*Matt.* xxvi 26. And as they were eating, Jesus took bread and blessed it, and brake it, and gave it to the disciples, and said, Take eat; this is my body.
4. *Christ is represented, by sensible signs, in the sacrament of baptism.*—*Rom.* vi. 3, 4. Know ye not that so many of us as were baptized into Jesus Christ, were baptized into his death? Therefore we are buried with him by baptism into death.
5. *Christ is represented, by sensible signs, in the sacrament of the Supper.*—1 *Cor.* xi. 24. This is my body which is broken for you: this do in remembrance of me.
6. *The benefits of the new covenant are represented in the sacraments.*—*John,* vi. 53, 54. Except ye eat the flesh of the Son of man, and drink his blood, ye have no life in you. Whoso eateth my flesh, and drinketh my blood, hath eternal life.
7. *Christ, and the benefits of the new covenant, are sealed to believers in the sacraments.*—*Rom.* iv. 11. He received the sign of circumcision, a seal of the righteousness of the faith, which he had, yet being uncircumcised.

8. *Christ and the benefits of the new covenant, are applied to believers in the sacraments.—John*, vi. 56, 57. He that eateth my flesh, and drinketh my blood, dwelleth in me, and I in him. As the living Father hath sent me, and I live by the Father: so he that eateth me, even he shall live by me.

What Lessons do you derive from the above Doctrines ?

I learn (1.) That the Romanists are wrong in declaring that the bread and wine used in the Lord's Supper, when consecrated by the priest, are converted into the real body and blood of the Lord, and cease to be bread and wine. My senses prove that this doctrine is false, and many arguments from Scripture overthrow it. (2.) That either having been baptized, or having also observed the Lord's Supper, I am under the more solemn engagement to devote my life to Christ. (3.) The great privilege to a believer, of properly receiving the sacrament; since Christ therein pledges himself to bestow all that he has promised in the New Testament, and actually bestows, to a greater or less extent, the several blessings purchased by his blood. (4.) That the sacraments should be observed with great reverence, with lively gratitude and hope, and with spiritual joy.

What Illustration can you relate ?

ROMISH ADMINISTRATION OF THE COMMUNION.—"KIRWAN," in one of his letters to Archbishop Hughes, says:—" I went into St. Peter's, in Barclay Street. The communicants drew around the altar upon their knees. With a little box in his hand, the priest passed from one to the other, taking a wafer, smaller than that used in sealing a letter, from the box, and placed it upon the extended tongue of the communicant. I was always taught that the teeth must not touch the wafer—that it must melt upon the

THE NEW TESTAMENT SACRAMENTS.

tongue. This I find to be the law of your church. I witnessed the ceremony, as I had often done before. I retired from the scene, asking these questions: Is that little wafer the real body and blood of Christ? Does the priest, in that little box, not as large as a snuff-box, carry two or three hundred real bodies of Christ? Do these communicants, each in their turn, eat the real body and blood of Christ? My dear sir, I cannot express to you the violence with which my mind rejected the absurdity."

Of the New Testament Sacraments.

Q. 93. WHICH ARE THE SACRAMENTS OF THE NEW TESTAMENT?

The sacraments of the New Testament are Baptism, and the Lord's Supper.

What Truths are embraced in this Answer?

1. *Baptism is a sacrament of the New Testament.*—*Mat.* xxviii. 19. Go ye, therefore, and teach all nations, baptizing them.

2. *The Lord's Supper is a sacrament of the New Testament.*—1 *Cor.* xi. 23. I have received of the Lord, that which also I delivered unto you, that the Lord Jesus, the same night in which he was betrayed, took bread, &c.

What Lessons do you derive from the above Truths?

I learn (1.) That the Jewish and Christian church are the same religious body, only under different modes of instruction, and with different advantages, both looking to Christ as the source of their richest blessings. (2.) That the Romanists have no authority for teaching that there are seven sacraments to be observed in the Christian church; to baptism and the Lord's Supper, adding confirmation, penance, ordination, marriage, and extreme unction. Though marriage and ordination are proper to be used, they have none of the qualities of a sacrament.

What Illustration is given?

SEVEN SACRAMENTS.—"What! seven! How is this? (asks the Rev. Dr. Nevins), I read in the Bible of only *two.* Whence have they the other *five?* O, they came from the other source of Christian doctrine (?)—*tradition.* It is true, the apostles *wrote* of only two sacraments; but Catholics would have us believe that they *preached* and *conversed* about five others; and those that heard them spoke of these sacraments to others; and they to others still; and so the story passed from lip to lip, until the Council of Trent (I believe it was) concluded that something had better be written about those five *extra* sacraments. I wonder that was never thought of before. It is surprising that it never occurred to the apostles, when they were writing their Epistles, to say a syllable about these *seven* sacraments. I may be very hard to please, but I cannot help feeling a desire to have *Scripture,* as well as *unwritten tradition,* in support of a doctrine or practice called Christian. I like to be able to trace a doctrine all the way back to the Bible, and to find it originating in the very oracles of God themselves."—*Thoughts on Popery.*

Of the Nature and Use of Baptism.

Q. 94. WHAT IS BAPTISM?

Baptism is a sacrament, wherein the washing with water, in the name of the Father, and of the Son, and of the Holy Ghost, doth signify and seal our ingrafting into Christ, and partaking of the benefits of the covenant of grace, and our engagement to be the Lord's.

What Truths are embraced in this Answer?

1. *Water is the sign to be used in Baptism.—Acts*, x. 47. Can any man forbid water, that these should not be baptized?
2. *Baptism is to be administered in the name of the Father, of the Son, and of the Holy Ghost.—Mat.* xxviii. 19. Baptizing them in the name of the Father, and of the Son, and of the Holy Ghost.
3. *The ingrafting of believers into Christ is signified by baptism.*—1 *Cor.* xii. 13. By one spirit are we all baptized into one body.
4. *Baptism seals the ingrafting of believers into Christ.* —*Gal.* iii. 27. As many of you as have been baptized into Christ, have put on Christ.
5. *Baptism signifies our having a right to the benefits of the covenant of grace.—Acts*, ii. 38. Repent and be baptized every one of you in the name of Jesus Christ, for the remission of sins, and ye shall receive the gift of the Holy Ghost.
6. *The Christian, in baptism, engages to be the Lord's.— Rom.* vi. 4. We are buried with him by baptism into death; that like as Christ was raised up from the dead by the glory of the Father, even so we also should walk in newness of life.

What Lessons do you derive from the above Doctrines?

I learn (1.) That the signification of baptism, as above described, relates only to believers, and not to all persons, infants or adults, that have been baptized. (2.) That it does not secure regeneration, or a religious and holy character, but is merely an outward symbol or sign of the necessity of the influence of the Holy Spirit to produce it. (3.) It implies, therefore, the doctrine that we are born depraved beings—or that we have a sinful nature, which requires *morally* to be made new, or regenerated. (3.) It is also regarded as showing the need of our being cleansed from the guilt of sin, or delivered from its condemning power, by the atoning blood of

Christ. (4.) It signifies that the baptized person is recognized as owing supreme love and devotion to the Father, Son, and Spirit; and if he be an adult person, solemnly promises to exercise such devotion and love. It is also a profession of faith in the doctrine of the Holy Trinity and of the several offices and relations of the persons of the Trinity, concerning man's salvation. (5.) It is a sign of admission into the visible church—an outward "engrafting into Christ"—into his "body"—the Church; and further, a pledge of future conformity to all the laws and institutions of Christ, for the conduct and sanctification of the church. (6.) The distinction between baptism as a *sign* and *seal*, is to be understood. To some it is a *sign* merely; to others, that is, to true believers, it is both a *sign and a seal*. (7.) That the rite of baptism does not possess an efficacy to remove *original sin*, as some falsely claim, for in that case all baptized persons would lead a holy life, and be free from the miseries that sin has introduced. (8.) That baptized persons, whether children or grown-up persons, should not be worldly-minded, unbelieving, and impenitent, but are justly expected to be sincere and cheerful followers and worshippers of Jesus Christ.

What Illustration can you relate?

IMPORT OF THE BAPTISMAL COVENANT.—The Rev. PHILIP HENRY, for the use of his children, prepared this short form of words, showing what is implied in baptism; taught it to his children, required them to repeat it every Sabbath evening, after their recitation of the Catechism, and was wont to add: "So say, and so do, and you are made for ever:"—"I take God the Father, to be my chiefest good and highest end. I take God the Son to be my Prince and Saviour. I take God the Holy Ghost to be my Sanctifier, Teacher, Comforter, and Guide. I take the

Word of God to be my rule in all my actions. And the people of God to be my people in all conditions. I do, likewise, devote and dedicate unto the Lord my whole self, all I am, all I have, and all I can do. And this I do deliberately, sincerely, freely, and for ever." He also took pains with his children to lead them into the understanding of it, and to persuade them to a free and cheerful consent to it. And when they grew up, he made them all write it over severally with their own hands, and very solemnly set their names to it, which he told them he would keep by him, and it should be produced as a testimony against them, in case they should afterwards depart from God, and turn from following after him.

Of the Subjects of Baptism.

Q. 95. TO WHOM IS BAPTISM TO BE ADMINISTERED?

Baptism is not to be administered to any that are out of the visible church, till they profess their faith in Christ, and obedience to him; but the infants of such as are members of the visible church are to be baptized.

What Truths are embraced in this Answer?

1. *Baptism is not to be administered to any who are not members of Christ's church, till they profess their faith in him.*—*Acts*, viii. 36, 37. What doth hinder me to be baptized? And Philip said, If thou believest with all thy heart, thou mayest.

2. *A profession of future obedience to Christ is necessary, previous to baptism.*—1 *Pet.* iii. 21. The like figure whereunto even baptism doth also now save us, (not the putting away of the filth of the flesh, but the answer of a good conscience toward God,) by the resurrection of Jesus Christ.

3. *Children of believing parents are proper subjects of*

baptism, as God bestows on many of them the blessings which it signifies.—*Luke,* xviii. 16. Suffer little children to come unto me, and forbid them not; for of such is the kingdom of God.

4. *Children of believing parents are entitled to the sign of the covenant, as God has given them the promises of it.*—*Acts,* ii. 39. The promise is unto you and to your children.

5. *Children are to be considered ceremonially holy, and are entitled to the sign of the covenant, by the profession and membership of only one of their parents.*—1 *Cor.* vii. 14. The unbelieving husband is sanctified by the wife, and the unbelieving wife is sanctified by the husband: else were your children unclean; but now are they holy.

6. *The infants of a family are entitled to the sign of the covenant, on the profession and baptism of their parent.*—*Acts,* xvi. 33. Was baptized, he and all his, straightway.

What Lessons do you derive from the above Doctrines?

I learn (1.) The nature of infant baptism. It is suited to remind the children that they belong to God, have been devoted to his service, and have no right to live a worldly and sinful life. (2.) It helps parents, and the church, and the pastor, to be faithful in their endeavors so to pray for, watch over, instruct, and guide them, that by God's grace they may become real disciples of Christ, and an honor to the Christian Church into which baptism openly admits them. (3.) No baptized person can remain an enemy of Christ, or impenitent, without a shocking violation of God's solemn ordinance.

What Illustrations are given?

1. THE ROMISH IDEA OF BAPTISM.—As stated by Challoner, a Roman Catholic writer, the effects of baptism, when duly administered, are these:—It washes away original sin; it remits all actual sin; it infuses the habit of divine grace into the soul; it gives a right and title

to heaven; it makes us children and members of the church. "Now, sir," (remarks "Kirwan" in his Letters to Archbishop Hughes,) "I have no sense by which I can perceive how the application of water by a priest, or a minister, or a curè, or a midwife, can accomplish all this, whilst testimony to the contrary addresses itself to all my senses. Christ died for the sins of all that believe in him; it is faith in Christ that secures the washing away of original and actual sin; and faith is the exercise of a heart renewed by the Holy Ghost. Being justified by faith we have peace with God, and a title to heaven. All this I can understand; but how your dipping three times in water can do all this, I see not. What the Bible attributes to the Holy Spirit, and to the exercise of true faith, you claim for the Sacrament of Baptism. If your doctrine of baptismal regeneration is true, what a singular commentary we have of it in the lives of your people! What singular manifestations of the habits of divine grace which your baptism infuses into the soul, you see daily among your people! I only wonder that the facts in the case have not long since exploded your doctrine, and led you back to the simplicity of the sacrament as taught in the Bible!"

2. *History of the Rite of Baptism.*—There never was any age, at least since Abraham, (says Dr. Wall,) in which the children, whether of Jews or proselytes, that were admitted into covenant, had not some badge or sign of such their admission. The male children of Abraham's race were entered by circumcision. The whole body of the Jews, men, women, and children, were, in Moses' time, baptized. After which, the male children of proselytes, that were entered with their parents, were, as well as their parents, admitted by circumcision, baptism, and a sacrifice—the female children by a baptism and a sacrifice. Now, after that circumcision and sacrifice were to

be abolished, under the Gospel dispensation, there was nothing left but baptism or washing, for a sign of the covenant, and of professing religion. This our Saviour took, probably as being the easiest and the least operose (laborious) of all the rest; and as being common to both sexes, making no difference of male or female, and enjoined it to *all who should enter into the kingdom of God*. And St. Paul does plainly intimate to the Colossians, (Col. ii. 11, 12,) that it served them instead of circumcision, calling it *the circumcision of Christ*, or *Christian circumcision.—Hist. Inf. Baptism*, v. 1, p. 90.

3. *Origen*, who possessed more information than any man of his day, and who lived near the time of the apostles, says: "The church received a tradition, or order, from the apostles, to give baptism to little children also." *Augustine*, who was born in the middle of the fourth century, affirms: "The whole Church practises infant baptism. It was not instituted by councils, it was always in use." *Pelagius*, who lived at the same time, and who had visited the most noted churches in Europe, Asia, and Africa, declares that he never heard of any one, even the most impious heretic, who asserted that infants were not to be baptized. Dr. Gill himself, one of the most learned of the Baptist writers, acknowledges that infant baptism was the practice of the church universally, from the third to the eleventh century.—*Cogswell's Theol. Class Book.*

Of the Nature and Use of the Lord's Supper.

Q. 96. WHAT IS THE LORD'S SUPPER?

The Lord's supper is a sacrament, wherein, by giving and receiving bread and wine, according to Christ's appointment, his death is showed forth;

and the worthy receivers are, not after a corporal and carnal manner, but by faith, made partakers of his body and blood, with all his benefits, to their spiritual nourishment and growth in grace.

What Truths are embraced in this Answer?

1. *Bread is appointed to be one of the elements of the Lord's Supper.—Luke*, xxii. 19. He took bread, and gave thanks, and brake it, and gave unto them.
2. *Wine is appointed as the other element to be used in the Lord's Supper.—Mat.* xxvi. 27. He took the cup, and gave thanks, and gave it to them, saying, Drink ye all of it.
3. *Christ's death is showed forth by giving and receiving bread and wine in the sacrament of the Supper.*—1 *Cor.* xi. 26. As oft as ye eat this bread, and drink this cup, ye do show the Lord's death till he come.
4. *It is not in a corporal or carnal manner that Christ's body and blood are received in the sacrament.*—1 *Cor.* x. 16. The cup of blessing which we bless, is it not the communion of the blood of Christ? The bread which we break, is it not the communion of the body of Christ?
5. *The body and blood of Christ in the sacrament are received by faith.—John*, vi. 35. I am the bread of life: he that cometh to me shall never hunger; and he that believeth on me shall never thirst.
6. *Christians in the sacrament are made partakers of Christ and all his benefits.—John*, vi. 51. I am the living bread which came down from heaven. If any man eat of this bread, he shall live for ever: and the bread that I will give is my flesh, which I will give for the life of the world.
7. *Spiritual nourishment is conferred in the sacrament.— John*, vi. 55. My flesh is meat indeed, and my blood is drink indeed.
8. *The Christian is enabled to grow in grace by worthily partaking of the Lord's Supper.—John*, iv. 14. The water that I shall give him, shall be in him a well of water springing up into everlasting life.

What Lessons do you derive from the above Doctrines?

I learn (1.) That in this sacrament Christians do not eat and drink the real body and blood of Christ, as the Romanists believe; and that the observance is useful, only as exciting the mind to an affectionate remembrance of the sufferings of Christ as the procuring cause of all our spiritual blessings. (2.) That those Christians who neglect, or do not take pains properly to observe this ordinance, are guilty not only of a great disrespect and want of love to Christ, but of a great disregard to their own spiritual welfare and comfort. (3.) That true love to Christ will prompt us to show forth the fact of his death, both in honor of him, and for the salvation of men. (4.) That this ordinance is not a sacrifice for sin, as the Romanists pretend, but a symbol or remembrance of the one sacrifice for sin, which Jesus offered once for all.

What Illustrations are offered?

1. THE MASS.—It never occurs to the Christian reader of the Scriptures that by the mass, Catholics can mean the transaction recorded by Matthew in his 26th chapter, and by three other sacred writers, and which we commonly speak of as the institution of the Lord's Supper. But that is what they mean by it. Then, they tell us, the first mass was said. In the Douay Catechism we find these questions and answers: *Q.* Who said the first mass? *A.* Jesus Christ. *Q.* When did he say it? *A.* At his last supper. Here it is, question and answer for it, if not *chapter and verse.* The Biblical reader will please to bear in mind, whenever hereafter he reads the narrative of the transaction, that the writer is giving an account of the first mass that was ever *said.* But what do they mean by the mass? The "Christian's Guide" says, on the subject: "I profess, likewise, that in the mass there

is offered to God a true, proper, and propitiatory sacrifice for the living and the dead." Christ offered it first when he said mass, and every priest now offers it when he says mass. * * * * * The Catholics say that when Christ performed these actions with the bread and wine, *he offered himself to God as a propitiatory sacrifice.* How does what he did bear the least resemblance to the offering of a propitiatory sacrifice? There was no bloodshed—no life taken—as was the case in all propitiatory sacrifices under the law; and in the sacrifice which Christ made of himself on the cross, and which has always, by Pagans, as well as the disciples of the true religion, been considered essential to a *propitiatory* sacrifice. I confess there was *something* offered. Bread and wine were offered. These might constitute a *eucharistic* sacrifice, but never a propitiatory one. * * * A sacrifice, to be a sacrifice, must be offered *to God*, as even the quotation from the "Christian's Guide" recognizes. But what was offered in this case was offered to the disciples. "Take eat," he said to them. It is true the bread and wine were offered to them as the memorial of a sacrifice in which the body of Christ was to be broken and his blood shed; but the memorial of a sacrifice is not a sacrifice. The emblematical representation of a thing is not the thing itself. Plainly there was no sacrifice in this transaction. But again, if Christ in the eucharist offered himself a sacrifice to God, as they affirm, and afterwards, as all admit, offered himself on the cross, then he *twice* offered himself; and if so, the writer of the Epistle to the Hebrews was under a great mistake, for he says, "Christ was *once* offered to bear the sins of many"—"we are sanctified through the offering of the body of Jesus Christ, *once for all.*" Here is a contradiction. Which shall we believe? The apostle of the Gentiles or the Catholic Church? * * * * But if the Catholic doctrine be true, Christ has been offered not twice only, but innumerable times. In every mass that ever has been said, he has been offered.—*Nevins' Thoughts on Popery.*

2. How do you remember Christ?—Some who profess respect, and indeed love, for Christ, remember Christ in their own way, but not in his way. They do some things in remembrance of him, but not that which he said "*do.*" I wonder, (says Dr. Nevin,) they do not adopt *his* way. I cannot help suspecting their love when I see they do not. It always appeared to me that such a benefactor as Christ ought to be remembered, and that sinners whom he died to save, should remember him in that way, even though it should not seem to them the most appropriate and reasonable manner of commemorating him.—*Practical Thoughts.*

3. His Last Wish.—It is enough for me, (says the Rev. Dr. Nevin,) that my Saviour inclined to this mode of being remembered, and *expressed such a wish:* the least I can do, is to comply with it. He did not express a great many wishes. I cannot help regarding it as unkind, that *this one wish* of Jesus should not be complied with; and especially when I consider what a friend he was—what a benefactor. * * * * * *All* his wishes, I think, should be complied with; but this was his *last.* He was going to suffer; he was to die in a few hours;—and *such* a death too! and *for them* of whom he made the request, that they might never die. * * * * * * I wonder those words, "broken for you," do not break the heart of every one who refuses.—*Practical Thoughts.*

4. Half a Sacrament!—Who ever heard of such a thing? A sacrament divided! Yes, even so. The authorities of the Roman Catholic Church, Pope, Council, &c., have divided the sacrament of the Lord's Supper, which our Lord instituted the same night in which he

was betrayed; and ever since the Council of Constance, they have allowed the people only half of it. * * * * * * But did not Christ give the cup, in the original institution of the sacrament, to as many as he gave the bread? Yes, *Christ* did. So say Matthew, Mark, Luke, and Paul. He took the cup, they tell us, and gave it to them; and Matthew adds that he said in giving it, "Drink ye *all* of it." Let not this be omitted by any disciple. It would seem as if Christ foresaw what the Constantine Council were going to do, and therefore said, "Drink ye *all* of it." Rome might, with much more plausibility, have denied her laity the other half of the sacrament—the bread. * * * There can be no such thing in reality as half a sacrament: to divide a sacrament, is to destroy it.—*Thoughts on Popery.*

Of the Proper Observance of the Lord's Supper.

Q. 97. WHAT IS REQUIRED TO THE WORTHY RECEIVING OF THE LORD'S SUPPER?

It is required of them that would worthily partake of the Lord's Supper, that they examine themselves of their knowledge to discern the Lord's body, of their faith to feed upon him, of their repentance, love, and new obedience; lest, coming unworthily, they eat and drink judgment to themselves.

What Truths are embraced in this Answer?

1. *Self-examination is required of all who would worthily partake of the Lord's Supper.*—1 *Cor.* xi. 28. Let a man examine himself, and so let him eat of that bread, and drink of that cup.

2. *Communicants should examine themselves as to their*

knowledge to discern the Lord's body.—1 *Cor.* xi. 29. Eateth and drinketh damnation (or judgment) to himself, not discerning the Lord's body.

3. *Communicants should examine themselves as to their faith.*—2 *Cor.* xiii. 5. Examine yourselves whether ye be in the faith.

4. *Communicants should examine themselves as to their repentance.*—*Lam.* iii. 40. Let us search and try our ways, and turn again to the Lord.

5. *Communicants should examine themselves as to their love.*—1 *John*, iv. 8. He that loveth not, knoweth not God; for God is love.

6. *Communicants should examine themselves as to their new obedience.*—1 *Cor.* v. 8. Let us keep the feast, not with old leaven, neither with the leaven of malice and wickedness; but with the unleavened bread of sincerity and truth.

7. *For communicants to neglect the duty of self-examination is dangerous.*—1 *Cor.* xi. 31. If we would judge ourselves, we should not be judged.

8. *Communicating unworthily, exposes us to the judgments of God.*—1 *Cor.* xi. 29. He that eateth and drinketh unworthily, eateth and drinketh damnation (or judgment) to himself.

What Lessons do you derive from the above Doctrines?

I learn (1.) That much careful thought should precede an attendance at the Lord's Table. (2.) That the public preparatory lecture may be highly useful. (3.) That I should pray much for God's presence and blessing at the ordinance, and should read such religious books, and such portions of Scripture, as treat of the sufferings of Christ, with a view to raise in my soul devout affections suited to the occasion.

What Illustrations can you relate?

1. The French, particularly the army, had great attachment to Bonaparte. Said he, "At Arcola, when I was advancing, Col. Meuron, my aide-de-camp, threw himself

before me, covered me with his body, and received the wound which was destined for me. He fell at my feet, and his blood spouted up in my face. He gave his life to preserve mine." What, then, should not the Christian soldier be willing to do for Christ, the Captain of his salvation, leading him on to no dubious victory?

2. THE PRESENCE OF CHRIST.—Jesus, at the right hand of the Father, is yet present with all his younger brethren and sisters in this vale of weeping. His *human nature* is at the right hand of God upon the throne—a lamb as it had been slain. But his *divine nature* is unlimited, fills all worlds, and is present in every dwelling of every disciple in this world. His Divine nature thus brings in continual information to his human heart of anything that is going on in the heart and history of his people; so that his human heart beats towards us just as if he were sitting by our side.—*M'Cheyne.*

3. After receiving the second time the Lord's Supper, *M'Cheyne* writes in his journal: "I well remember when I was an enemy, and especially abhorred this ordinance *as binding me down;* but if I be bound to Christ in heart, I shall not dread any bands that can draw me close to him."

4. Says the Rev. *Thomas Adam*, "I do not go to the Lord's Table to give, but to receive; not to tell Christ how good *I* am, but to think how good *he* is. The words are, 'Do this in remembrance of me,' as if the Saviour said: 'Remember who I am, and what thou art; remember me as thy Saviour—as thy Master; remember my love, and thy obligations; remember me as hating thy sin, as bearing thy sin; remember me, and fear not; remember me, and sin not; remember me to live *for* me, *by* me, *with* me.'"

Of the Nature of Prayer.

Q. 98. WHAT IS PRAYER?

Prayer is an offering up of our desires unto God for things agreeable to his will, in the name of Christ, with confession of our sins, and thankful acknowledgment of his mercies.

What Truths are embraced in this Answer?

1. *Prayer is the offering up of our desires.—Psal.* lxii. 8. Pour out your heart before God.
2. *Prayer must be offered up to the true God.—Isa.* xlv. 22, 23. Look unto me, and be ye saved, all the ends of the earth: for I am God, and there is none else.—I have sworn by myself, and the word is gone out of my mouth in righteousness, and shall not return, That unto me every knee shall bow, every tongue shall swear.
3. *Prayer must be sincere.—Jer.* xxix. 13. And ye shall seek me and find me, when ye shall search for me with all your heart.
4. *Prayer must be frequent.*—1 *Thess.* v. 17. Pray without ceasing.
5. *Prayer must be offered up for things only which are agreeable to God's will.*—1 *John,* v. 14. If we ask anything according to his will, he heareth us.
6. *Prayer must be offered up in the name of Christ.*— *John,* xvi. 23. Whatsoever ye shall ask the Father in my name, he will give it you.
7. *Prayer must be offered up with confession of sin.*— *Dan.* ix. 4. I prayed unto the Lord my God, and made my confession.
8. *Prayer must be offered up with thanksgiving.—Phil.* iv. 6. By prayer and supplication with thanksgiving let your requests be made known unto God.

What Lessons do you derive from the above Doctrines?

I learn (1.) That the words of prayer, however proper and scriptural, do not amount to prayer if they do not express the feelings of my heart. (2.) That it is a great insult to God to address him in the language of prayer, without corresponding desires; in the language of confession, without humility and penitence for the sins confessed; in the language of praise, without an adoring sense of the divine goodness and condescension for the mercies acknowledged. (3.) That I can obtain blessings by prayer only through the mediation and grace of Christ. (4.) That they who do not pray in the method required above, practically deny their dependence on God, their indebtedness to God, their sinfulness and their need of Christ's favor. (5.) That not only private, but family prayer, is a duty and a privilege.

What Illustrations are offered?

1. CAUSE FOR THANKSGIVING.—At a meeting of ministers, as they were inquiring after each other's welfare, one said, "I feel that I have peculiar occasion for thanksgiving that I am here, for my life was brought into great peril by an accident on the way." "And I," said another, "have surely still greater cause for thanksgiving, seeing that I was brought all the way hither *without any accident at all.*"

2. *M'Cheyne on Confession.*—He says: "I am persuaded that I ought to confess my sins more. I think I ought to confess sin the moment I see it to be sin; whether I am in company, or in study, the soul ought to cast a glance of abhorrence at the sin. If I go on with the duty, bearing the sin unconfessed, I go on with a burdened conscience, and add sin to sin. * * * * * I ought to confess often the sins of my youth, like David and Paul—my sins before conversion, my sins since conversion—sins against light and knowledge—against love and grace—against each person of the Godhead. I ought to look at my sins in the light of the Holy Law—in the

light of God's countenance—in the light of the Cross—in the light of the Judgment-seat—in the light of Hell—in the light of eternity." He further says: "I ought to examine my dreams, my floating thoughts—my predilections—my often-recurring actions—my habits of thought, feeling, speech, and action—the slanders of my enemies—and the reproofs and even banterings of my friends—to find out traces of my prevailing sin—matter for confession. I ought to have a number of Scriptures marked, to bring sin to remembrance. I ought, on Sabbath evenings, and on Communion Sabbath evenings, to be especially careful to confess the sins of holy things.—*Memoir*, p. 135.

3. PRAYER OF A ROOM-MATE.—The celebrated English preacher and writer, JOHN ANGEL JAMES, owed his conversion, in the way of means, to the sight of a companion, who slept in the same room with him, bending his knees in prayer on retiring to rest. "That scene, so unostentatious, and yet so unconcealed," says he, "roused my slumbering conscience, and sent an arrow to my heart; for though I had been religiously educated, I had restrained prayer, and cast off the fear of God: my conversion to God followed, and soon afterwards my entrance upon college studies for the work of the ministry."

4. DR. CHALMERS AND HIS DAUGHTER.—The Rev. Dr. Fletcher, of London, having preached with great acceptance to children in Glasgow, Dr. Chalmers invited him to breakfast on the following morning. After breakfast, and family worship, Dr. Chalmers said to him, "Sir, it was not an invitation founded on mere compliment that I gave you last evening to meet me this morning; nor was it to enjoy your conversation. I have a daughter who appears still to have no part or lot with the people of God. If there be any human instrumentality, under God, which can impress her mind, I believe it must be wielded

by yourself. I will call her in; and while you are speaking to her, *an agonized father will be speaking to his God.*" The result was her hopeful conversion.

5. LUTHER'S PRAYERS.—"No day passes," said a German pastor in 1530, "in which he does not devote at least three hours to prayer and meditation. I once succeeded in hearing him pray. What energy, what faith in his words! He prays earnestly as a man communing with God; and with such trust and faith as a man conversing with his father."

Of the Rule of Direction in Prayer.

Q. 99. WHAT RULE HATH GOD GIVEN FOR OUR DIRECTION IN PRAYER?

The whole word of God is of use to direct us in prayer; but the special rule of direction is that form of prayer which Christ taught his disciples, commonly called The Lord's Prayer.

What Truths are embraced in this Answer?

1. *The young and unskilful should be taught to pray.*—*Luke*, xi. 1. Lord, teach us to pray, as John also taught his disciples.
2. *We have need to be directed in prayer.*—*Rom.* viii. 26. We know not what we should pray for as we ought.
3. *The whole word of God is of use to direct us in prayer.* —*John*, xv. 7. If ye abide in me, and my words abide in you, ye shall ask what ye will, and it shall be done unto you.
4. *The Lord's prayer is the special rule given us for our direction in prayer.*—*Mat.* vi. 9. After this manner, therefore, pray ye, "Our Father," &c.

What Lessons do you derive from the above Doctrines?

I learn (1.) The propriety and advantage of using the

Lord's Prayer as a daily help in my devotion. (2.) To make myself familiar with all those other parts of the Bible which may both supply me with suitable thoughts and expressions to be used in prayer, and show with what dispositions and aims I am to approach my God in this service. (3.) That I am not required to confine myself to any particular form or forms of prayer. (4.) That having the Bible as a guide and help, all should learn to pray with propriety and acceptance. (5.) Those who do not thus pray, are without excuse.

What Illustrations are given ?

1. *Matthew Hale*, once Chief-Justice of England, in his Letters to his Children, says: "If I omit praying and reading a portion of God's blessed word in the morning, nothing goes well with me all day."

2. *Dr. Doddridge* used often to say, "that he never advanced well in human learning without prayer, and that he always made the greatest progress in his studies when he prayed with the greatest fervency."

3. Towards the close of her last illness, and when able only to speak in short sentences, Mrs. *Hannah More* said to a little girl, in whom she was interested: "God bless thee, my dear child; love God; serve God; *love to pray to God more than to do any other thing.*"

4. Says PHILIP HENRY: "Let prayer be the *key of the morning,* and the *bolt of the night.*"

Of the Preface to the Lord's Prayer.

Q. 100. WHAT DOTH THE PREFACE OF THE LORD'S PRAYER TEACH US?

The preface of the Lord's prayer, (which is, "Our Father which art in heaven,") teacheth us to draw near to God with all holy reverence and confidence, as children to a father, able and ready to help us: and that we should pray with and for others.

What Truths are embraced in this Answer?

1. *We are, in prayer, to approach God with holy reverence.—Psal.* cxlv. 19. He will fulfil the desire of them that fear him: he also will hear their cry, and will save them.
2. *We are, in prayer, to approach God with holy confidence.—Eph.* iii. 12. In whom we have boldness and access with confidence.
3. *We are, in prayer, to approach God as our Father.—Rom.* viii. 15. Ye have received the spirit of adoption, whereby we cry, Abba, Father.
4. *We are, in prayer, to approach God as being able to help us.—Eph* iii. 20. Unto him who is able to do exceeding abundantly above all that we ask or think.
5. *We are, in prayer, to approach God as being willing to help us.—Mat.* vii. 11. How much more shall your Father which is in heaven give good things to them that ask him.
6. *We are to join with others in prayer.—Acts,* xii. 12. Many were gathered together, praying.
7. *We are to pray for others.—*1 *Tim.* ii. 1. I exhort therefore, that, first of all, supplications, prayers, intercessions, and giving of thanks be made for all men.

What Lessons do you derive from the above Doctrines?

I learn (1.) That to use this prayer with sincerity, I must be a child of God, and as I am not such by nature, I must be "born again" of the Spirit. (2.) That I should esteem it the greatest privilege to speak to such a Father as this prayer addresses, and to come to him as a child. (3.) Though He is said to be in heaven, yet he also fills immensity, so that he is always near me, and able to help me. (4.) I must learn to confide in my Heavenly Father as able and ready to help his children when they call upon him.

What Illustrations can you give?

1. AN AGED POOR MAN.—One of the members of Christ's flock was reduced to great poverty in his helpless old age, and yet he never murmured. A kind-hearted neighbor who met him on the road, said to him, "You must be badly off. I cannot tell how you maintain yourself and your wife; and yet you are always cheerful." "Oh, not so," replied the old Christian; "we are not badly off. We have a rich Father, and he does not suffer us to want." "Your father not dead yet! he must be very old indeed." "My Father never dies, and he always takes care of me." That aged Christian was a daily pensioner on the providence of his merciful and covenant-keeping God.

2. "AH, MASSA, YOU NO UNDERSTAND IT!" A few years since, in one of our large cities, lived a poor colored woman, named Betty, who had been confined by sickness for near twenty years. She had long been blind, and was said to be 105 years old; was noted for her good sense and warm-hearted piety. Mr. B——, a man of wealth and large business, in the same city, often took time to call and see her. His voice, and even his step, had become familiar to her, and always lighted up a smile on her dark and wrinkled face. He would often say some pleasant thing to cheer this lonely pilgrim on her way to Zion. One day, Mr. B—— took a friend from the country to see Betty. As he entered the cottage door, he said, "Ah, Betty, you are alive yet." "Yes, tank God," said Betty. "Betty," said he in a half sportive tone and manner, "why do you suppose God keeps you so long in this world, poor, and sick, and blind,

when you might go to heaven, and enjoy so much?" Betty assumed her most serious and animated tone, and replied: "Ah, Massa, you no understand it. Dere be two great tings to do for de church; one to pray for it—toder be to act for it. Now, Massa, *God keeps me alive to pray for de Church*, and he keeps you alive to act for it. *Your great gifts no do much good, Massa, without poor Betty's prayers.*" For a few moments Mr. B—— and his friend stood silent and astonished. They felt the knowledge and the dignity of this short sermon. "Yes, Betty," replied Mr. B——, in the most serious and subdued tones, "your prayers are of more importance to the church than my alms." This short sermon, preached by poor Betty, was never forgotten by Mr. B—— or his friend. It made them more humble, more prayerful, and more submissive in afflictions.—Abd. from *Parents' Magazine.*

Of the First Petition in the Lord's Prayer.

Q. 101. WHAT DO WE PRAY FOR IN THE FIRST PETITION?

In the first petition, which is, "Hallowed be thy name;" we pray that God would enable us and others to glorify him in all that whereby he maketh himself known, and that he would dispose all things to his own glory.

What Truths are embraced in is Answer?

1. *Without God we are of ourselves unable to glorify him.*—2 Cor. iii. 5. Not that we are sufficient of ourselves to think anything as of ourselves; but our sufficiency is of God.
2. *We should pray that God would enable us to glorify him.*—Psal. li. 15. O Lord, open thou my lips, and my mouth shall show forth thy praise.

3. *We should pray that God would enable others to glorify him.—Psal.* lxvii. 3. Let the people praise thee, O God; Let all the people praise thee.

4. *We should pray that God would dispose of all things for the glorifying of himself.—John,* xii. 28. Father, glorify thy name.

What Lessons do you derive from the above Doctrines?

I learn (1.) That without divine help I cannot entertain sufficiently great, and noble, and devout thoughts of God, nor act with due respect and awe before Him. (2.) The sin of hastily and without some preparation of mind, calling upon God in prayer. (3.) By the "name" of God, I am to understand God himself, by whichever of his names he may be addressed, or thought of. (4.) The great and shocking sin of a profane use or mention of any of the names by which God is made known to us.

What Illustrations can you give?

1. Childhood's Prayer.—A lady, in advanced life, thus writes of herself: "I left home at the age of eleven, alone and unaided, to gain my own livelihood. I went to sea among such as were sailors sixty years ago; and all that prevented me from ruin was the prayer which my mother had taught me nightly. And old as I now am, not a night passes in which I do not offer the Lord's Prayer; scarcely a night without the simple petition of the child—'Now I lay me down to sleep,'" &c. Such and so powerful were the early teachings of a mother, and such the influence of this prayer.

2. David Brainerd.—Among the dying sayings of this heavenly-minded man, President Edwards has recorded the following: "My heaven is to please God, and to glorify him, and give all to him, and to be wholly devoted to his glory; that is the heaven I long for; that is my religion; and that is my happiness, and

always was, ever since I suppose I had any true religion; and all those that are of that religion shall meet me in heaven. I do not go to heaven to be advanced, but to give honor to God. It is no matter where I shall be stationed in heaven, whether I have a high or a low seat there; but to love, and please, and glorify God is all."

Of the Second Petition.

Q. 102. WHAT DO WE PRAY FOR IN THE SECOND PETITION?

In the second petition, which is, " Thy kingdom come;" we pray, That Satan's kingdom may be destroyed; and that the kingdom of grace may be advanced, ourselves and others brought into it, and kept in it; and that the kingdom of glory may be hastened.

What Truths are embraced in this Answer?

1. *The kingdom of the universe is God's.*—Psal. ciii. 19. His kingdom ruleth over all.
2. *Satan has a kingdom in this world.*—John, xiv. 30. The prince of this world cometh, and hath nothing in me.
3. *We should pray for the destruction of Satan's authority and kingdom.*—Psal. lxviii. 1. Let God arise, let his enemies be scattered: let them also that hate him flee before him.
4. *God has in Christ established a kingdom of grace in the world.*—Luke, i. 33. He shall reign over the house of Jacob for ever; and of his kingdom there shall be no end.
5. *We should pray for the advancement of the kingdom of grace.*—Isa. lxii. 7. Give him no rest till he establish, and till he make Jerusalem a praise in the earth.

6. *We should pray that we ourselves be made subjects of Christ's kingdom.—Luke,* xxiii. 42. Lord, remember me when thou comest into thy kingdom.

7. *We should pray that others be brought into the kingdom of grace.—Rom.* x. 1. Brethren, my heart's desire and prayer to God for Israel is, that they might be saved.

8. *We should pray that God would keep us in his kingdom of grace.—Psal.* cxix. 117. Hold thou me up, and I shall be safe: and I will have respect unto thy statutes continually.

9. *We should pray that God would keep others in his kingdom of grace.—*1 *Thes.* v. 23. I pray God your whole spirit, and soul, and body, be preserved blameless unto the coming of our Lord Jesus Christ.

10. *There is approaching for the people of God a kingdom of glory.—Rev.* xxii. 5. There shall be no night there; and they need no candle, neither light of the sun ; for the Lord God giveth them light: and they shall reign for ever and ever.

11. *We should pray that the kingdom of glory should be hastened.—Rev.* xxii. 20. He which testifieth these things saith, Surely I come quickly, Amen. Even so, come, Lord Jesus.

What Lessons do you derive from the above Doctrines ?

I learn (1.) To pray that the gospel may be everywhere preached, believed, and obeyed, so that the power of Satan may become less and less in every heart, and that the power of Christ may become greater, and even supreme. (2.) That all men may yield themselves to Christ as their rightful sovereign and Saviour. (3.) That the full effects of the religion of Christ as experienced in heaven are worthy of my earnest desire and prayer.

What Illustrations can you give ?

1. Rev. Dr. Griffin.—In his diary he says: "The three strongest desires which have habitually influenced me for years are: (1.) To be delivered from sin. If this

could be, I could bear anything, and be happy in poverty and disgrace. (2.) To enjoy God. I think I surely long more for this than riches or honors, and would give up everything for it. (3.) That God's kingdom may come. When I hear of any appearance favorable to Zion, my heart is glad."

2. Rev. Dr. Charles Hall.—He had devoted his children to God. He most earnestly desired to see them all not only Christians, but eminently useful Christians. In a letter to one of his sons, after a vivid sketch of the peculiarities of the age, this passage follows:—" You will soon come, if your life is spared, upon the stage, right in the *forenoon* of a day of action, such as the world never saw. I would fain impress you with the idea, that you are to live in an *uncommon era;* and that you owe it to your own character, to God, and to the interests of human nature, to *be* more, and *do* more, than if you had lived at another time.—[*Dr. Smith's Discourses.*]

3. Jonathan Edwards.—In his account of his views and feelings soon after he received the hope of salvation, President Edwards says: "My heart was knit in affection to those in whom were appearances of piety, and I could bear the thoughts of no other company, but such as were holy, and disciples of the blessed Jesus. I had a great longing for the advancement of Christ's kingdom in the world. My secret prayer used to be in great part taken up in praying for it. If I heard the least hint of anything that happened in any part of the world, that appeared to me in some respect or other, to have a favorable aspect on the interest of Christ's kingdom, my soul eagerly catched at it, and it would much animate and refresh me. I used to be earnest to read public news letters, mainly for that end; to see if I could find some news favorable to the interest of religion in the world." He regarded (says the *Puritan*) the history of the world as

the history of redemption. Every event furnished him with an occasion of thanksgiving or of prayer.—The same was true of the apostolic ELLIOT. When incidents had been related in his hearing, and had formed the subject of conversation, he used to say, "Now let us turn all this into prayer."

4. A TOO COMMON INCONSISTENCY.—If persons who have money to spare for a thousand superfluities, or even for a thousand mischievous indulgences, do almost nothing for the spiritual welfare of others, what a condemning contrast do they exhibit between their prayers and their conduct! *Either let men live to promote the kingdom of God, or cease to pray that it may come* If they will live so as to promote the world's sensuality, scepticism, and ungodliness, then let them never more utter the petitions which they do not mean; and if they will not labor for the world's conversion, let them not pretend to pray for it.—*Noel.*

Of the Third Petition.

Q. 103. WHAT DO WE PRAY FOR IN THE THIRD PETITION?

In the third petition, which is, "Thy will be done in earth, as it is in heaven;" we pray, That God by his grace, would make us able and willing to know, obey, and submit to his will in all things, as the angels do in heaven.

What Truths are embraced in this Answer?

1. *We are of ourselves unable to know or to do the will of God.*—1 Cor. ii. 14. The natural man receiveth not the things of the Spirit of God: for they are foolishness unto him: neither can he know them, because they are spiritually discerned.

THE THIRD PETITION.

2. *God only can make us able and willing to obey and submit to his will.—Phil.* ii. 13. It is God which worketh in you both to will and to do of his good pleasure.

3. *We ought to pray that the will of God may be known and obeyed over all the earth.—Psal.* lxvii. 2. That thy way may be known upon earth, thy saving health among all nations.

4. *We ought to pray that God would make us able and willing to know his will.—Eph.* i. 18. The eyes of your understanding being enlightened; that ye may know what is the hope of his calling, and what the riches of the glory of his inheritance in the saints.

5. *We ought to pray that God would make us able and willing to obey his will.—Psal.* cxix. 35. Make me to go in the path of thy commandments; for therein do I delight.

6. *We ought to pray that God would make us able and willing to submit to his will.—Acts,* xxi. 14. The will of the Lord be done.

7. *We ought to obey the will of God in all things.—Psal.* cxix. 5, 6. O that my ways were directed to keep thy statutes! then shall I not be ashamed when I have respect unto all thy commandments.

8. *We ought to submit to the will of God in all things.*—1 *Sam.* iii. 18. It is the Lord, let him do what seemeth him good.

9. *We ought humbly to obey and submit to the will of God as the angels do in heaven.—Job,* i. 21. The Lord gave, and the Lord hath taken away; blessed be the name of the Lord.

10. *We ought cheerfully to obey and submit to the will of God.—Psal.* c. 2. Serve the Lord with gladness: come before his presence with singing.

11. *We ought diligently to obey the will of God.—Psal.* cxix. 37. Quicken thou me in thy way.

12. *We ought constantly to obey and submit to the will of God.—Psal.* cxix. 112. I have inclined my heart to perform thy statutes always, even unto the end.

What Lessons do you derive from the above Doctrines?

I learn (1.) That it is my duty to study the Scriptures that I may obtain a better knowledge of what God desires me to do, and to be. (2.) To submit to the calamities and privations that are divinely appointed to me, with a cheerful patience, that shall prompt me to say, as Christ said, "Not as I will, but as thou wilt." (3.) To labor to send the Gospel to all men, and to pray for its success, that all men may be in a condition to be prepared to act in proper obedience to the will of God. (4.) There is deplorable need for putting up, daily and earnestly, this third petition of the Lord's prayer, for almost universally men are seen doing their own will in opposition to the will of their heavenly Father.

What Illustrations are given?

1 How to do God's will.—A Sabbath-school teacher, instructing his class in this portion of the Lord's Prayer, said to them: "You have told me, my dear children, *what* is to be done—*the will of God;* and *where* it is to be done—*on earth;* and *how* it is to be done—*as it is done in heaven.* How do you think the angels and happy spirits do the will of God in heaven, as they are to be our pattern?" The first child replied: "They do it *immediately;*" the second, "They do it *diligently;*" the third, "They do it *always;*" the fourth, "They do it *with all their hearts;*" the fifth, "They do it altogether." Here a pause ensued, and no child appeared to have an answer; but, after some time, a little girl arose and said, "Why, sir, they do it *without asking any questions.*"

2. Submission to Circumstances.—Dr. Johnson used to say that a habit of looking on the best side of every event is better than a thousand a year. Bishop Hall quaintly remarks: "For every bad there might be a worse; and when a man breaks his leg, let him be thankful it was not his neck."

3. As the late Rev. Dr. Charles Hall was near the end of life, a friend asked him: "Do you really feel that

your heavenly Father is about to call you to rest from your labors?" "I do not know," he answered, "for substance, how that may be; nor do I feel solicitous to know. I leave all that, with all my interests, however great or dear, to the disposal of infinite wisdom and goodness." The last Sabbath but one before his death, his daughter read to him the lines:

> "My times are in thy hand;
> My God I wish them there:
> My life, my friends, my soul I leave,
> Entirely in thy care."

Having given the closest attention to the end, he then remarked, with emphasis: "I think I can say that."

4. THE WIDOW'S GRIEF.—*Ebenezer Adams*, an eminent member of the Society of Friends, on visiting a lady of rank, whom he found, six months after the death of her husband, on a sofa covered with black cloth, and in all the dignity of woe, approached her with great solemnity, and gently taking her by the hand, thus addressed her: "So, friend, I see then, thou hast not yet forgiven God Almighty." This reproof had so great an effect upon the lady, that she immediately laid aside her violent grief, and again entered on the discharge of the duties of life.

5. THE DYING BOY.—The son of a Baptist minister, in Massachusetts, aged five and a half years, being asked, when near his death, whether he chose to live with his parents and friends here, or die and be with Jesus in heaven, cheerfully answered: "I would rather die, and be with Jesus in heaven, and WAIT THERE TILL YOU COME."

6. DR. DODDRIDGE, being found in tears, when just about to embark for Lisbon, in pursuit of health, remarked: "I am weeping, but my tears are those of joy. I can give up my country, my relations, my friends, into the hands of God; and as to myself, I can as well go to HEAVEN from Lisbon, as from my own study at Northampton."

7. The Rev. John Newton, in his seventy-fifth year, thus writes to Rev. Samuel Pierce: "I am waiting for my dismission. I desire to leave the *how*, and the *when*, and the *where*, to him who does all things well. My prayer is, that while I live I may live to Him; that when the summons shall arrive, I may be found ready; and that if He sees fit to lay me aside, I may be preserved from the weakness which sometimes clouds old age, even of good men; that I may not disparage my profession or ministry, by impatience, peevishness, or jealousy; but may retire with a good grace, truly thankful that others are coming forward to serve him, I hope, better, when I can serve Him no longer."

8. To an afflicted mother, at the grave of her dead child, it was said, "There was once a shepherd, whose tender care was over his flock day and night. One sheep would neither hear his voice nor follow him; so he took up her little lamb in his arms, and then the sheep came after him."

9. Difficulty of submitting to present circumstances.— When I am well, I think I could die contentedly: when I am sick, I am impatient to be well again.—*Adam.*

Of the Fourth Petition.

Q. 104. What do we pray for in the fourth petition?

In the fourth petition, which is, "Give us this day our daily bread;" we pray, That of God's free gift we may receive a competent portion of the good things of this life, and enjoy his blessing with them.

What Truths are embraced in this Answer?

1. *Temporal good things may be made a subject of prayer.*

—*Gen.* xxviii. 20. If God will be with me, and will keep me in this way that I go, and will give me bread to eat, and raiment to put on.

2. *Every good thing we enjoy is undeserved by us, and is a free gift from God.—Gen.* xxxii. 10. I am not worthy of the least of all the mercies, and of all the truth, which thou hast showed unto thy servant.

3. *We are to seek only what may be necessary for the present day and not be over anxious for the future.—Mat.* vi. 34. Take therefore no thought for [or, be not over anxious about,] the morrow: for the morrow shall take thought for the things of itself. Sufficient unto the day is the evil thereof.

4. *We are to ask for such a portion of the good things of life as God, in his wisdom, sees to be best for us.—Prov.* xxx. 8. Feed me with food convenient for me.

5. *We are to seek God's blessing on what we receive, which alone makes temporal good things valuable.—Prov.* x. 22. The blessing of the Lord, it maketh rich, and he addeth no sorrow with it.

What Lessons do you derive from the above Doctrines?

I learn (1.) That God is mindful of my wants in this life, as well as those of the life to come. (2.) That for present mercies of each day I owe him my thanks. (3.) That I should look to God for the needful supplies of each day and hour.

"This day be bread and peace my lot;
All else beneath the sun,
Thou knows't if best bestowed or not,
And let thy will be done."

What Illustration can you relate?

THE SCANTY MEAL.—A traveller, overtaken in a storm, sought shelter in a dilapidated and lonely dwelling. Before entering, however, he looked through the gaping crevices, and saw a woman seated at a table, on which was placed a coarse and scanty meal. Her hands and eyes were uplifted. Her lips moved; and, as he listened, he heard her say, "ALL THIS, AND HEAVEN TOO?"

2. Hebdomadal Devotions.—Some never unite in any form of social prayer but on the Sabbath. To suit their hebdomadal devotions this (fourth) petition should have run: "Give us this *week* our *weekly* bread." But as it now is, we have the supplies of the other six days unasked for. We acknowledge our dependence on God for only a seventh portion of our time.—*Dr. Nevins.*

3. Asking Blessings upon Food.—"I was on one occasion," says George Pritchard, "dining on board an English ship of war, with Queen Pomare, other members of the royal family, and several chiefs. A large table was prepared on the quarter-deck. All being seated, the plates were soon abundantly supplied, but not one of the natives attempted to eat. The captain was greatly surprised at this, and said to me: "Mr. Pritchard, I fear we have not provided such food as the natives like: I don't see one of them begin to eat." I replied: "You could not have provided anything that the natives would like better; the reason why they do not commence eating, is simply this: they are accustomed always to ask a blessing." Before I could say anything more, the captain, evidently feeling a little confounded, said: "I beg your pardon, Mr. Pritchard; please to say grace." I immediately "said grace," when the natives soon gave proof that they liked the food which had been provided. One of the officers from the end of the table looked at the captain very significantly, and said: "We have got it to-day!" and then addressing himself to me, said: "Mr. Pritchard, you see what a *graceless* set we are." All the gentlemen seemed to feel the rebuke thus unintentionally given.—*The Missionary's Record.*

Of the Fifth Petition.

Q. 105. What do we pray for in the fifth petition?

In the fifth petition, which is, "And forgive us

THE FIFTH PETITION.

our debts, as we forgive our debtors;" we pray, That God, for Christ's sake, would freely pardon all our sins; which we are the rather encouraged to ask, because by his grace we are enabled from the heart to forgive others.

What Truths are embraced in this Answer?

1. *We should pray for the pardon of sin.—Hos.* xiv. 2. "Take away all iniquity, and receive us graciously.— *See also Ps.* li. 1.
2. *Pardon of sin is to be expected only through Jesus Christ.—Eph.* i. 7. "In whom we have redemption through his Word, the forgiveness of sins, according to the riches of his grace."
3. *We must forgive others.—Col.* iii. 13. "Forbearing one another, and forgiving one another."
4. *God alone can enable us, from the heart, to forgive others.—Gal.* v. 22, 23. "The fruit of the Spirit is love, joy, peace, long-suffering, gentleness, goodness, faith, meekness, temperance; against such there is no law."
5. *Our being enabled to forgive others, encourages us to ask forgiveness for ourselves.—Luke,* xi. 4. "Forgive us our sins; for we also forgive every one that is indebted to us."
6. *Unless we forgive others, we ourselves shall not be forgiven.—Mat.* xviii. 35. "So likewise shall my heavenly Father do also unto you, if ye from your hearts forgive not every one his brother their trespasses."—*See also Mal.* vi. 14, 15.

What Lessons do you derive from the above Doctrines?

I learn (1.) That ill-will, a spirit of revenge, or even a want of kind regard, towards any of my fellow-men who may have wronged me, will justly stand in the way of my receiving pardon and love from my heavenly Father, and will shut me out of heaven. (2.) Not only the danger but the moral evil of an unkind and unforgiving disposition, which renders one so unlike God. (3.) My constant need of divine help, to keep my mind and heart in this undisturbed, meek, loving frame towards all with whom I have to do. (4.) That if I am not inclined to forgive others, I ought to be ashamed to ask God to forgive my greater sins against him. (5.) I should never cease to thank the Redeemer, that he, by offering himself to die in our stead, made full satisfaction to the justice of God for my sins; yet, so far as I am concerned, pardon is a matter of grace. I have done and suffered nothing, to entitle me to claim the remission of punishment as a right.

> "Consider this,—
> That in the course of justice, none of us
> Should see salvation: we do pray for mercy;
> And that same prayer doth teach us all to render
> The deeds of mercy."
> "How shalt thou hope for mercy, rend'ring none?"
> —SHAKSPEARE.

What Illustrations are offered?

1. THE LITTLE BLIND BOY.—A little blind boy was asked what forgiveness is. His beautiful reply was: "It is the odor that flowers breathe when trampled upon."

2. "WHO ARE THE MEEK?" was a question put by a missionary in Jamaica, when questioning some little black boys on *Mat.* v. One of them very pertinently answered: "Those who give soft answers to rough questions."

3. Rev. CHARLES SIMEON, says: "To pass by a transgression is more becoming the Gospel than to resent it." "A man strikes me with his sword, and inflicts a wound. Suppose, instead of binding up the wound, I am showing it to everybody; and after it has been bound up, I am taking off the bandage continually, and examining the depth of the wound, and making it to fester, till my limb

becomes greatly inflamed, and my general health is materially affected; is there a person in the world who would not call me a fool? Now, such a fool is he also, who by dwelling upon little injuries, or insults, or provocations, causes them to agitate and influence his mind. How much better were it to put a bandage over the wound, and never look at it again?"

4. GENERAL OGLETHORPE AND JOHN WESLEY.—In the course of a voyage to America, Mr. Wesley heard Gen. Oglethorpe, with whom he sailed, making a great noise in the cabin, upon which he stepped in to know the cause. The General immediately addressed him, saying: "Mr. Wesley, you must excuse me, I have met with a provocation too great for man to bear. You know the only wine I drink is Cyprus wine, as it agrees with me best of any; I therefore provided myself with several dozens of it, and this villain (the servant, who was present, almost dead with fear) has drank up the whole of it. But I will be revenged on him. I have ordered him to be tied hand and foot, and to be carried to the man-of-war which sails with us. The rascal should have taken care how he used me so, for I never forgive." "Then, sir," said Mr. Wesley, looking calmly at him, "I hope you never sin." The General, confounded at the reproof, threw his keys to the servant, and bade him do better in future. Here, then, is the point. If we would never forgive, we must never sin. The very proneness to sin which we find in ourselves, should be a most powerful incentive to the cultivation of a spirit of forgiveness.—*Rel. Herald.*

Of the Sixth Petition.

Q. 106. WHAT DO WE PRAY FOR IN THE SIXTH PETITION?

In the sixth petition, which is, "And lead us not into temptation, but deliver us from evil," we pray that God would either keep us from being tempted to sin, or support and deliver us when we are tempted.

What Truths are embraced in this Answer?

1. *We should pray that God, if consistent with his will, would keep us from being tempted into sin.*—*Mat.* xxvi. 41. "Watch and pray that ye enter not into temptation."—See also 2 *Chron.* xxxii. 31.

2. *We should pray for support under temptation.*—*Psal.* cxix. 133. "Let not any iniquity have dominion over me."

3. *We should pray for deliverance from temptation.*—2 *Cor.* xii. 8. "For this thing I besought the Lord thrice that it might depart from me."

What Lessons do you derive from the above Doctrines?

I learn (1.) That I am constantly exposed to sin as well as to suffering, and that on God alone I must rely for grace to feel and act right. (2.) That it is a wicked and a dangerous thing, for any, after uttering this prayer, to put themselves, unless duty calls, in a situation where they know they will be strongly tempted or inclined to violate God's commands. (3.) To withstand temptation, I must impress my heart with a sense of God's presence and holiness; with my obligation to obey him in all things, and even by the greatest effort; with the evil nature of sin, and the misery consequent upon indulging in it; and with the fact that Christ died to induce me to abandon all sin, and to save me from the power of temptation and from the malicious arts of the Tempter.

What Illustrations are given?

1. "Go to dark Gethsemane,
   Ye that feel the Tempter's power,
Your Redeemer's conflict see,
   Watch with him one little hour;
Turn not from his griefs away,
Learn of Jesus Christ to pray."

2. The Rev. CHARLES HALL, while in Stratford-upon-Avon, writes: "The great enemy has this day sorely buffeted me, so that my joy has been turned unto mourning. I go to my bed looking to Jesus, or *towards* him, for Oh, I do not perceive his smiling face. 'Return, O holy Dove return.'"

Of the conclusion of the Lord's Prayer.

Q. 107. WHAT IS THE CONCLUSION OF THE LORD'S PRAYER?

The conclusion of the Lord's Prayer, which is, "For thine is the kingdom, and the power, and the glory, for ever, Amen," teacheth us to take an encouragement in prayer from God only; and in our prayers to praise him, ascribing kingdom, power, and glory to him; and in testimony of our desire and assurance to be heard, we say, Amen.

What Truths are embraced in this Answer?

1. *We should take our encouragement in prayer from God only.*—*Dan.* ix. 18. "We do not present our supplications before thee for our righteousness, but for thy great mercies."

2. *In our prayers we should join thanksgiving and praise.* —1 *Chron.* xxix. 10. "David blessed the Lord before all the congregation; and David said, Blessed be thou, Lord God of Israel, our Father, for ever and ever."

3. *In our prayers we should ascribe the kingdom or universal dominion to God.*—1 *Chron.* xxix. 11. "All that is in the heaven and the earth is thine; thine is the kingdom, O Lord; and thou art exalted as head above all."

4. *In our prayers we should ascribe all power and glory unto God.*—1 *Chron.* xxix. 11. "Thine, O Lord, is the greatness, and the power, and the glory, and the victory, and the majesty."

4. *In prayer we should earnestly desire that God would*

hear us.—Dan. ix. 19. O Lord, hear; O Lord, forgive; O Lord, hearken and do; defer not, for thine own sake, O my God."

5. *We should pray with a hope and an humble assurance that God will hear us.—Heb.* x. 22. "Let us draw near with a true heart, in full assurance of faith."

6. *Our prayers should be concluded with an "Amen."—Psal.* cvi. 48. "Let all the people say, Amen."

What Lessons do you derive from the above Doctrines?

I learn (1.) That this prayer should be used with confidence, and assurance of hope, since Christ, the infallible Teacher, who best knows what God's will is, and what he may be pleased to grant, has authorized and directed me to use it. (2.) In prayer I am to have reference to the glory of God as the chief end to be attained by prayer, since it is the chief end for which God made me and all other beings and things. (3.) I should entertain large conceptions of the power of God to confer upon me and others all needed good. (4.) I should call to mind the great supremacy of God, his exalted rank as the King of kings, that I may promptly yield him the deepest reverence, and most largely desire that worship and obedience may be rendered to Him by all his creatures.

What Illustration follows?

THE JANEWAY FAMILY, of England, is remarkable in the annals of piety, for the fervor of their devotion and the joyful and even exulting state of mind in which they passed from the scenes of time into eternity. As illustrative of the subject in hand, the following expressions of feeling are taken from the record of their last hours: The Rev. WILLIAM JANEWAY (the father) said to his son: "My heart is full; I can hold no more. I know now what that sentence means, 'The peace of God which passeth understanding.' I cannot express what glorious discoveries God hath made of himself to me. Oh, help me to bless the Lord!"

His second son, the Rev. JOHN JANEWAY, observed: "Death has lost its terribleness—it is nothing. I say, death is nothing, through grace, to me. I can as easily die as shut my eyes, or turn my head and sleep: I long to be with Christ; I long to die." When Christians came to see him, he would beg of them to spend all the time with him in praise. "O help me to praise God! I have now nothing else to do, from this time to eternity, but to praise and love God. I have what my soul desires upon earth. I want but one thing, and that is, a speedy lift to heaven. O praise, praise, praise that infinite boundless love, that hath, to a wonder, looked upon my soul, and has done more for me than thousands of his dear children. Come, help me with praises, all that's little; come help me, O ye glorious and mighty angels, who are so well skilled in this heavenly work of praise! Praise him, all ye creatures upon the earth! Praise is now my work, and I shall be engaged in that sweet employment for ever. Let us sing a psalm of praise. Come let us lift up our voice in the praise of the Most High: I with you as long as my breath doth last, and when I have none, I shall do it better." A little before he died, in the prayer, or rather in the praises, he was so wrapt up with admiration and joy, that he could scarce forbear shouting for joy. In the conclusion of the duty, with abundance of faith and fervency, he said aloud, "Amen! Amen!"

The Rev. JAMES JANEWAY (the third son), just before he died, was also in a remarkably happy and devout frame of mind. Though very weak in body, he broke forth with a loud voice, "Amen! Hallelujah!" and desired others to join with him; but as they did not immediately do it, he added, "James Janeway is the only singer." Soon he was transported with joy again, and thus gave expression to it: "Millions of praises to the Most High Jehovah! Heaven and earth praise him! Ye mountains and hills praise him! All ye saints bless Him, who hath visited us in our low estate, and redeemed us, by grace, unto himself!"

THE END.

CPSIA information can be obtained
at www.ICGtesting.com
Printed in the USA
LVHW082244060820
662595LV00022B/964